Leading Issues in Information Warfare and Security Research

Edited by

Julie Ryan

Leading Issues in Information Warfare and Security Research
Volume One

First published April 2011 by
Academic Publishing International Ltd, Reading, UK
http://www.academic-publishing.org
info@academic-publishing.org

ISBN: 978-1-908272-08-9

Note to readers.

Some papers have been written by authors who use the American form of spelling and some use the British. These two different approaches have been left unchanged.

Printed by Goodnewsdigitalbooks in the UK.

Contents

i-Warfare Some Introductory Remarks

It is tempting to look at the subject of information warfare as simply a matter of technology. While technology is vitally important to the understanding of the concept, simply looking at the technology in isolation leads to missing the more important problems. These problems include the nature of competition, emerging changes in the way we live, and how we protect and defend ourselves, individually and jointly, against threats to our security. There are no easy answers or even good definitions, but the conversation is well underway and this book introduces that conversation.

Information is the currency of the realm. As with any currency, it is subject to competition, manipulation, nurturing, theft, destruction, and governance. Hence, it is important to consider a concept of warfare that both uses information and the systems upon which information is gathered, husbanded, distributed, and controlled. The papers offered in this anthology are presented in a logical progression designed to take the reader through a thought process that begins with the historical antecedents of our current environment and ends with provoking questions regarding the nature of conflict and self-defence.

The context of this conversation is one of security: the right to be safe in one's person, the safety and continued value of one's possessions, the mutual security of one's environment, the elements of security for one's community (including economic and national security), and the communal security of the international environment. These issues have never been easy to delineate so it should not be terribly surprising that the emergence of information security as a landscape for competition should be any less than extraordinarily complex.

To introduce this book, a brief overview of the changes emerging in the current environment is provided. These changes include the death of distance, a new plurality, and the changes in political power bases. And of course, all of these changes are taking place in a competitive framework, which is what causes information warfare to be a matter of concern.

Finally, an overview of potential ways of considering cyber warfare is provided. There are at least three ways in which the concept can be considered: that of from a legal response perspective, that of a doctrinal issue, and that of a functional problem space. The papers presented cover all three of these perspectives.

The Death of Distance and a New Competitiveness

Changes are occurring in the definition of security for both countries and individuals. We are in the midst of a social and economic revolution, akin to the industrial revolution, which has been called the information revolution. Just as the industrial revolution changed the way people lived, where they lived, how capital was created and how it was distributed, and how governance worked, so too is the information revolution changing all those elements of life. Because the information infrastructure upon which this revolution depends knows no geopolitical boundaries, this revolution extends across the domains of diplomacy and its extension, warfare, engendering a new dimension to warfare - information warfare.

Much has been written about information warfare in the past decade. Information warfare is generally described as encompassing those actions designed to gain information superiority and to deny the advantages of information superiority to the enemy. That information superiority is desirable is an unquestioned assumption, and the meaning of information superiority is described as more, better and faster information –whether obtained by exploiting your own technological capabilities or by attacking your opponent's information and information systems to make them less, worse and slower than your own.

These definitions are so broad that they fail to completely satisfy almost everyone, as evidenced by a pervasive unease permeating the national security community that is responsible for determining what the threats are and how the nation should best prepare to defend itself. Clearly something is missing – a vital ingredient that will make all the pieces fall into place and allow forward progress in the development of information warfare strategy, tactics, doctrine and procedures.

This missing link is the geopolitical context of the postulated struggle. It is possible that the existing regime of geopolity is changing. As it has evolved in the past, perhaps it is evolving now. The world in which information warfare must be waged is one that is characterized as transnational in nature, with highly intertwined interests caused and reinforced by the explosive growth of information technologies. While it is recognized conceptually that the global playing field has changed in both form and substance, this recognition is rarely evident yet in discussions of national security means and ends. And yet it is this fundamental change in form and substance that defines the future of our nation's security and our way of life. Rather than laboriously assessing the implications of information in all its myriad forms applicable to a nation's security needs, what must be assessed is the implication of information technology on the cooperative communal relationship that is currently instantiated as the nation-state.

Certainly it is not without utility to study the application of the latest technologies to the protection and achievement of national goals and security. The history of warfare is, in one sense, a story of the evolution of technologies and their application to geopolitical struggles. The introductions of the longbow, the crossbow, the machine gun, and the thermonuclear bomb all changed the nature of warfare. The use of horses, tanks, airplanes, and spacecraft each had a fundamental impact not only on the tactics of battles, but on the very nature of the battlefield itself. The advent of telegraphy, radio, radar, and multispectral sensing revolutionized warfare. Now solid state electronics, computers, networks, and fiber optics enable new ways to project power. In 1994, the US Joint Security Commission stated: "Networks are already recognized as a battlefield of the future. Information weapons will attack and defend at electronic speeds using strategies and tactics yet to be perfected. This technology is capable of deciding the outcome of geopolitical crises without the firing of a single weapon[1]."

But a more broad-ranging analysis of the impact of technology on the character and discourse of nation-states reveals much deeper issues. Since

---

[1] The Joint Security Commission, "Redefining Security"; a report to the Secretary of Defense and the Director of Central Intelligence; Washington D.C., February 28, 1994.

before the dawn of recorded history, mankind has been enslaved to the physical reality described by the grade-school equation:

rate times time equals distance
R x T = D

As the speed of transportation and communications increased, the distance that could be covered in a unit of time decreased. As a result, individual attention was taken from the village to a larger yet still local area, then to the nation, and eventually the world. The notions of "We" versus "They" have always been based on the realities of speed, time and distance. This seems to no longer be strictly true, particularly to denizens of virtual worlds such as Second Life[2].

In this universe of information systems and networks, both the concepts of speed and location are modified. In a very real sense, there are two speeds: one which is conventionally bound by physical movement and which is applied to people and things; and another, which applies to the movement of information and ideas, which is bounded only by the rate pulses of light can move through optical fibers and the speed at which electrons can move between thin layers of silicon. And there are two locations: a physical location and a cyber location. The cyber location may in fact span many different physical locations.

In such a world, distance loses some of its meaning. A new pluralism is enabled by modern telecommunications systems. Since Saigon is as close to Brooklyn as Chicago is to Gdansk, that is to say no distance at all in cyberspace, the old geopolitical boundaries that defined -- and protected -- us no longer fully work. When currency and intellectual capital, as well as philosophies and bigotries, move at the speed of light, those who find commonality in beliefs and aspirations can band together in virtual communities more easily than in cities, counties and countries. When weapons move at similar speeds and the battlefield exists in systems and networks, with the targets being information assets and infrastructure and a potential goal the crippling of a state's ability to respond with force or the de-

---

[2] Second Life is a product of Linden Research, Inc. Players inhabit worlds of their own and mutual creation, in bodies of their own imagination. As stated on the website, "Anything is possible." http://secondlife.com/

struction of an economy or way of life, it becomes necessary to rethink what is meant by "national security", both in term of the nation and in terms of the security.

Just as aviation, and more lately space travel, opened the third dimension to both commerce and warfare, and conquest of the electromagnetic spectrum opened a new and previously invisible domain for exploitation, the creation of world-spanning computer networks opens a new realm for exploration on behalf of both commerce and conflict. Each of these changes required a new vision of our world and a re-evaluation of who we are as individuals, families, tribes and geopolitical entities, and how we can and must relate to one another. Faster transportation and faster communications open our world to new experiences, new ideas, and new threats.

This, then, is the challenge: to develop an understanding of the emerging information-based world and to understand the challenges to our socio-economic and geopolitical entities in that future. A forecast of that future must encompass all dimensions of human life, to include the technological, economic, managerial, political, social, cultural, intellectual, religious and ethical, and ecological dimensions.

Thinking About Competition and Warfare

"These things know no national boundaries…." This statement applies to global organized crime, global terrorism groups, and global information networks. Although rarely stated and even more rarely considered, the statement that no one owns the Internet is very true and very applicable – while large entities, some states and some corporations, control major portions of it, it has long since passed out of any one entity's control. This "cyberspace" of systems and networks has truly become a global resource, analogous to the seas and the sky.

Just as legal agreements have emerged regarding international interactions on the seas and in the sky, some codified rules of behavior are beginning to emerge for conduct in cyberspace. While these rules, including ethics, morality, etiquette and laws, are yet to be fully developed they are needed to mediate behavior on-line and resolve conflicts that arise there. The challenge that faces us is to determine what the community itself is becoming, what communal security is becoming, and to determine how to preserve concepts such as personal freedom and even meaningful democracy in this future.

Because it is so new and so amorphous, operationally defining the competitional concept referred to variably as "information warfare", "cyberwarfare", "information operations", and "computer network operations" can be an exercise in madness. Are classic electronic warfare techniques included or not? Are psychological operations included or not? These are the types of arguments that quickly arise when one tries to develop a definitive construct of information warfare. Therefore, in this book, we acknowledge but avoid that quagmire. Instead, we present here thought-provoking issues that are intended to help the reader think about the hard problems associated with competition between geo-political states in the information era.

The papers included here are purposefully selected to reflect global perspectives, the countries of origin represented including the USA, Australia, Sweden, South Africa, Romania, France, Kuwait, Greece, and Estonia. For that is a fundamental and important point that truly separates whatever information warfare may be from conventional competition: the global interconnectedness of the informationenabled society erodes physical boundaries and ensnares each of us into the global web. What strategists in Nepal think impacts how strategists in Australia must think, and vice versa.

So, what are we to think about information warfare? At its most fundamental conceptual level, it must be warfare. Therefore, we must think about the strategies, goals, and tactics of war waging activities. But information warfare may occur in a dimension that is as equally poorly defined as the term "information warfare": that of cyberspace. So when we think about warfare in cyberspace, we need to have analogies to consider in order to develop a common understanding of what it is we are talking about.

Carl von Clausewitz is often quoted as saying that 'war is a mere continuation of policy by different means'[3]. It is instructive to consider his fuller contextual discussion of the topic:

The war of a community—of whole nations and particularly of civilised nations—always starts from a political condition, and is called forth by a political motive. It is therefore a political act. Now if it was a perfect, unrestrained and absolute expression of force, as we had to deduce it from its mere conception, then the moment it is called forth by policy it would step into the place of policy, and as something quite independent of it would set it aside, and only follow its own laws, just as a mine at the moment of explosion cannot be guided into any other direction than that which has been given to it by preparatory arrangements. This is how the thing has really been viewed hitherto, whenever a want of harmony between policy and the conduct of a war has led to theoretical distinctions of the kind. But it is not so, and the idea is radically false. War in the real world, as we have already seen, is not an extreme thing which expends itself at one single discharge; it is the operation of powers which do not develop themselves completely in the same manner and in the same measure, but which at one time expand sufficiently to overcome the resistance opposed by inertia or friction, while at another they are too weak to produce an effect; it is therefore, in a certain measure, a pulsation of violent force more or less vehement, consequently making its discharges and exhausting its powers more or less quickly, in other words conducting more or less quickly to the aim, but always lasting long enough to admit of influence being exerted on it in its course, so as to give it this or that direction, in short to be subject to the will of a guiding intelligence. Now if we reflect that war has its root in a political object, then naturally this original motive which called it into existence should also continue the first and highest consideration in the conduct of it. Still the political object is no despotic lawgiver on that account; it must accommodate itself to the nature of the means, and through that is often completely changed, but it always remains that which has a prior right to consideration. Policy therefore is interwoven with the whole action of war, and must exercise a continuous influence upon it as far as the nature of the forces exploding in it will permit[4].

---

[3] Clausewitz, Carl von. On War. Chapter 1, Item 24. Available online at http://www.clausewitz.com/readings/OnWar1873/BK1ch01.html.
[4] ibid, part 23.

Even though the world has changed dramatically since von Clausewitz penned these sentiments in his book On War in 1832, there are important points made in this analysis which very much bear on the conceptualization and understanding of information warfare. The linkage between politics and strife is key.

There are four general venues in which geopolitical relationships are negotiated and competed. Each of these has in times past led to situations where the politics of the situation wound up being decided through war. These venues are economic competition, cultural competition, religious competition, and competition for resources. Often, in history, competition in more than one of the venues has led to war between competing parties. Over time, human society has developed an increasing number of tools to mediate the natural competition in ways that reduce tension and increase the potential for fairness in the competition. The tools include laws that both prohibit and require certain types of behavior, international treaties that mediate and moderate competition, and international conventions on behaviors. Despite the fact that the post-World War II era has seen a number of armed conflicts, arguably the conflicts have been fewer in number than potentially might have been and have been less destructive than unmoderated conflict.

In considering the concept of information warfare, it is important to consider these venues for competition and established means for moderating competition and preventing conflict. In other words, simply considering the technology potential is not enough. The politics, the impacts on people, the role of extra-national organizations, the competition of ideas: all of these must be considered, because at the end of the day, it is not the technology that wages war, it is the people. Serious questions abound, including the following:

- What types of action in cyberspace rise to the level of act of armed aggression? Does it matter if these acts are carried out by nations, corporations, ad hoc groups, or individuals?
- What is the relationship between information warfare and cybercrime? Should there be a distinction or is one even possible?
- Should information warfare actions that rise to the level of act of armed aggression even be allowable? Or should they be treated in a way similar to nuclear or biological weapons?

- Is it possible to control the technologies to prevent the proliferation of information warfare capabilities, or would that put an undue constraint on information dependent economies?
- Are the asymmetries associated with information warfare so great that unleashing the potential might in fact recraft the geopolitical landscape?
- What are the rights of nonstate actors to defend themselves from either being used as conduits for information warfare (such as the large network companies) or being the target of information warfare attacks? Should they be allowed to defend themselves or should defense be the sole provence of the geopolitical entity?
- What are the rights of individuals to defend themselves? What are the duties of a citizen to assist in defending his nation? Do these rights and obligations exist, or should they?

These are not easy questions, nor are there easy answers to these questions. The papers in this selection have been chosen in order to lead the reader though a structured consideration of these issues, starting with some concept exploration, then delving into organizational issues, next touching on the technologies, and then finally looking into the legal and ethical issues. The papers have been lightly edited to provide additional context to the reader, mostly through the use of footnotes that provide the reader with pointers to additional resources. Finally, some concluding thoughts are offered.

A New Calculus of Competition

Most analysts agree that the thermonuclear-focused superpower confrontation we call the Cold War was not won through military might but largely through the diplomatic and economic efforts fronting the strong military. The historic themes of that global competition were anchored in territory (distance), population and resources, and were strongly influenced by huge nuclear weapons arsenals that were the monopoly of the superpowers. Lesser states were dependent on superpowers' protection and joined blocs led by one or the other. Additionally there was direct economic competition between the superpower blocs, but it was always associated with and modified by the security arrangements that were the centerpiece of global affairs.

That comfortable calculus has been replaced by the newly emerging power of IT networking which permits and enables a vastly more complex matrix of ethnic, economic, political and social alliances and enmities -- in short, a new pluralism.. This pluralism exists not only among nation-states, but pervades them, with individuals and groups with like interests joining on-line in virtual communities that need not and do not recognize traditional geopolitical boundaries.

In recent years, virtually all major institutions and organizations, from nation-states to religions and from transnational commercial enterprises to military alliances, are exploiting the increased functionality, efficiency, and productivity promised by IT connectivity. Unfortunately, with increased connectivity also comes increased vulnerability. Absent appropriate policies, technologies, practices and procedures to protect information, connectivity means that anyone with access to these information networks has the power to access, manipulate, misuse or destroy the information resident on or transiting over the networks. Many public and private sector organizations have yet to take the time to consider either the nature or magnitude of this problem. This is a legitimate cause for concern but not a new concern. In fact, this dilemma was recognized well over a decade ago:

The United States relies for its very existence economically, socially, and politically on an extraordinarily sophisticated and intricate set of longdistance networks for energy distribution, communication, and transportation. Because these networks also rely upon each other, a truly serious disruption in any one will cascade quickly through the others, rending the vital fabric of our nation at its most crucial points. Under these circumstances the ability to respond to national security crises will at least be severely constrained and may be completely interrupted for some crucial interval[5].

Communication networks, an essential tool for the management of national crises, of other types of networks, and of commerce, are particularly susceptible to human interference. Electronic funds transfers (EFT) have

---

[5] Kluepfel, H. "Countering Non-Lethal Information Warfare: Lessons Learned On Foiling The Information Superhighwayman Of The North American Public Switched Telephone Network" Proceedings IEEE 29th Annual 1995 International Carnahan Conference on Security Technology, 1995. 18-20 Oct 1995, page(s): 474 - 479

become the vital arterial network of the international banking communities upon which all domestic business and foreign trade depend. The sheer amount of
money transferred every hour over these networks is staggering.

It's not just money, either. Networks and their infrastructure components, their functions, and their uses have greatly proliferated and diversified. Their complexity has increased. The competitive pressures for economic growth and rapid implementation of new technical capabilities have not been balanced by demand for adequate technical, legal, regulatory, and managerial protective measures. The result, in some areas, has been an increased potential for disruptive failure, as well as the overall appearance of a much greater number of inadequately protected, attractive targets for purposeful abuse and unwanted exploitation.

The opportunities and full implications of the information technology revolution are gradually being recognized and acted upon by the broad range of state actors as well as by non-governmental organizations for whom connectivity on a global scale has meant increases in access and influence. Connectivity also results in the bypassing of traditional governing hierarchies and the diffusion of power. In all cases, these nations and organizations are led to conclude that information has power, in and of itself, independent of the technologies that were used to create, store, process and communicate the information. This power exists in contrast to classic metrics such as strategic location, raw material resources, population, etc. In fact, information, even without any substance, may arguably be the most important commodity in assessing the true strength of any group in the coming age.

Our dependency on information and IT gives rise to profound vulnerability. Traditional barriers of time and distance that have permitted us to hold trouble at arm's length have been rendered irrelevant. The information-based infrastructures that we depend upon for our security, and which are omnipresent in our workplaces and daily lives, have become vectors for assaults on our information-rich lifestyle.

A Revolution in Relationships

In the 1980s and 1990s, a critical area of debate was what was termed a Revolution in Military Affairs (RMA). Today we are dealing with something much more complex, which might be termed a Revolution in Relationships, or the birth of a new polity: the cyber-polity.

Today, every aspect of an individual's daily existence is intertwined with information technology. Microprocessor-controlled products, such as cars and planes, robotics, expert systems, wired buildings, intelligent transportation systems, and network management systems surround us. From facsimile machines to satellite communications, information technology is enabling humans to communicate faster and further than ever before. As more individuals become networked to each other, the value of the network increases exponentially. When there were only a few telephones, they were a laboratory curiosity. Millions of telephones became an intrinsic and vital component of our economy. Similar results apply to computer networks. This phenomenon was identified by Dr. Robert Metcalfe, who defined what he calls the "Law of the Telecosm." This law links "the power of a network--literally how much it can do--to the square of the number of connected machines: P(n)=n[squared]"[6].

In the global community, this leveraging power of information technology provides previously ineffective marginalized groups with additional means for both direct challenges to authority as well as indirect media for intra-group communications, planning, and management. Recent cases include the B-92 radio station in Bosnia[7], the use of the Internet by the Chiapas

---

[6] McCann, John M. "Digital Dawn CyberTrends", Duke University, http://www.duke.edu/~mccann/q-ddawn.htm, quoted as being originally drawn from Pablo Bartholomew-Gamma, "The Networked Society: Welcome to the Wired World," Special Report from Time Inc. concerning the World Economic Forum in Davos, Switzerland, February, 1997

[7] See for example "Preserving the Free Flow of Information on the Internet: Serbs Thwart Milosevic Censorship" at http://www.usip.org/events/preserving-free-flow-information-internet-serbs-thwart-milosevic-censorship-round-two

revolutionaries to marshal global attention to their cause[8], the use of tape-recorded messages by the Ayatollah Khomeini while in exile in Paris, the use of Twitter in the Iranian election protests, and the use of Facebook during the Egyptian protests[9]. These examples illustrate the breakdown of boundaries, both physical and customary. Where the cracks in the wall appear, the ideas of the possibilities become apparent to all observers, thus leading to more cracks.

Recognizing the effect that information technology has on globalization trends as well as on individual capabilities, it is logical to assume that more information will be shared more widely. As that information is shared, each participant in an authority relationship is able to compare his situation with those of others in the same or other authority relationships. This comparison will affect the perceived value of the services in the authority relationship, and in those cases where defects or derogation are perceived, may cause a loss of equilibrium.

Attempting to close down the channels of communication is a short sighted and probably futile effort; recognizing the effects and working with them is much more likely to stave off catastrophic challenges to authority. The most recent government to learn this lesson was Syria10, but the lesson has been learned over and over again throughout history. Unfortunately, the availability of the internet and other channels of communication is no guarantee that the information sent or received is truthful, in any of the senses of that word.

---

[8] See for example "Rebellion in Chiapas: insurrection by Internet and public relations" by Jerry W. Knudson from Temple University, available online at http://www.bsos.umd.edu/aasp/chateauvert/rebellio.pdf

[9] See for example "The dark side of Internet for Egyptian and Tunisian protesters", which discusses many of these events. By Evgeny Morozov for the Globe and Mail, published Jan. 28, 2011. Available online at http://www.theglobeandmail.com/news/world/africa-mideast/the-dark-side-of-internet-for-egyptian-and-tunisian-protesters/article1887170/print/

[10] *"Syria protest intensifies; Internet access is cut off: Rage continues over torture, death of teen"* By Liam Stack and Katherine Zoepf, New York Times / June 4, 2011; followed by "Syria's Internet is back up… for now" By Steven J. Vaughan-Nichols | June 6, 2011, 10:04am, ZDNet, http://www.zdnet.com/blog/networking/syria-8217s-internet-is-back-up-8230-for-now/1139

The growth of the media and network technology permits the generation and dissemination of information much faster than has ever been possible up to this time. These factors, taken together, now pose a significant new consideration for nation-state governments as well as for civic minded individuals: the velocity at which new and destabilizing ideas can be disseminated. Governments are still composed of people who need a human time scale to consider factors presented and then act. The traditional time available to gather data and to deliberate is now being compressed, and the window available within which authorities can act is expressed in the same near-real-time context as the ceaseless flow of information within the new wide area networks that pervade our countries and continents. Failure of governments to first catch up, and then keep up, with the "refresh rate" of destabilizing information is self-reinforcing as groups challenging the traditional authority structures discern that they now have the ability to affect public awareness and sentiment out of proportion to their size, budgets, and geographical hegemony. The initiative is clearly in the hands of those who are proactively controlling the nature, timing and mechanisms of information dissemination -- in essence, the tempo of crises.

The use of information technologies for direct and indirect challenges is not limited to the Internet and related data networks. Destabilizing information may be spread by the media as well. When contemplating the role of the media in an IT-enabled pluralist world, we must consider several dynamics: manipulation of the media and manipulation by the media.

Manipulation of the media.

This can take the form of manipulating or withholding access, or of selective cooperation by traditional authorities or challengers in story generation and transmission. In an environment of heavy dependency on media information sources, political, military, or popular reaction to reported events could be significantly affected. This is true in every aspect of media performance, including the timeliness, precision, and slant of the message. The media may be duped by those seeking to present a deliberately misleading message (a concept known as disinformation). The Allied Forces in the Gulf War provided the media with ready access to amphibious forces which appeared to be readying for an attack on Iraq, when in fact no such attack was intended, and which was duly reported in international news broadcasts known to be reviewed by the Iraqi command.

Alternatively, the media may be used as an agent of influence by those presenting an accurate picture of events, but one which is calculated to foster a specific reaction within an influential sector of the viewing public. The case that is seared into the mind of the American public is the portrayal of U.S. Army casualties being dragged through the streets of Somalia. By dutifully beaming these viewpoints to global audiences in crisis-real-time, the "free and independent media" can be co-opted as an active agent of a belligerent power, who may be working in direct opposition to U.S. national interests at that moment. In so doing, the newsman's camcorder provides a "bully pulpit" for bit players who would otherwise find it impossible to directly resist western political or military efforts.

Media organizations known or believed to be "favorable" to the local authority's position may receive special privileges of access to key leadership figures or facilities. In so doing, these privileged groups appear to have a more detailed, timely or better documented story to tell, thereby gaining viewer support and strengthening the credibility of their news and editorial positions. This particular mechanism of controlling media message output -- actively aiding cooperative organizations in their efforts to outshine their competitors -- is the bridge to the second, and even more serious area of concern.

Manipulation by the media.
This type of manipulation can be used to deliberately support or oppose a particular viewpoint, based on the news organization's national affiliation, sponsorship, or political stance of the owners. This is an insidious danger, and one that is, on the surface, difficult to confront in a free society. The fact that the media has enormous influence on the masses and their leaders is unarguable. The presumption that those individuals who control large and pervasive media organizations have views and commitments that place them at a particular point on the political and ideological spectrum is similarly unavoidable. Given that, how can we be surprised that these "media barons" might use their considerable influence to build constituency for positions with which they are sympathetic, while denigrating those they oppose?

This is hardly a new phenomenon. William Randolph Hearst was singularly influential in precipitating the Spanish American War, at least in part as a means to boost circulation for the benefit of his newspaper empire. Within the context of this discussion, it would be completely proper to credit him with manipulating public opinion -- and national policy -- by means of substantially controlling the flow of information within American society of that time[11].

Any attempt to frame solutions to the problems associated with the media and its role in Information Warfare gets very sensitive, very quickly. In the West, it is readily acknowledged that the freedom of expression and of the press are bedrock principles of society. In fact, the existence of a free press is usually held up as a leading test of the maturity of democratic institutions and principles in emerging democracies -- and very properly so. Notwithstanding that, we feel it is reasonable -- even necessary -- to note and characterize the dangers that manipulation of the press can bring.

As with many other aspects of the Information Age, the sword cuts two ways. Instant, global reporting brings us insight, access and cultural exposure that most could never achieve otherwise. On the other hand, a society which digests information and forms opinions largely on the basis of 20-second sound bites is one that is vulnerable to manipulation through the medium of those sound bites. A government whose real-time intelligence fusion and analysis centers prominently display, and routinely rely on, privately-owned media reporting to supplement official means of data gathering is one which has an obligation to think carefully about the integrity (i.e. editorial backdrop) of that data stream in various scenarios.

The Growing Issue of Non-State Actors

The term "non-state actors" refers to those persons or groups who are acting independently of national agendae, as opposed to those who may be apparently independent, but who are in fact significantly engaged in

---

[11] "The Spanish-American War is often referred to as the first "media war." During the 1890s, journalism that sensationalized—and sometimes even manufactured—dramatic events was a powerful force that helped propel the United States into war with Spain. Led by newspaper owners William Randolph Hearst and Joseph Pulitzer, journalism of the 1890s used melodrama, romance, and hyperbole to sell millions of newspapers--a style that became known as yellow journalism." Crucible of Empire: The Spanish American War. Great Projects Film Company, 1999. http://www.pbs.org/crucible/frames/_journalism.html

advancing nation-state interests. Seen through this lens, we are once again forced to confront the unpleasant reality that the current and future problem is significantly more complex than the one we faced during the Cold War. The investment needed to acquire significant capability to exploit, disrupt, degrade or destroy information and information systems or networks does not require large amounts of cash, personnel, space, technology, industrial base or unique expertise. There are no critical or raw materials or significant industrial precursor processes that may be detected, traced or regulated (in contrast, say, to the acquisition and refinement of Plutonium, for example). The skills, tools and techniques required for effective use of the relevant equipment are easily obtained in ways that leave no audit trail. The small and inexpensive amount of terminal equipment required to achieve global network access is readily available from legitimate commercial sources and is lost within the legitimate development of information infrastructures in support of commercial enterprise.

Rational nation-states can usually be trusted to act in furtherance of interests which can generally be identified and predicted. However, in the new technology-enabled cyberpluralism, non-state actors will be much less visible and consequently less predictable as to the nature, timing or location of their actions. When we recognize that non-state actors can be seen as embracing acts of political, ethnic or religious terrorism, vandalism and wanton destructiveness, theft, or a complex set of motivations, we must acknowledge that responding to the magnitude and unpredictability of this problem will prove challenging. There will also undoubtedly continue to be rogue nation-states that are similarly motivated; however, these states normally can be identified and singled out for especially cautious treatment by the international community.

The conclusions we must draw from this broadened list of motives and actors point to an expanded potential for compromising or destroying our critical systems and processes, including those which provide for the welfare and security of our nation. The result is a great broadening of our vulnerability to destabilization.

Non-state actors need not be fanatical ethnic or religious factions or terrorist groups. Some of the most powerful and IT-capable non-state actors are transnational commercial organizations. As consolidation of industries and firms proceeds, independent commercial enterprises reach the size of nation-states in terms of gross revenues, capital resources, personnel, facilities and production capacity. Moreover, these transnational companies owe allegiance to no nation-state or bloc, but act to maximize revenues and profits while lowering tax liabilities to traditional governments. This allows moderate- to large-scale companies to become global in scope and influence while, at the same time, weakening the traditional nation-state.

In some cases, the interests of nation-states and transnational enterprises converge, while in others nation-states have been co-opted. In either case, we can see the power, influence and capabilities of the state, such as national intelligence capabilities, being harnessed to influence the outcome of commercial negotiations in favor of certain transnational commercial enterprises. Where the transnational non-states are illicit, their interactions with nation-states can impact a wide range of national diplomatic and security concerns. As we examine the question of Global Organized Crime in all its manifestations, it is essential that the United States consider the whole range of actors, even states themselves, as potential perpetrators of industrial espionage, organized crime and terrorism in the information age.

A logical conclusion is that the responsibility of a government to ensure the welfare and security of the citizens certainly must include securing the information infrastructure of the nation. This challenge is easier stated than accomplished, when the vast majority of the infrastructure is not only privately owned but administered privately on a global basis.

A New Look at Security and The Rise of the Cyber Polity

Historically, the central role of the military has been to protect the society from which it springs and to project power abroad in pursuit of geopolitical strategies. As threats to the nation-state have evolved, so have the capabilities and responsibilities of the military. The military has been bound by the notions of distance and time with the rest of society, and defense was understood and planned and operated in spatial and temporal terms. Early on, when the perceived threat was to the sanctity of the actual territory of a homeland, military forces defended at the shoreline and border, a Navy built and operated a near-coastal capability, and there were essentially no forces stationed outside of countries. This had to change when the strategic threat posed by long-range bombers, intercontinental ballistic missiles, and missile-capable submarines became apparent, and of necessity included strategies of deterrence.

In a world pervaded by computer systems and networks, the notions of time and space that formed the foundation of prior strategies and tactics have to be reconsidered. The topography of cyberspace is very different from that of the geopolitical units with which our diplomatic and military forces have prepared to deal.

Geopolitical boundaries are not reproduced, and cannot be reproduced, in the universe of networks. Information and information weapons move across those networks at electronic speeds. Attacks can occur without warning and it may not be immediately apparent even that an attack is taking place, much less its source. Electrons wear no uniforms and carry no flags. Nevertheless, a full-scale strategic attack on one country could conceivably affect every aspect of the global computer-enriched economy. Targets might include a telephone system, the power grid, air traffic control and other transportation systems, the financial community, law enforcement, and an ability to recall reserves and mount a military response. The effects of a successful attack might involve few deaths directly, although many deaths could result indirectly, but would have profound consequences for the economy and way of life. In fact, there have been no deaths attributed directly to the cyber-attack waged on Estonia in 2007, but the effects were dramatic, as will be discussed in several of the presented papers in this anthology.

The emergence of the new cyber-political pluralities offers additional concerns for communal security. It is important to note that the emergence of cyber-political units (CPUs) do not eliminate geopolitical threats but add cyber-political complexities to the existing litany of potential problems. How established geopolitical entities react to the emergence of this new class of problem may determine in great measure the success in continued security at home and protection of global interests. Attempting to repress or contain these emergent units is likely to be counter-productive..

The challenges proffered by these entities are simultaneously internal and external. The security of the nation is threatened both by the evaporation of containing and protecting borders and by the diffusion of power enabled by widespread information networks. To modify the national security infrastructure in a meaningful manner that best relates to the emerging cyber-political realities requires an analysis of the authority relationship and how it is being diffused and weakened. With that understanding, a new view of security can be developed and strategies employing that view can be adopted.

There are several elements that need to be revisited:

-
- The composition of the authorities: Who are they? What value do they provide? Why are they empowered to lead? What are the limitations on their power?
- The composition of the new cyber-pluralities: Who are they? What support do they provide to the authorities, if any? What services do they expect to be provided by the authorities? What limitations do they place on authorities' actions?
- The composition of the relationship between the two: How is it negotiated? How are changes made and disputes resolved?

By "authorities" we mean those who have been empowered to lead, manage, issue commands and enforce obedience. They obtain that power in a variety of ways: strength of arms, personal charisma or expertise, tradition or organizational position, persuasive rational argument, or by being chosen by an electorate with the power to appoint its leaders. Life or death power and its ability to extract absolute obedience is, however, rarely possible for individuals, and purely coercive power cannot exist in complex societies where the exercise of authority can only be accomplished through the organized behavior of groups. Obedience and cooperation are not inevitable, and even in the most repressive and tyrannical governments there are factions and subgroups, in which pluralism lies the possibility of dissent, disobedience, rebellion and revolution. The new information technologies diffuse the power of traditional authorities and enable the activities of these pluralities, the "new cyber-pluralities" which, because of the borderless nature of cyberspace are not completely within the boundaries and hegemony of any single nation-state. Just as authorities must provide services to their subjects in return for their right to rule and command the services of the subjects, or they will not long retain their exalted positions, authorities must learn to deal with the new cyber-pluralities with whom they must coexist, be they ethnic, religious or political in nature or transnational commercial enterprises.

Whether an authority will be able to successfully exercise control in this new arrangement will depend on the perception and judgment of the new cyber-pluralities' as to whether obedience or cooperation will lead to the rewards expected (or lack of the punishment promised), and whether this reward will satisfy a fundamental need for safety and security, social affiliation, esteem or prestige, autonomy or power, or feelings of competence and achievement. The new cyber-pluralities' willingness to be governed will be great if they value need satisfaction, think that the authority's rewards will be instrumental in satisfying those needs, and deem it likely that the services they provide will satisfy the authority's objectives so that the reward will follow. Lacking assurance of any one of these factors undermines the authority's influence and leads to a challenge to the authority.

Influence is always reciprocal. To control, one must allow oneself to be controlled to some extent. The coercive dictator must punish subordination or suffer the loss of credibility. Tradition-based systems must offer loyal, obedient supporters warmth and security. Even charismatic leaders must give of themselves, allowing followers to see, hear and touch the authority. Such reciprocal systems tend toward equilibrium if they are to survive for any length of time. Changes to that equilibrium result from either extrinsic or intrinsic changes to the authority, the new cyber-pluralities, the services either provides, or the environment in which they relate to each other. Some changes can enhance the rewards both the authority and the non-authorities receive from their relationship, and both can mutually benefit from the change. Other changes reduce the actual or perceived value of the services provided by the authority, the services provided by the new cyber-pluralities, or both. The resulting dissonance challenges the authority and leads to either realignment of the services to re-achieve equilibrium or shatters the relationship entirely.

The constriction of time and subsequent decrease in the significance of distance between peoples adds to the ability of ideas, concepts, methods and technologies used in external situations to creep into the knowledge bases and skills repertoires of both the authority and the new cyber-pluralities. The constriction of time and distance leads to increasing contact between different authorities, nation-states and cyber-pluralities, which in turn often leads to increasing tendencies to interfere either purposefully or accidentally in those other authority relationships.

The impact of the increasing interfaces among authority relationships is also significant in the realm of negotiations regarding the authority relationship boundaries. In the new reality, the authority relationship boundaries are not necessarily physical, but lie where the ability of the authority to exert influence over the new cyber-pluralities fades into subservience to another authority relationship. This boundary may, in fact, be a fluid and unstable zone, changing with context.

The impact of information technology and globalization has been to increase the number of authority relationships it is possible to participate in and thereby create more boundaries to be negotiated. Each boundary intersection creates friction. The more often the boundaries come into contact, the more friction is created. This energy must be released in some manner. Traditional means of expending this energy have included warfare, police action, and lawsuits.

Evolutionary advances and revolutionary leaps occurring in technology, trade and politics are causing a redefinition of identity and relationships. The cause and effect is that national interests are intertwined almost to the point that there are essentially no such things as strictly internal policies anymore. Internal policies affect businesses, which are increasingly international and, in any case, trade internationally. Unfavorable policy brings international pressure for change. Internal policies also affect people, who are increasingly able to communicate with sympathetic supporters in other parts of the world. A nation's political and industrial leadership is continually pressured by such supporters to change its policies regarding dealings with other countries. Similarly, transnational organizations have encountered pressures by their consumers to change operations (or even eliminate them) in other parts of the world.

Imposing a structure that does not work and/or does not reflect accurately the way individuals operate effectively hamstrings an organization. People who are motivated to get the job done will work outside of the organization chart, and as a result will cause confusion and challenge authority within the established chain. People who are motivated to play by the rules will become increasingly frustrated and will lose any initiative for finding solutions to problems, becoming moribund in their attempts to fit into the structure. The value of the authority service will decline in the eyes of the not-authority, creating a situation conducive to a challenge to that authority.

With the emergence of cyberpolitical units, the traditional hierarchies -- the authority relationships of the industrial age -- are diminished in power and ability to exercise hegemony unless positive action is taken to include the members of the virtual community in an active participation in governance and protection of communal security.

Effective Information Assurance

In this emerging cyber-political world with complex interconnectivities in information systems and content, assuring effective information assurance is a non-trivial challenge. In this environment, mutual defences are truly mutual. When your systems are connected to a network, they are connected to every other system as well as other networks connected to that network. The weaknesses in defences at any node on that network can endanger your systems and information. Yet disconnecting from the network is not a viable option, either.

It may well be, in the emerging cyberpolitical era, that economic competition overshadows direct military competition. These economic competitions, as practiced by modern, market-economy organizations, bridge private and governmental interests. Information-based technologies are being eagerly employed by all sectors of society, including business, government and private sector. Information-based competition, focused on achieving an economic advantage by acquiring confidential and proprietary business information such as design secrets, proprietary technologies and market plans is a key piece of current international affairs. Such competition, being naturally linked to classic national objectives and interests, including trade, diplomatic, and security-related issues, fosters some degree of active collaboration between commercial and state entities, depending upon the extent to which their interests coincide. In some cases, the cooperation is very visible and extensive.

Detailed understanding of the technology by its users is often limited, and in fact a design goal known colloquially as user-friendliness. Those who have knowledge, access, and motivation may exploit unknown, undocumented, and even deliberately hidden flaws. In addition to vulnerabilities inherent in information networks and systems, information itself is a powerful weapon made more so by the explosion of paths through which information can be disseminated.

To understand information assurance in this context requires an appreciation for the exposure caused by networking, the practical applications of security technologies and practices, and the mutual dependence for robust security.

The ability to assign value to information (as well as the importance of even trying to do so) is a critical outcome of this situation. Identifying a specific, dollar value for some piece of information can be difficult, with answers ranging from very simple and rigorous dollar amounts to completely emotional and non-reproducible. However difficult to value, it is clear that information has value from a security point of view. The content of the information, its veracity, and availability all contribute to its value. Concomitantly, its unavailability, doubtful reliability, or limited content all detract from its value. The banking and finance community provide us with clear examples of direct value of information, both in terms of availability and in terms of content, since the products and processes of that industry are assessed in terms of monetary value.

Valuing information content and infrastructure is necessary in order to justify the investment in information assurance. The ability to have information assurance is directly related to expenditure of effort in associated technologies, policies and methodologies. There are existing technologies, practices and methodologies that provide significant levels of information assurance to those who invest the time and effort to avail themselves of those resources, but the protection does not come inexpensively. Effective information assurance is a well-balanced mix of technological and non-technological solutions. Technology alone can't provide robust information assurance. It must be augmented by practices and policies covering every aspect of the operational environment, including personnel hiring practices, physical access constraints, and business continuity planning.

There are several existing trends that underscore the importance of awareness and education, as well as cooperation.

First, information and recipes for both writing malicious software (such as viruses) and exploiting vulnerabilities (such as how to execute a SYN flood attack) are widely available, published both electronically and in "dead tree" format. This information allows even neophytes with little technical expertise to become threats.

Second, just as scientists stand on the shoulders of giants to see further, so do social misfits. As the basis of knowledge grows, so does the complexity of the attack capabilities. Thus it is that automated programs that assist in creating virus programs now offer additional features, such as encryption and polymorphism. It would be naïve to believe that there might be any loss in capability or complexity in threat capabilities against information systems; to the contrary, a very sound assumption is that this body of knowledge and capabilities will continue to grow. As threats with significant resources (such as criminal syndicates or national governments) enter this field of research, the body of knowledge will increase commensurately.

Third, maintaining a capable defensive posture against threats requires continuous commitment of resources and energy. This is complicated by the fact that expenditure of effort by one node in a network can be undermined by lack of effort by one or more other nodes in the network. The requirement for cooperative attention to common security practices is fundamental to collective security capabilities. If done correctly, it could enable further efficiencies in the information sphere by enabling economies of scale in technology investment. However, full effort would still be required in the non-technological aspects of information security and assurance, such as good practices and policies.

A thoughtful mix of capabilities provides robust information assurance. It begins with risk assessment, a process that must be revisited periodically, since no organizational environment ever remains in stasis. The risk assessment takes into consideration every aspect of the environment, examining it for vulnerabilities. These vulnerabilities are not limited to those existing in information systems but also include vulnerabilities in personnel practices, physical security and other aspects of the environment.

A second aspect of the risk assessment is an examination of potential threats. The assessment of threats again is not limited to those who would solely act against the information systems but includes all potential threats, such as forces of nature and accidents. Focusing on threat alone can be detracting: proving the existence of an actual threat can be impossible. A threat consists of both the capability to act and the motivation to act. Malicious acts against information systems can be performed with ordinary capabilities, thus eliminating the capability as a distinguishing feature of a threat. Motivation can change in a nanosecond, thereby changing a non-threat into a threat almost instantaneously. Advance notification of hostile intent is clearly not a distinguishing characteristic of threat either, then. Since threats cannot be completely identified in advance, postulation of threats is a useful tool. Considering every type of threat that may take action provides a comprehensive assessment of the potential dangers that exist. This understanding can underscore assessment of value and aid decision processes related to assignment of resources.

With an understanding of vulnerabilities and threats comes the opportunity to incorporate safeguards and countermeasures into the operational environment. These countermeasures also contribute to the risk assessment, both for the protections they offer and the new vulnerabilities they may introduce into the environment. An example of a vulnerability introduced by a countermeasure is that of the compromised password: the password is a countermeasure to a vulnerability, but contains its own vulnerabilities that must be assessed and understood. Finally, the value of elements within the environment must be assessed in order to give context to the risk assessment. The impact of a compromise of a school lunch menu is markedly different from the impact of compromise of an electronic payment system, and the measures to mitigate such impact commensurate with that value.

Once the risk assessment has provided a comprehensive understanding of the operational environment, then decisions can be made on how protective measures will be incorporated into the environment. The protective capabilities include both technological and non-technological aspects, as mentioned previously. Technologies can include firewalls, cryptography and automated audit capabilities, while non-technological capabilities include enforcing practices, setting policies and operating with due diligence.

The protections must be assumed to be less than 100% certain, however. Protection is only the first part of a continuity of capabilities planning activity. Once protective measures are in place, detective measures must be incorporated. It does no good to lock a door if the lock is never checked for integrity; neither does it do any good to have a fence if the fence is never checked for holes. Similarly, the protective measures in an operational environment must be checked for correctness and continued viability through detection capabilities. This then places the enterprise in a position to respond when a breach of security is detected in order to correct the situation.

The ability to manage the implementation and ongoing operations of a comprehensive Protect-Detect-Correct capability is obviously much more than computer science. It requires managerial skills, operational security skills, physical security skills, and system engineering skills as well. This leads to the inevitable conclusion that effective information assurance requires more than skilful computer scientists and more than stand alone technology solutions.

Succeeding the Nation-State?

The rise of the city state as the dominant geopolitical entity in an information rich environment is predicted by more than one futurist. Paul Saffo, in some speeches, provides evidence that this change is already underway. He stated at the 2007 World Economic Forum that "There's less than 50 percent chance that the United States will exist as a nation by the middle of this century. And that that is actually a good news." He then used Silicon Valley as a case study to explore the future of what he terms the modern city-state that will not supplant nations but eclipse nations in importance to every day people[12]. Should Saffo be correct or even close in his prediction, the whole notion of competitiveness and warfare will probably need to change as well.

What would a "war" between San Francisco and Shanghai look like? Probably very different than a "war" between the US and China. But we know from history that geopolitical structures evolve and change according to what is going on in the world. So possibly this is an important element to consider when contemplating cyber warfare.

---

[12] "See, for example, Saffo, Paul, in the video at this link. http://www.wired.com/epicenter/2007/09/paul-saffo-pred/

Another issue is how "money" is issued and controlled. In memory, the role of issuing and guaranteeing a currency has been the role of a national government. The currency movements have been taxed in order to fund the workings of the state (roads, military, etc). Yet today we see the rise of non-state currencies, including frequent flyer miles, virtual gold, game points, and even virtual currencies such as BitCoin[13], all of which are out of the direct control of national governments. When governments no longer have exclusive authority and control over the creation and transfer of wealth, how will governments fund state functions and how ultimately will they control the people who inhabit their territory? It's an interesting question, particularly when one considers the fact that the currency innovations mentioned above all exist exclusively in cyberspace. This then potentially creates a conflict of interest between a government and its citizens.

Going Forward

In reading through the papers that comprise this book, the reader is asked to consider several questions, all of which have no answers at this point in time. However, it is both the consideration of the concepts and the subsequent discussion that are critical to the development of mutual agreements on civil behavior and legitimate competition.

There are three aspects that the reader is asked to consider:

1) Legal: how should acts of aggression in cyberspace be considered from a legal perspective?

2) Doctrinal: how should acts of aggression in cyberspace be considered from a doctrinal perspective?

---

[13] From Wikipedia: "Bitcoin is a digital currency created in 2009 by Satoshi Nakamoto. The name also refers both to the open source software he designed to make use of the currency and to the peer-to-peer network formed by running that software. Unlike other digital currencies, Bitcoin avoids central authorities and issuers. Bitcoin uses a distributed database spread across nodes of a peer-to-peer network to journal transactions, and uses digital signatures and proof-of-work to provide basic security functions, such as ensuring that bitcoins can be spent only once per owner and only by the person who owns them."
http://en.wikipedia.org/wiki/Bitcoin

3) Functional: how should the functional aspects of cyber warfare be considered in terms of functionality?

With these questions in mind the papers in this book will pose and focus the challenges to academics, their students and practitioners.

Julie Ryan, D.Sc.
Associate Professor and Chair
Engineering Management and Systems Engineering
George Washington University
1776 G. St. NW Suite 101
Washington, DC, 20052
jjchryan@gwu.edu

How the Pride Attacks

Sabah Al-Fedaghi
Kuwait University, Kuwait

Editorial Commentary

In this paper, Sabah al-Fedaghi addresses a fundamental question that of targeting and executing attacks. Taking his inspiration from the lion, he develops a flow model of attack execution that is quite intriguing. He leads through a conceptual analysis of attack progression, and in doing so provides both indicators as to where 'indications and warning' data might be captured and where intercession might be possible. Understanding attack patterns is, of course, a critical component to effective defense. If information warfare is to be a real component of geopolitical conflict, then attack patterns will develop and will be seen. Proactively putting sentinels to detect and alert on such attack activity would be critical. This type of analysis provides the type of proactive and probabilistic detection structure needed for effective defense.

Abstract: The aim of this paper is to develop a general conceptual model for attack progression that can be applied to modeling of computer and communication threat risks. An attack is a group of activities including actions carried out by an adversary, the attacker, on a potential victim. The paper focuses on attacks that aim at overpowering the victim/prey to gain some benefit. This type of attack seems the most common in the field of computers. A brief review is given of various forms of modeling of information-security attacks with emphasis on use cases, and diagrams of misuse cases. Three kinds of attacks are examined from very diverse domains: (1) those in the animal world, where lion prides exhibit one of the most powerful tactics for overcoming prey, (2) those In the United States Air Force, where pilots use an Attack Cycle that includes detect, locate, identify, decide, execute, target, and assess, and (3) those in computer systems, where an attack has recently been described as comprising six phases: Reconnaissance, Weaponization, Delivery, Compromise/Exploit, Command-and-control, and Exfiltration. The paper examines existing models of the last two and introduces a new flow model to facilitate development of a general conceptual model of attacks. The flow model is defined in terms of a transition graph comprising five states. The flow model is a uniform method for representing things that "flow," i.e., things that are received, processed, created, released, and/or transferred. Examples of "things that flow" (flowthings) include information, materials (e.g., in manufacturing), and money. A basic principle of the model is separation of various flowthings and identification of their flows. Accordingly, the conceptual picture of a pride's attack includes streams of flows of signals (from the environment), information, plans, decisions, and actions. These flows can trigger each other. The conceptual description includes the spheres of the attacker and those of the defender. Matters located in the defender's sphere are necessary for completely specifying the progression of the attack. We claim that such a methodology of attack modeling provides a more effective analysis in the fields of threat modeling and secure software development.

Keywords: conceptual model, attacks, information flow, security, threat risk

1. Introduction

Remember how the pride attacks the pack, Not the group at front but one from the back, This is the only way the devil can succeed, Entering your mind at its greatest time of need —*Luke Easter*

http://en.wikipedia.org/wiki/Lion

Information-security attack modeling has been developed in various forms, e.g., attack trees, use cases, misuse cases, scenarios and services, and asset analysis (Gordon et al. 2005), and have been applied for many purposes, e.g., security requirements specification and identification of commonly occurring attack patterns. As a sample method of description, attack trees are used to analyze attacks through identification of security vulnerabilities and of compromises caused by attackers. An attack tree represents a damaging event. Branches of the tree elaborate the methods by which that event could occur.

These types of descriptions are complemented by (security) use cases and misuse cases that have been used to identify security requirements, for documentation purposes, and to stipulate high level security patterns. Misuse (abuse) cases are extended use cases utilized in the specification of security threats. They include such additional relationships as *prevents*, *detects*, and *threatens*. Figure 1 shows sample use and misuse cases.

Nevertheless, this type of description does not describe an attack; rather, it identifies basic entities and relationships involved in security threats. In this paper we propose a more elaborate conceptual picture that allows visualization of the activities involved in the attack phenomenon.

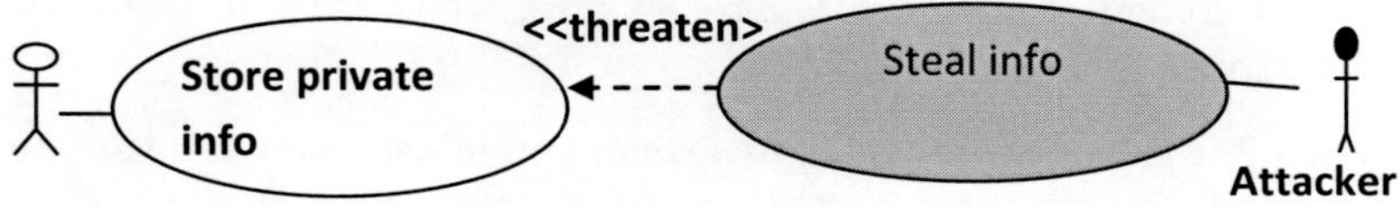

Figure 1: Sample use case/misused case (partially from Røstad, 2006)

Here we define an attack as a group of activities including actions carried out by an adversary, the attacker, on a potential victim/prey. To reduce the domain of study we focus on attacks aimed at overpowering the victim/prey to gain some benefit. This type of attack seems the most common type of attack in the area of computers. According to Cloppert (2009b),

By far and away, the goals of the most sophisticated adversaries in 2009 are focused on the surreptitious acquisition of sensitive information for the purposes of competitive economic advantage, or to counter, kill, or clone the technologies of one's nation-state adversaries.

We also notice that in many attack-related studies, the focus of analysis is on improving decision making. The Observation-Orientation-Decision-Action (OODA) model offers synthesized conceptualization of information warfare for use in the Air Force (Schechtman 1996; Brumley 2006). Information is analyzed and combined with existing knowledge during the Orientation step, to produce a model for decision making.

Decision making is an important factor in construction of a rationality-based model that allows choosing from alternatives by moving through a series of steps. In contrast, our approach provides a descriptive model encapsulating structured knowledge captured from the real-world phenomenon of attacking. "Descriptive" here refers to identifying the "attack progression" though its various phases intertwined with causal relationships (e.g., detection of the prey triggers locating it). This type of model facilitates understanding of and communication about the notion of attack.

In the next section we examine attacks in three different contexts:

- In the animal world, where a lion pride exhibits one of the most powerful tactics for overcoming prey
- In the U.S. Air Force, where pilots use Attack Cycle
- In computer systems, where an attack has recently been described in terms of six phases

In section 3, a new flow model is reviewed, and in section 4 it is used to model or redesign the three contexts of attacks mentioned above. Section 4 ends with introduction of a general attack model incorporating these various types of attacks.

2. Three kinds of attacks

To draw a general conceptual picture of an attack, we examine three attacks from very diverse domains: animals, military, and computers.

2.1. Prides attack

Lions are predators that live in a group called a pride that occupies a pride area. Lionesses take the role of hunters in the majority of coordinated hunting efforts by the pride. They proceed as a coordinated group in effectively monitoring, selecting, pursuing, and bringing down the kill. Lionesses plan the attack by encircling the herd from different points and targeting the closest prey. Before initiating the attack, they sneak up close to their prey, taking advantage of factors such as cover and reduced visibility. The attack involves catching the victim, and killing it (mostly) by strangulation, especially of large prey, by enclosing the animal's mouth and nostrils in its jaws.

This sequence of actions by lionesses involves processes that can be used as a template for modeling attacks. A conceptual model of this pride attack will be developed after our flow model is introduced. The model represents an initial version of an attack description that will then be enriched with details from the other two complex attack environments.

2.2. USAF attack model

The United States Air Force Intelligence Targeting Guide (USAF 1998) uses the attack cycle functions shown in Figure 2. The six mission functions of the cycle interact continuously at the decision stage in target analysis.

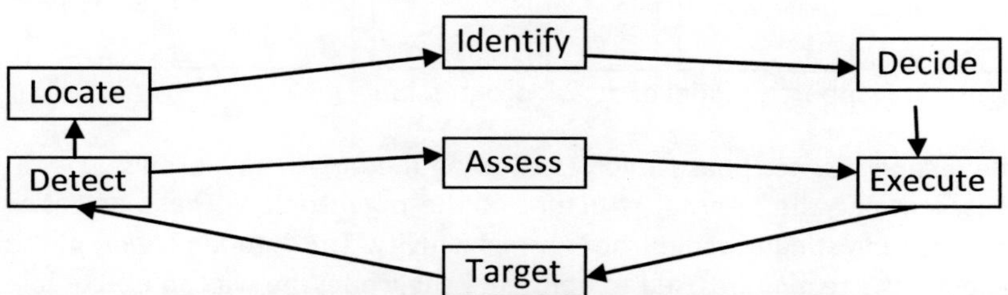

Figure 2: USAF Intelligence Targeting Guide attack cycle functions (USAF 1998).

Comparing this model with lionesses' attack methodology, the following can be observed.

- The first step for lionesses seems to be "awareness" of something in their pride area. This can be considered detection in the USAF model.
- Accordingly, a locating process is activated.
- The next crucial step for lionesses is identification of the intrusion "thing": is it potential food (e.g., wildebeest, impala, zebra, buffalo), or a challenge (adult rhinoceros, elephant)?
- The next step is not deciding as in the USAF model; rather, it is collecting information about the target such as density of the pack, presence of small or weak members, etc.
- Lionesses also depart from the USAF model in the next step, which is planning the attack before deciding. Each lioness plays a role and takes a position, encircling the herd while "calculating" even the direction of the wind during the planned attack.

Contrasts in the two methodologies will become clearer when the pride attack is described in terms of our flow model.

2.3. Cloppert's model

In the context of computer forensics, Cloppert (2009) conceptualizes the phases of an attack in six sequential stages (Figure 3). Some phases may occur in parallel, and the order of phases can be interchanged.

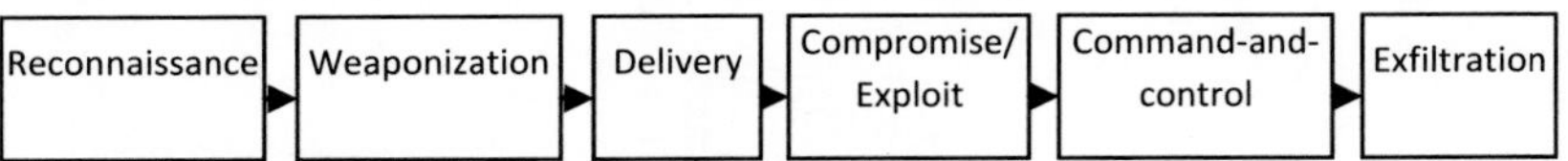

Figure 3: Cloppert's model of attack progression

The *reconnaissance* phase involves knowing the target, e.g., browsing websites, learning the internal structure of the organization. These activities are often indistinguishable from normal activity. The *weaponization* phase reflects "the technique used to obfuscate shellcode, the way an executable is packed into a trojaned document, etc. Only by reverse engineering of delivered payloads is an understanding of an adversary's weaponization achieved" (Cloppert 2009). *Delivery* is the phase where "the payload is delivered to its target such as an HTTP request containing SQL injection code or an email with a hyperlink to a compromised website." The *compromise* phase includes elements of software, human, or hardware vulnerabilities. This phase results in "the compromised host behaving according to the attacker's plan as a result of the execution of the delivered payload (e.g., running an EXE attachment to an email)." This phase may include subphases such as "the delivery of shellcode that pull down and execute more capable code upon execution." The *command-and-control* phase represents the period after which adversaries leverage the exploit of a system. Communication back to "the adversary often must be made before any potential for impact to data can be realized."

Cloppert's (2009) phases lump a great deal of semantics. The basic ingredients we conceptualize as necessary to describe an attack differ drastically from Cloppert's phases. First, in an attack we must identify what is being "transferred" between adversaries. In fencing, the duelists exchange thrusts, and in boxing, they transfer punches. Attacks in fencing and in boxing are first described in terms of thrusts and punches, respectively, that *flow* between the attacker and the defender. These *things that flow* between adversaries are explained in terms of the way in which they are created (generated), received, transferred, released, and processed (twisted, strong, etc.). Things that flow from/to an attacker may be of different kinds. The attacker receives information, transfers a punch, creates a (fault) signal. Each kind has its own sphere of flow. For example, to describe a cheating card player, we must examine his/her information, signals, and actions. For example, we can observe that Cloppert's reconnaissance phase includes signals (communication carriers), information (knowledge), and actions dimensions. This phase, in Cloppert's words, includes "knowing Internal structure of the organization"; hence it may include eavesdropping (signals), browsing of Web sites (information), and actual visits to the organization (actions).

In the next section we introduce our specification methodology — called the flow model (FM) — which allows a greater opportunity to scrutinize previous descriptions in terms of our standpoint.

3. Flow model

The flow model is basically a lifecycle specification of things that flow (e.g., information). Lifecycle and flow are familiar notions (Al-Fedaghi 2006). The Air Force Information Resources Management system (Department of the Air Force 1995; Schechtman, 1996) specifies cradle-to-grave information management in terms of the information lifecycle:

Create→Use→Store→Destruct.

This lifecycle is conceptually incomplete. Suppose a piece of information is created that is then transmitted. Transmission in the channel means it enters a different stage of its life that is different from states of being created, used, stored, or destroyed. The information can be destroyed while being transferred, but is this different from being destroyed while stored? What is needed is a "state transaction" model for life cycle that includes exclusive (i.e., being in state A excludes being in any other state) and complete states of information.

The Flow Model (FM) was first introduced by Al-Fedaghi (1946) nd has been used since then in several applications such as software requirements, communication, and business processes (2009a, 2009b) This section provides a review of the basic model as it has been described in other publications, and it includes new aspects of the model.

A flow model is a uniform method for representing things that "flow," i.e., things that are exchanged, processed, created, transferred, and communicated. "Things that flow" include information, materials (e.g., manufacturing), and money.

To simplify this review of FM, we introduce a method of describing *information* flow (Al-Fedaghi, 2006). There are five states of information: transferred, received, processed, created, and released, as illustrated in Figure 4. The model can also be defined in terms of a transition graph with five states, as we describe later in the paper. Information can be stored, copied, destroyed, used, etc. in any of the five generic stages. As a flow structure, the model is characterized by five stages: receiving, processing, creating, releasing, and transferring. In Figure 4, flows are denoted by solid arrows and may trigger other types of flow, denoted by dashed arrows.

The environment in which information exists is called its infosphere (e.g., computer, human mind, organization information system, department information system). The infosphere is described in terms of the five-stage schema (hereafter, "schema").

The schema is reusable because a copy of it is assigned to each entity. An entity may have multiple subspheres, each with its own flow schema.

In Cloppert's reconnaissance phase, we first identify "things that flow." Through "browsing websites, pulling down PDF's, learning the internal structure of the target organization," the attacker receives, processes, creates, releases, and transfers signals, information, and actions. Thus, he/she has signal spheres, information spheres, and action spheres where flowthings (signals) move in their stream.

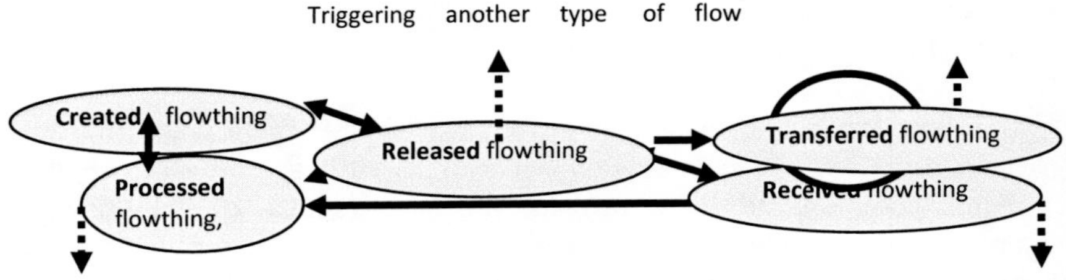

Figure 4: State transition diagram for FM with possible triggering mechanism

While the pride is sleeping under the tree, lionesses *receive* signals (e.g., noise) of something in the pride area. They process the *signals* and take (*create*, *release*, and *transfer*) actions to inspect the intruder. They collect (receive), and process more data (*signals*) to *create* information that is *processed* to *create* more information.

Identifying flowthings in the conceptualized system is a fundamental first step in FM. Flowthings are things that can be received, processed, created, released, or transferred. A conceptualization of a stream of flowthings may not necessarily contains all stages. For example, conceptualization of a physical airport can model the flow of passengers: arriving (received), processed (e.g., language and passports), released (waiting for boarding), and transferred (to planes); however, airports do not *create* passengers. In this case, the schema includes only the stages received, processed, released, and transferred.

The states shown in Figure 4 are exclusive in the sense that if information is in one state, it is not in any of the other four states. Consider a piece of information σ in the possession of a hospital. Then, σ is in the possession of the hospital and in one of the following states:

- 1. σ has just been collected (received) from some source, patient, friend, agency, etc. and stored in the hospital record waiting to be used. It is received (row) information that has not been processed by the hospital.
- 2. σ has been processed in some way, converted to another form (e.g., digital), translated, compressed, etc. In addition, it may be stored in the hospital information system as processed data waiting for some use.
- 3. σ has actually been created in the hospital as the result of doctors' diagnoses, lab tests, and so forth. Thus, σ is in the possession of the hospital as created data to be used.
- 4. σ is being released from the hospital infosphere. It is designated as released information ready for transfer. Analogous to a factory environment, σ represents materials designated as ready to ship outside the factory. It may actually be stored for some period waiting to be transported; nevertheless, its designation as "for export" keeps it in such a state.

- 5. σ is in a transferred state where it is being transferred between two infospheres. It has left the released state and will enter the received state, where it will become received information in the new infosphere.

It is not possible for processed information to directly become received information in the same infosphere schema. Processed information cabecome received information in another infosphere by first becoming released information, then transferred information, in order to arrive (be received) at the other environment.

Consider the seller and buyer information spheres shown in Figure 5 (Al-Fedaghi 2009a). Each contains two schema: one for the flow of orders, and the other for the flow of invoices. In the seller's infosphere, processing of *Order* triggers the creation of *Invoice* in the seller's infosphere, thus initiating the flow of invoices.

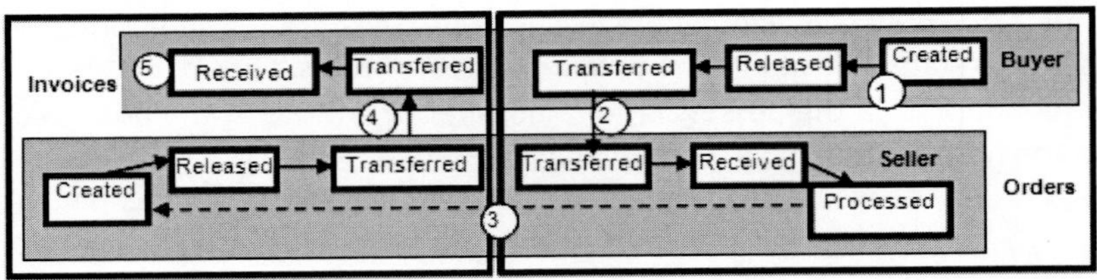

Figure 5: Order flow triggers invoice flow

The reflexive arrow of the communicated state in Figure 4 (state transition diagram) denotes the flow from transfer stage to another transfer stage of another infosphere. In Figure 5, the *Buyer* creates an *Order* that flows by being released and then transferred to the *Seller*. The "transfer components" of the Buyer and the Seller can be viewed as their transmission subsystems, while the arrow between them represents the actual transmission channel.

Figure 5 also illustrates the triggering mechanism between flows of orders and invoices. An important principle in FM is the separation of flows. Orders trigger invoices, and each has its schema in the actor's information sphere.

Formally, FM can be specified as

FM = {Receive*, Process*, Create*, Release*, Transfer*},

where the asterisks indicate secondary stages (Al-Fedaghi 2009b). For example, {Copy, Store, Delete, and Destroy} can represent these secondary stages, as illustrated in Figure 6. We can define the flow between the five generic stages as the directed graph:

{(Receive, Process) (Receive, Release), (Release, Receive), (Process, Create), (Create, Process), (Process, Release), (Release, Process) (Create, Release), (Release, Create), (Release, Transfer)}

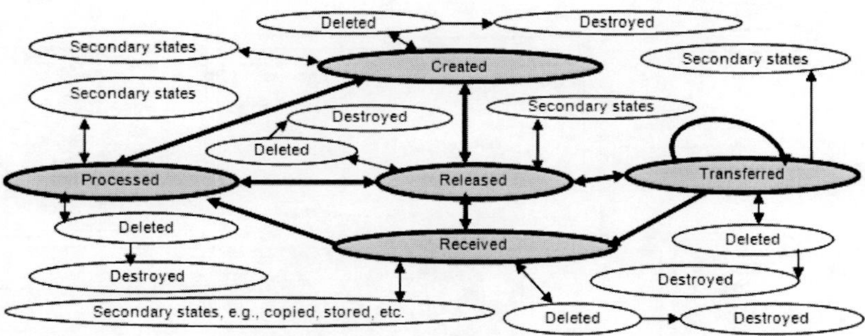

Figure 6: Detailed state diagram for the flow model

One "inaccuracy" in this formalization is the arrows (Release, Receive), (Release, Process), and (Release, Create). Each arrow denotes a "return" flow. For example, if the communication channel is down for a long time, it may be decided to return the "message" to the sender (creator, processor, or receiver) who previously released it. For simplicity's sake, our formalization does not guarantee that the released message is "returned" to its previous state, i.e., an internal sender. If the schema represents a company, then receiving, processing, and creating information are three different departments.

The formalization can be complemented with rules and constraints that permit flow from one state to another.

4. FM Attack model

Consider the pride's attack described previously, conceptualized as shown in Figure 7. Signals are received (detected) in the pride area (circle 1), triggering creation of information (circle 2) that is processed and produces the first type of action (circle 3) of seeking more data. Such a process reaches a threshold (point 4) of creating a plan, making a decision, and taking action to realize the actual attack.

A simplified version is shown in Figure 8 in terms of flows triggering flows. Mapping this pride attack to Cloppert's, we identify similarities and missing elements, as follows.

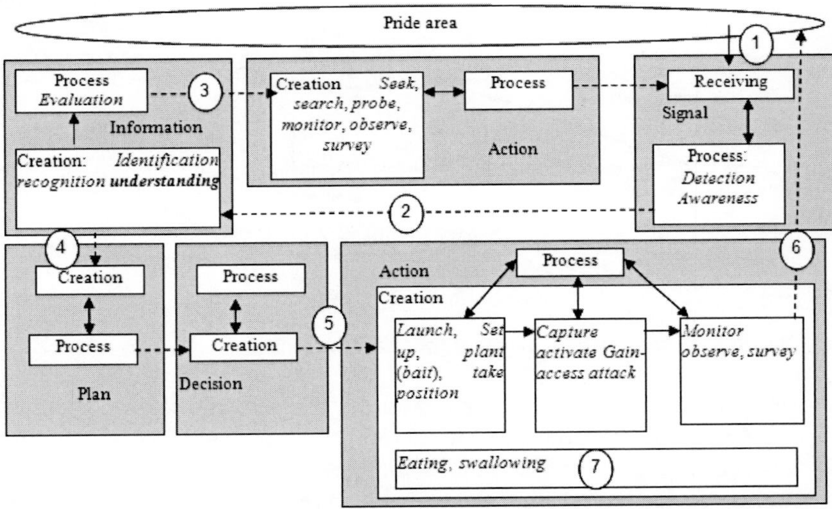

Figure 7: Conceptual model of pride attack

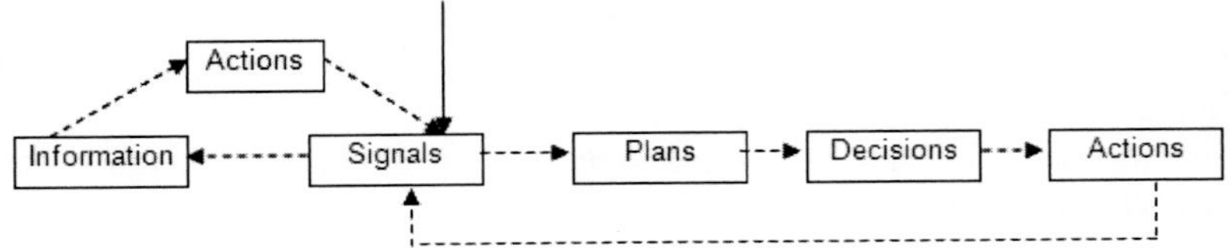

Figure 8: Pride attack modelled in terms of flows triggering flows

In the next subsection, the military-based USAF model and computer-based Cloppert model are inspected to reveal additional operations that can be incorporated into the pride attack model.

4.1. Revisiting the USAF attack model

Cross-examining the FM and USAF attack model, we observe the following with respect to USAF model steps.
Detect, Locate, Identify: These steps fall in the signal-information-actions triangle of Figure 8. Detect denotes the process of receiving signals about an object in the attacker sphere. Locate and identify indicate processing and creating of information triggered by received data. These steps seem to be elements in what the USAF calls *intelligence*.

Decide: These steps are suddenly followed by "decide." This is reasonable since the model represents an air attack where an attack is a reflexive action. In addition, according to USAF (1998), "the attack cycle works on four assumptions ... [including that] there must be direction and guidance provided for each of the six steps. . . . Execution planning prepares input for and supports the actual tasking, construction, and subsequent execution by weapon systems."

The real reflexive action comes from the defender. As we will explain later, upon receiving a sudden attack action, the defender reacts in two ways: reflexive reaction, and a settled reaction involving the signal-information-action triangle and planning. These notions will be incorporated into a more refined conceptual picture than Figure 2.

Execute: This phase represents actions in FM. Thus, in general, "decide-execute" and "decisions-actions" in FM are aligned consecutively in the two models.

Target: This term includes the meanings "capture or destruction" and "disruption, degradation, neutralization, and exploitation, commensurate" (USAF, 1998). These are classified as actions in FM and performed after initiating the attack. Attackers come in different kinds. In addition, the term "exploitation" is used in the Cloppert attack model. These issues will be discussed in the next section.

The USAF (1998) report discusses at length the term "targeting" as an intersection of intelligence and operation. It talks about types of targets and target development, and relates targeting to enemy, goal, objectives, and so forth. In FM this means that some account of the "target or victim, or defender" enters the attack conceptual description. This seems reasonable since the offensive activities are interwoven with defensive activities. Some attack aspects may be well described from a defensive point of view, and, vice versa, some forms of resistance can be viewed well from the perpsective of the attacker.

Assess: This phase in USAF can be mapped in the FM model by the arrow from actions to the signal-information triangle. According to USAF (1998) "After mission execution, the quality of the whole process is assessed. Improvements in force employment, munitions design and situation assessments emerge from this appraisal of post- strike data... The product of this phase is tailored to the decision makers."

"Assess" may also indicate a high-level judgment such as that the attack is successful. Handling of this additional aspect in FM will be discussed later.

4.2. Revisiting Cloppert's attack model

Reconnaissance phase: From the attacker's perspective, reconnoitering is an offensive operation designed to obtain information *before* a battle; however, collection of information usually continues during battle. The three flows to the left—signals, information, and actions—reflect a more general view than the "Reconnaissance phase," as will be described later.
Weaponization phase: This phase is missing from the pride's attack. It can be pictured as a detour that leads to actions in plans in Figure 8.

Delivery phases and Compromise/Exploit: Delivery phase is the action (attack) phase. We note that actions are of different types. Actions in the *Reconnaissance phase* are directed toward the outside environment, including the potential target (e.g., lionesses move closer to a specific kind and size of prey). The action in the delivery phase is directed at the prey itself. In "delivery," "compromise," and "exploit," the semantics become clearer as we specify who is doing what to whom. The direction of the action is also important. In "Delivery," actions are created by the attacker and received by the defender. "Compromise" seems to indicate that the defender does something. "Exploit" seems to indicate that the attacker does something. We view Cloppert's "Compromise/Exploit" phase as an action by the attacker toward the defender.

In attacks such as the pride's attack, however, actions are reciprocal between the attacker and the defender. From the defender's point of view, such action is called resistance. An attack is met with resistance. By "Compromise," it seems that Cloppert shifts from the attacker sphere to the defender sphere. "The compromise phase will possibly have elements of a software vulnerability, a human vulnerability aka 'social engineering,' or a hardware vulnerability" (Cloppert 2009). This implies for us that to completely draw a conceptual picture of an attack, it is necessary to extend the description to the defender sphere. This is what we do when we redraw Figure 8 to include aspects of Cloppert's model.

The command-and-control phase: This phase seems to encompass all elements previously discussed. It includes collecting information during the attack, processing it, planning of the next move in the field, making decisions, and taking the next action.

Exfiltration: This phase involves, in Cloppert's words, "taking the data." This indicates "pulling" flow from the defender to the attacker.

4.3. Revisiting the FM attack model

Taking these additional details into consideration, Figure 9 shows the resulting conceptual picture. The figure includes the spheres of the attacker and those of the defender. Including matters related to the defender is necessary to completely model attacks. This principle was implicitly indicated in the USAF model (Figure 2) in the discussion about "targeting" and types of targets, relating targeting to enemy, goal, objectives, and so forth. These terms refer to the object under attack. The same Idea is embedded in Cloppert's "compromise phase," where the focus shifts to the defender. Surprisingly, many processes can be found in the conceptualization of attacks and resistance to attacks. The first of such processes is the signals-information-action triangle in FM that corresponds partially to intelligence in USAF and to reconnaissance in Cloppert's model.

Dotted oval A contains streams of signals, information, and actions. These three streams of flow are circles 1, 2, and 3 in Figure 7 describing the pride's attack. Initially, the attacker receives signals from its environment (outside), but during the attack it also receives signals from the defender itself. Lionesses who receive buffalo noise "pull up" updated signals about the buffalo's condition. In military battles, communication signals are continuously analyzed. Cloppert's command-and-control phase involves collection of signals-information during the attack. Hence, in Figure 9, signals flow between the attacker and the defender.

The defender has the counter part of oval A: oval E. The defender also receives signals from the environment and processes them. They trigger information that, in turn triggers more signal-action (e.g., who is attacking me? size? direction?, how heavy?). Oval E is the signal-information-action of the defender.

Returning to the attacker sphere, we see that Cloppert's Weaponization phase can be attached to the "plan" flow (oval B) as a type of action in preparation for the attack. These actions involve creation of a weapon.

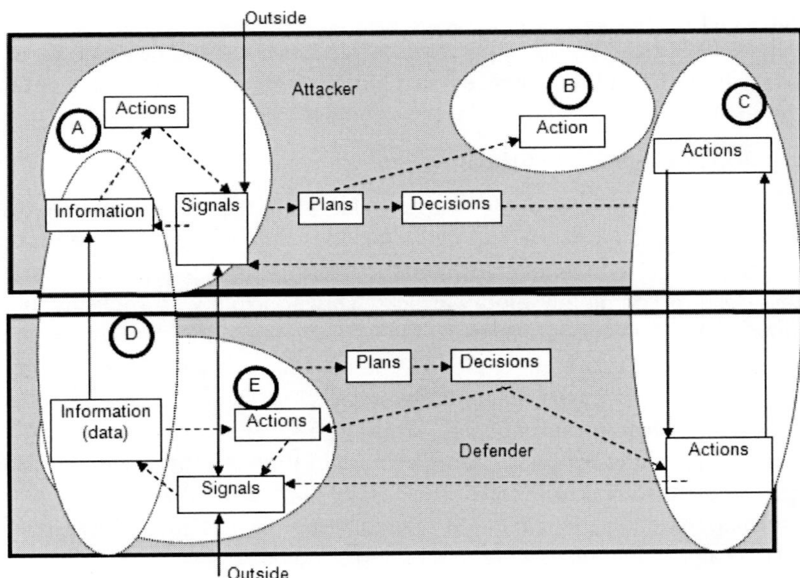

Figure 9: Streams of flow of attacker and defender

After the decision to attack, it is time to take action, where the action (attack) flows from the attacker to the defender (oval C). This flow is indicated by a solid arrow from oval C to oval A. This corresponds to "Delivery phases" and partially to "Compromise/Exploit phase" in Cloppert's model; however, Figure 9 indicates that the defender may in its turn deliver reflexive counter actions. This is shown in oval C by a solid arrow from the defender to the attacker.

Alternatively, the defender may respond in a settled way: upon receiving the action, it triggers "pull up" signals in oval E (strength of the attack, time frequency, and so forth). Here we complete the cycle, with the defender receiving signals and processing them for information that triggers defensive action. The defender processes data from its environment and from the attack itself.

Finally, dotted oval D represents Cloppert's Exfiltration, where the attacker "pulls up" data from the defender's information sphere.

5. Conclusion

This paper proposes a general conceptual model for attack progression that can be applied to modeling of computer and communication threat risks. Three kinds of attacks are examined from very diverse domains: the animal world, the U.S. Air Force, and computer systems. Accordingly, a flow model for attacks has been developed. The conceptual description includes the spheres of the attacker and the defender. Such attack description provides the possibility of more elaborate analysis in the fields of threats modeling and secure software development. Further work would apply the resulting model to description of actual computer attacks.

References

Al-Fedaghi, S. (2009a) "Conceptualization in state machines, statecharts, and flow model," Int. Rev. Comput. Software (IRECOS).

Al-Fedaghi, S. (2009b) "Conceptualization of business processes," IEEE Asia-Pacific Services Computing Conference (IEEE APSCC 2009), Dec 7-11, 2009, Biopolis, Singapore.

Al-Fedaghi, S. (2006) "Some aspects of personal information theory," 7th Annual IEEE Information Assurance Workshop (IEEE-IAW 2006), United States Military Academy, West Point, NY. http://ieeexplore.ieee.org/stamp/stamp.jsp?arnumber=01652066

Brumley, L., Kopp, C., and Korb, K. (2006) The Orientation step of the OODA loop and Information Warfare.

http://www.csse.monash.edu.au/courseware/cse468/2006/Lectures/OODA-Loop-BKK-IWC7-2006.pdf

Cloppert , M. (2009a) Security Intelligence: Attacking the Kill Chain, SANS Institute Computer Forensic Blog, October 14. https://blogs.sans.org/computer-forensics/2009/10/14/security-intelligence-attacking-the-kill-chain/

Cloppert , M. (2009b) Security Intelligence: Introduction, SANS Institute Computer Forensic Blog, July 22. https://blogs.sans.org/computer-forensics/2009/07/22/security-intelligence-introduction-pt-1/

Department of the Air Force (1995, August) Vistas: Air Force Information Resources Management Strategic Plan. Washington: HQ USAF.

Gordon, D., Stehney, T., Wattas, N., and Yu, E. (2005) System Quality Requirements Engineering (SQUARE): Case Study on Asset Management System, Phase II, Carnegie Mellon University http://www.cert.org/archive/pdf/05sr005.pdf

Røstad, L. (2006) "An extended misuse case notation: Including vulnerabilities and the insider threat," 12th REFSQ conference. http://www.di.unipi.it/REFSQ06/Papers/01%20Rostad.pdf

Schechtman, G. M. (1996) Manipulating the OODA loop: The overlooked role of information resource management in information warfare. Accessed December 2009. http://www.au.af.mil/au/awc/awcgate/afit/schec_gm.pdf

USAF Intelligence Targeting Guide. (1998) "Chapter 1: Targeting and the Target." Air Fiorce Pamphlet 14-210 Intelligence, 1 February. http://www.fas.org/irp/doddir/usaf/afpam14-210/part09.htm

Towards An Intelligent Software Agent System As Defense Against Botnets

E. Dembskey and E. Biermann
School of Computing, CSET, UNISA, Pretoria, South Africa
and French South African Institute of Technology
Cape and Peninsula University of Technology, Cape Town, South Africa

Editorial Commentary

It is useful to consider the notion of information competition without the distraction of technology in order to really appreciate the fundamentals. Information is a critical part of human existence: the ability to imagine, to project one concept onto another, to communicate ideas, and to coerce, deny, and distract others. Appreciating how information competition occurred in a previous age provides context to an analysis of technologically based competition in the information age.

Abstract: Computer networks are targeted by state and non-state actors and criminals. With the professionalization and commoditization of malware we are moving into a new realm where off-the-shelf and time-sharing malware can be bought or rented by the technically unsophisticated. The commoditization of malware comes with all the benefits of mass produced software, including regular software updates, access to fresh exploits and the use of hack farms. To an extent defense is out of the hands of the government, and in the hands of commercial and private hands. However, the cumulative effect of Information Warfare attacks goes beyond the commercial and private spheres and affects the entire state. Thus the responsibility for defense should be distributed amongst all actors within a state. As malware increases and becomes more sophisticated and innovative in their attack vectors, command & control structures and operation, more sophisticated, innovative and collaborative methods are required to combat them. The current scenario of partial protection due to resource constraints is inadequate. It is thus necessary to create defence systems that are robust and resilient against known vectors and vectors that have not previously been used in a manner that is easy and cheap to implement across government, commercial and private networks without compromising security. We argue that a significant portion of daily network defence must be allocated to software agents acting in a beneficent botnet with distributed input from human actors, and propose a framework for this purpose. This paper is based the preliminary work of a PhD thesis on the topic of using software agents to combat botnets, and covers the preliminary literature survey and design of the solution. This includes a crowd sourcing component that uses information about malware gained from software agents and from human users. Part of this work is based on previous research by the authors. It is anticipated that the research will result in a clearer understanding of the role of software agents in the role of defence against computer network operations, and a proof-of-concept implementation.

Keywords: Information Warfare, Botnet, Software Agent

1. Introduction

We propose to use distributed software agents (SA) as a method for overcoming botnets and other malware in the area of Information Warfare (IW). This area of research is important due to the growing threat posed by malware. This research addresses some of the long term research goals identified by the US National Research Council (National Research Council (U.S.). Committee on the Role of Information Technology in Responding to Terrorism et al. 2003) and four of the ten suggested research areas in (Denning, Denning 2010). It is an extension and refinement of research undertaken to determine if an IW SA agent framework is viable (Dembskey, Biermann 2008).

Malware is a reality of networked computers and is being increasingly used by state, criminal and terrorist actors as weapons, vectors for crime and tools of coercion. While it is debatable whether a digital Pearl Harbour is a genuine possibility (Smith 1998), it is agreed that malware is on the increase and is being commoditized (Knapp, Boulton 2008, Microsoft 2010, Dunham, Melnick 2009), though there is some dissent on this point (Prince 2010). Technically unsophisticated users can purchase time on existing botnets to accomplish some goal, e.g. phishing attacks, spamming, or the denial, destruction or modification of data.

A botnet is a distributed group of software agent-like bots that run autonomously and automatically, usually without the knowledge of the computers owner. Botnets are usually, but not necessarily, malicious. The purpose of botnets is not necessarily destructive; it is often financial gain, which results in a very different approach to development and Command & Control. An effective process of prevention, detection and removal will mitigate botnets regardless of their purpose.

IW is warfare that explicitly recognises information as an asset. Computer Network Operations (CNO) is a form of IW that uses global computer networks to further the aims of warfare. CNO is divided into Computer Network Attack (CNA) and Computer Network Defence (CND). Increasingly, politically motivated cyber attacks are focusing on commercial and not government infrastructure (Knapp, Boulton 2008). Also, money from online scams may be used to fund terrorist and further criminal activity.

SA are a form of software that have the properties of intelligence, autonomy and mobility. We define SA as programs that autonomously and intelligently acquire, manipulate, distribute and maintain information on behalf of a user or another software agent.

Intrusion prevention is the Holy Grail of security. This goal is currently unobtainable; there will be intrusions. The literature shows that traditional defences such as firewalls, antivirus and intrusion prevention are not effective against botnets (Ollmann 2010). Some researchers believe that anti-malware software is less effective than in the past (Oram, Viega 2009). Researchers at Microsoft (Microsoft 2010) assert that malware activity increased 8.9% from first to second half of 2009. This is probably an overly conservative figure. Some researchers estimate that botnet infections are up to 4000% higher than reported (Dunham, Melnick 2009). One major problem in prevention is that social engineering (Bailey et al. 2009) is a major cause of infection, which defeats many prevention systems and undermines detection.

One development that will likely impact the malware threatscape is the arrival of broadband access to Africa. For an analysis of the impact see (Jansen van Vuuren, Phahlamohlaka & Brazzoli 2010). It is estimated that there are 100 million computers available for botnet herders to use (Carr, Shepherd 2010). However, we are of the opinion that, due to a range of socio-economic factors, Africa may be a source of volunteers for botnets similar to Israel's Defenderhosting.

2. Malware

Malware is a term encompassing all the different categories of malicious software, which include amongst others Trojans, viruses, worms and spyware. The advancements in technology and especially the ability to be 24/7 connected to people and resources across the globe have hugely increased the volumes of malware circulating global networks. This is evident from the large amount of spam constantly and increasingly being delivered to mailboxes. According to Damballa (2009) the success of spamming botnets has led to the commoditization of spam in which volume has become the primary means to generate cash.

Malware are created and initiated in countries across the globe with different websites listing different statistics regarding the country of origin, on a weekly basis. For example the USA, China and Russia are being listed by The Spamhaus Project[14] as the countries where the largest percentage of spam are created and exported, while M86 Security Labs[15] list the US, India and Brazil as the recent largest contributors.

Creating or obtaining malware has become relatively easy with the evolution of technology and especially the commoditization of malicious code. Different types of malware can be obtained via malware kits or through specialists offering their services to design and develop unique pieces of malicious code for different platforms or forums. Some of the more famous examples include *Webattacker*, *Smeg*, *Fragus*, *Zeus* and *Adpack.*

The evolution and spread of malware is directly related to the number of entities being connected, with the increase in not only the amount but also the different types of malware being evident today. With the increase in malware also came constant research and development to combat these unwanted software, which in turn leads to the creators of malware to be more innovative. According to Chiang & Lloyd (2007), the traditional method of using the Internet Relay Chat (IRC) protocol for command and control made way for new methods of hiding the command and control

---

14 http://www.spamhaus.org/statistics/countries.lasso

15 http://www.m86security.com/labs/spam_statistics.asp

communication such as HTTP based communications, encryption and peer-to-peer networks as it became easier to detect and block IRC traffic. This became evident in the creation and re-invention of botnets such as *Agobot* (Wang, 2009), *Rustock* (Chiang & Lloyd, 2007) and *Conficker* (Porras, 2009).

The impact of the advances, commoditization and the DIY culture for the creation of malware on global networks and especially global security is huge. Malware is being used to amongst others steal personal data, conduct espionage, harm government and business operations, deny user access to information and services and according to the report conducted by the International Organization for Economic co-operation and Development (OECD, 2007) poses a serious threat to the Internet economy. Securing networks is not only depended on security vendors and security specialists but also rely on normal users of the networks to protect their stations. The increasing use of social networks such as Facebook, Twitter and MySpace as well as mobile generation provide increasing grounds for malware to access contact details and personal information.

It is vital for the Internet economy that robust and resilient counter systems needs to be constantly in operation, while adapting to changing conditions.

3. Current Malware Detection Techniques

The first hint of a malware infection may be the receipt of an email stating that a system appears to be infected and has abused a different system; the convention is that administrative contacts of some form are listed at global regional information registry sites such as AfriNIC, ARIN, APNIC, LAPNIC and RIPE to assist in communication. The abuse may take the form of spam, scanning activity, DDoS attacks, phishing or harassment ((Schiller, Binkley & Harley 2007).

It is a poor security method indeed that relies on informants only. A better approach is the use of network-monitoring tools such as wireshark or tcpdump as malware activity results in data that can be analysed. Examples of prevalent data types are (Bailey et al. 2009):

- DNS Data: Data regarding name resolution can be obtained by mirroring data to and from DNS servers and can be used to detect both botnet attack behaviour.

- Netflow Data: Netflow data represents information gathered from the network by sampling traffic flows and obtaining information regarding source and destination IP addresses and port numbers. This is not available on all networks.
- Packet Tap Data: Packet tap data, while providing a more fine grained view than netflow but is generally more costly in terms of hardware and computation. Simple encryption reduces this visibility back to the same order as netflow.
- Address Allocation Data: Knowing where hosts and users are in the network can be a powerful tool for identifying malware reconnaissance behaviour and rapid attribution.
- Honeypot Data: Placed on a network with the express intention of them being turned into botnet members, honeypots can be a powerful tool for gaining insight into botnet means and motives.
- Host Data: Host level data, from OS and application configurations, logs and user activity provides a wealth of security information and can avoid the visibility issues with encrypted data.

An even better method is an Intrusion Detection System (IDS). An IDS can either be Host-Based Detection System (HIDS) or Network-Based Detection System (NIDS). Both of these are further categorised by the type of algorithm used, namely anomaly- and signature-based detection. Anomaly–based techniques develop an understanding of what normal behaviour is on a system, and reports any deviation. Signature-based techniques use representations of known malware to decide if software is indeed malicious. A specialised form of anomaly-based detection, called specification-based detection makes use of a rule set to decide if software is malicious. Violation of these rules indicates possible malicious software.

A NIDS sees protected hosts in terms of the external interfaces to the rest of the network, rather than as a single system, and gets most of its results by network packet analysis. Much of the data used is the same as discussed using the manual methods above. A HIDS focuses on individual systems. That doesn't mean each host runs its own HIDS application, they are generally administered centrally, rather it means that the HIDS monitors activity on a protected host. It can pick up evidence of breaches that have evaded outward-facing NIDS and firewall systems or have been introduced by other means, such internal attacks, direct tampering from internal users and the introduction of malicious code from removable media (Schiller, Binkley & Harley 2007).

Malware can also be detected forensically. Though this occurs after damage has been incurred, it is important for a number of reasons including legal purposes. Forensic aims can include identification, preservation, analysis, and presentation of evidence. Digital investigations that are or might be presented in a court of law must meet the applicable standards of admissible evidence. Admissibility is a concept that varies according to jurisdiction (Schiller, Binkley & Harley 2007).

Two techniques that are essentially forensic in nature are darknets and honeynets, though the knowledge gained from their use helps to prevent, detect and remove botnets. A darknet is a closed private network used for file sharing. However, the term has been extended in the security sphere to apply to IP address space that is routed but which no active hosts and therefore no legitimate traffic. Darknets are most useful as global resource for sites and groups working against botnets on an Internet-wide basis (Schiller, Binkley & Harley 2007). A honeypot is a decoy system set up to attract attackers and study their methods and capabilities. A honeynet is usually defined as consisting of a number of honeypots in a network, offering the attacker real systems, applications, and services to work on and monitored transparently by a Layer 2 bridging device (honeywall). A static honeynet can quickly be spotted and blacklisted by attackers, but distributed honeynets attempt to address that issue and are likely to capture richer, more varied data (Schiller, Binkley & Harley 2007). In contrast to honeynets, darknets do not advertise themselves.

Botnets, the malware we are interested in, are difficult to combat for the following reasons (Bailey et al. 2009):

- All aspects of the botnet's life-cycle are all evolving constantly.
- Each detection technique comes with its own set of tradeoffs with respect to false positives and false negatives.
- Different types of networks approach the botnet problem with differing goals, with different visibility into the botnet behaviours, and different sources of data with which to uncover those behaviours.

A successful solution for combating botnets will need to cope with each of these realities and their complex interactions with each other.

4. Software Agents

A software agent is a program that autonomously acquires, manipulates, distributes and maintains information on behalf of some entity. We reject the trend of labeling software utilities such as aggregators and download managers as SA; we base our definition on the properties of the software. The literature defines a large number of agent properties. Not all properties are found in all agents, but an in order to be termed Agent software must satisfy some minimum set of these properties. Bigus and Bigus (Bigus, Bigus 2001) suggest that these are autonomy, intelligence and mobility. These properties are defined as follows:

- Autonomy - The autonomous agent exercises control over its own actions and has some degree of control over its internal state. It displays judgment when faced with a situation requiring a decision, and makes a decision without direct external intervention.
- Intelligence - This does not imply self-awareness, but the ability to behave rationally and pursue a goal in a logical and rational manner. Intelligence varies between simple coded logic and complex AI-based methods such as inferencing and learning.
- Mobility- Mobility is the degree to which agents move through the network. Some may be static while others may migrate as the need arises. The decision to move should be made by the agent (Murch, Johnson 1999), thus ensuring the agent has the property of autonomy.

From these properties we can judge that SA have potential applications in dealing with tasks that are ill-defined or less structured. It is also apparent that SA interact with their task environments locally; the implication of this is that the same agent can exhibit different behaviour in different environments (Liu 2001). Padgham & Winikoff ((Padgham, Winikoff 2004)) provide a list of reasons why agents are useful, including loose coupling, decentralisation, persistence, better functioning in open and complex systems and reactiveness as well as proactivness.

The use of SA to combat botnets is not unprecedented. It had already been suggested that AF.MIL should be purposely made part of a botnet (Williams 2008). Some researchers see botnets as types of SA (Bigus, Bigus

2001). Other researchers ((Stytz, Banks 2008)) have begun to work on the problem of implementing such an approach.

5. Proposed System

Vulnerabilities are introduced in software deliberately or accidently during development, or via software or configuration changes during operation. Botnets are not typically introduced during software development and thus require later introduction, and usually unintentionally. Possible vectors of infection are viruses, worms and Trojans. These may be introduced via email, download, drive-by download, network worm or some external storage device. According to (Cruz 2008) the majority of infections occur due to downloads (53%) and infection via other malware (43%). Email and removable drives account for 22% of infections. Instant Messaging, vulnerabilities, P2P, iFrame compromises, other infected files and other vectors account for 27% (the total is higher than 100% because some malware uses multiple vectors). The vast majority of infections are as a result of downloads, suggesting this should be the primary threat to mitigate. This is the attitude adopted in this research, with the recognition that this could change at any time, temporarily or permanently, thus necessitating a system that is flexible enough to cope with this change.

Several methods to detect and deter botnets have been proposed such as incorporating data mining techniques as well as incorporating methods to detect communication between the bot and the master (Massud *et al.,* 2008).

Massive multiplayer online role playing games (MMORPG) battle to differentiate between human and bot players. Yampolskiy & Govindaraju (2008) studied running processes and network traffic as a method to distinguish between humans and bots. Chen *et al* (2009) identified bots in MMORPG through traffic analysis. They showed amongst others that traffic is distinguishable by (1) the regularity in the release time of the client command; (2) the trend and magnitude of traffic burstiness in multiple time scales; and (3) the sensitivity to different network connections. Thawonmas *et al* (2008), conduct behaviour analysis within this gaming environment and implement methods focusing on resource gathering and trading behaviour.

Traffic classification is also proposed and done by Li *et al* (2009), with Lu *et al* (2009) proposing a hierarchical framework to automatically discover botnets. They first classify network traffic into different application communities by using payload signatures.

Virtual bots are also introduced as a method to create uncertainties in the botnet market. Li *et al* (2008) followed a different perspective by looking at botnet disabling mechanisms from an economic perspective. This links to methods looking at collective behaviour of bots, i.e. studying the focus and deriving solutions from there (Pathak *et al.*, 2009; Stone-Gross *et al.*, 2009).

Xie *et al* (2008) characterize botnets by leveraging spam payload and spam server traffic properties. They identify botnet hosts by generating botnet spam signatures from emails. Ramachandran. & Feamster (2008) studied the network level behaviour of spammers. They identified specific characteristics, such that spam is being sent from a few regions of IP address space. They also propose that developing algorithms to identify botnet memberships need to be based on network level properties. Staying on the network level, Villamarín-Salomón & Brustoloni (2009) propose a Bayesian approach for detecting bots based on the similarity of their DNS traffic to that of known bots.

A detailed look into the solutions summarized above, led us to propose a design incorporating the use of intelligent SA as a counter to botnets. Our design incorporates the different aspects and required characteristics as detailed in the literature. Our design is also a next step in detailing our proposed framework (Dembskey, Biermann 2008)

As stated in (Dembskey, Biermann 2008), we propose three layers, namely IDS, Observer and Communication.

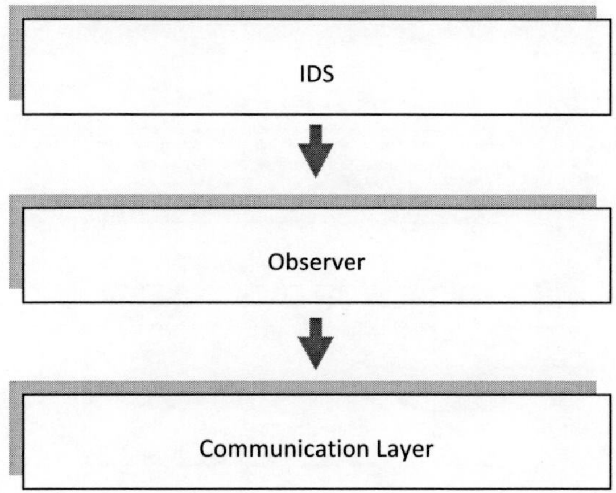

Figure 1: Three layers of IDS, Observer and Communication

Using these layers as our starting point we introduce sub-layers and descriptions as depicted in Figure 2. We only focus on the Observer and IDS layers.

The observer layer consists of five sub-layers all focusing on gathering information:

- Collective Behaviour
- Communication Analysis
- Resource Gathering
- Spreading & Growth Patterns
- Network Traffic Analysis

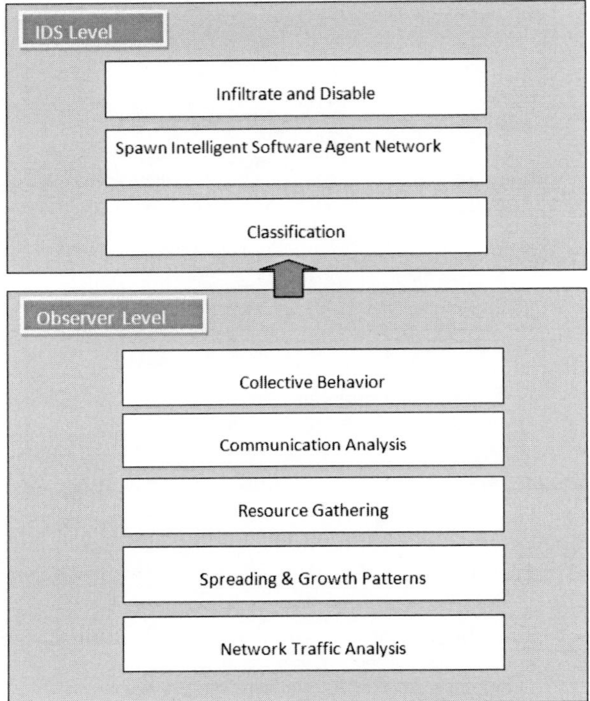

Figure 2: Sub-layers of the design

Each of these sub-layers focuses on particular aspects of gathering information through observation. This observation is conducted through a focused software agent network.

Within network traffic analysis, intensive signature analyses are conducted in order to provide data to the IDS layer. From these analyses, information on spreading and growth patterns is gathered and models proposed. Resource gathering focused on observing specifics such as bandwidth depletion and resource utilizations. Communication analysis refers to the communications taking place between bots and masters and the analysis thereof. This will assist in determining the collective behaviour or focus of the botnet as well as assist in detailing the economic focus.

The information gathered within the observer layer is used as input to the IDS layer. The IDS layer will function as both a HIDS and a NIDS; that is, it will have operational agents on hosts and servers. The IDS layer includes the following:

- Infiltrate and disable
- Spawn Intelligent Software Agent Network
- Classification

The information gathered within the observer level are use to classify the botnet and according to the classification an intelligent software agent network is spawned to infiltrate and ultimately disable the botnet.

Agentification of email client and server software, host and server monitoring software, host and server firewall and AV software, network monitoring software, user monitoring software is required, or at least, the capability to interface with these applications.

It is anticipated that the crowd sourcing component will function on two layers. Firstly, SA from different organizations will communicate threats amongst themselves with minimal supervision. Secondly, information will be sourced from human beings. Both open and proprietary sources should be used, but the following two points must be kept in mind. The use of proprietary systems will have a cost implication and the use of that data may not legally be allowed to propagate through the entire SA system. Secondly, the possibility of attack vectors being introduced is a real concern – if crowd sourcing results in false positives through the means of concerted and purposeful false reporting, then a DoS attack may occur, with the system's SA falsely identify normal activity as malicious and halt it. A robust and up-to-date system that can share data on the safety of web sites and software will mitigate the risk from the primary sources of infection discussed above. The CYBEX (X.1500) is in the opinion of the authors the correct path to follow to implement this system.

As part of this research we will implement and test a model of the proposed system against a variety of botnets. The model will not be comprehensive and will focus on mitigating threats launched via drive-by downloads and locally installed software. The network of NIDS and HIDS with the crowd sourcing component will be implemented.

We must also consider the impact of virtualization and the trend towards cloud and grid computing, which we think will continue. It is also not the intention that this system is entirely automated, as the effect of systemic failure may be worse than anticipated and human intervention may serve to mitigate this risk.

In summary, we propose to model and implement a proof-of-concept of an integrated SA botnet defense system. Some challenges of developing such a system are its complexity and human privacy requirements and laws. Rather than be daunted by this, we instead believe that the effort will be well rewarded and will identify future areas of research.

References

Bailey, M., Cooke, E., Jahanian, F., Xu, Y. & Karir, M. 2009, "A survey of botnet technology and defenses", Proceedings of the 2009 Cybersecurity Applications & Technology Conference for Homeland Security-Volume 00, IEEE Computer Society, pp. 299.

Bigus, J.P. & Bigus, J. 2001, Constructing intelligent agents using Java, Wiley New York.

Carr, J. & Shepherd, L. 2010, Inside cyber warfare, 1st edn, O'Reilly Media, Inc., Sebastopol, Calif.

Chen, K., Jiang, J., Huang, P., Chu, H., Lei, C. & Chen, W. 2009. Identifying MMORPG Bots: A Traffic Analysis Approach. EURASIP Journal on Advances in signal Processing. Volume 2009, Article 3.

Chiang, K. & Lloyd, L. 2007. A Case Study of the Rustock Rootkit and Spam Bot. Proceedings of the First Workshop on Hot Topics in Understanding Botnets, Cambridge, MA.

Cruz, M. 2008, , Most Abused Infection Vector. Available: http://blog.trendmicro.com/most-abused-infection-vector/ [2010, 9/27/2010].

Damballa Inc. 2009. Upate on the Enemy: A deconstruction of who profits from botnets. Available: http://www.damballa.com/downloads/d_pubs/WP%20Update%20on%20the%20Enemy%20(2009-05-13).pdf

Dembskey, E. & Biermann, E. 2008, "Software agent framework for computer network operations in IW", Proceedings of the 3rd International Conference On Information Warfare And Security, ed. L. Armistead, ACL, pp. 127.

Denning, P.J. & Denning, D.E. 2010, "Discussing cyber attack", Commun.ACM, vol. 53, no. 9, pp. 29-31.

Dunham, K. & Melnick, J. 2009, Malicious Bots: An Inside Look Into the Cyber-Criminal Underground of the Internet, Auerbach Publications.

Jansen van Vuuren, J., Phahlamohlaka, J. & Brazzoli, M. 2010, "The Impact of the Increase in Broadband Access on South African National Security and the Average citizen", Proceedings of the 5th International Conference on Information Warfare and Security, ed. L. Armistead, ACL , pp. 171.

Knapp, K.J. & Boulton, W.R. 2008, "Ten Information Warfare Trends" in Cyber Warfare and Cyber Terrorism, eds. Kenneth Knapp & William Boulton, IGI Global, US; Hershey, PA, pp. 17-25.

Li, Z., Liao, Q & Striegel, A. 2008. Botnet Economics: Uncertainty Matters. Workshop on the Economics of Information Security (WEIS 2008), London, England.

Li, Z., Goyal, A., Chen, Y. & Paxson, V. 2009. Automating Analysis of Large-Scale Botnet Probing Events. Proceedings of the 4th International Symposium on Information, Computer and Communications Security. Sydney, Australia.

Liu, J. 2001, Autonomous agents and multi-agent systems: explorations in learning, self-organization, and adaptive computation, World Scientific.

Liu, J., Xiao, Y., Ghaboosi, K., Deng, H. & Zhang, J. 2009. Botnet: Classification, Attacks, Detection, Tracing and Preventive measures. EURASIP Journal on Wireless Communications and Networking, Volume 2009. Hindawi Publishing Corporation.

Lu, W. Tavallaee, M. & Ghorbani, AA. 2009. Automatic Discovery of Botnet Communities on Large-Scale Communication Networks. Proceedings of the 4th International Symposium on Information, Computer and Communications Security. Sydney, Australia.

Masud, MM., Gao, J., Khan, L., Han, J. & Thuraisingham, B. 2008. Peer to Peer Botnet Detection for Cyber-Security: A Data Mining Approach. In: Proceedings of the 4th annual workshop on Cyber security and information intelligence research: developing strategies to meet the cyber security and information intelligence challenges ahead. Oak ridge, Tennessee.

Microsoft, 2010. Download details: Microsoft Security Intelligence Report volume 8 (July - December 2009). Available: http://www.microsoft.com/downloads/details.aspx?FamilyID=2c4938a0-4d64-4c65-b951-754f4d1af0b5&displaylang=en [7/21/2010].

Murch, R. & Johnson, T. 1999, Intelligent software agents, prentice Hall PTR.

National Research Council (U.S.). Committee on the Role of Information Technology in Responding to Terrorism, Hennessy, J.L., Patterson, D.A., Lin, H. & National Academies Press 2003, Information technology for counterterrorism: immediate actions and future possibilities, National Academies Press, Washington, D.C.

OECD (Organization for Economic Co-operation and Development). 2007. Malicious Software (Malware): A Security Threat to the Internet Community. Ministerial Background Report [Online]. Available: http://www.oecd.org/dataoecd/53/34/40724457.pdf

Ollmann, G. 2010, "Asymmetrical Warfare: Challenges and Strategies for Countering Botnets", The 5th International Conference on Information-Warfare & SecurityACI, Reading, England, pp. 507.

Oram, A. & Viega, J. 2009, Beautiful security, 1st edn, O'Reilly, Sebastopol, CA.

Padgham, L. & Winikoff, M. 2004, Developing intelligent agent systems: a practical guide, Wiley.

Pathak, A., Qian, F., Hu, Y.C., Mao, ZM. & Ranjan, S. 2009. Botnet Spam Campaigns Can Be Long Lasting: Evidence, Implications, and Analysis. Proceedings of the 11th International Joint Conference on Measurement and Modeling of Computer Systems. SIGMETRICS / Performance'09, June 15-19, 2009, Seattle, WA.

Porras, P. 2009. Reflections on Conficker: An insider's view of the analysis and implications of the Conficker conundrum. CACM 52 (10). October.

Prince, B. 2010,, Russian Cybercrime: Geeks, Not Gangsters | eWEEK Europe UK. Available: http://www.eweekeurope.co.uk/knowledge/russian-cybercrime-geeks-not-gangsters-9182/2 [2010, 8/30/2010].

Ramachandran, A. & Feamster, N. 2006. Understanding the Network Level Behavior of Spammers. Proceedings of the 2006 Conference on Applications, Technologies, Architectures and Protocols for Computer Communications, SIGCOMM'06, September 11-15, 2006, Pisa, Italy.

Schiller, C.A., Binkley, J. & Harley, D. 2007, Botnets: the killer web app, Syngress Media Inc.

Smith, G. 1998,, Issues in S and T, Fall 1998, An Electronic Pearl Harbor? Not Likely. Available: http://www.issues.org/15.1/smith.htm [2010, 8/16/2010].

Stone-Gross, B., Cova, M., Cavallaro, L., Gilbert, B. & Szydlowski, M. 2009. Your Botnet is My Botnet: Analysis of a Botnet Takeover. Proceedings of the 16th ACM Conference on Computer and Communications Security. CCS'09, November 9–13, 2009, Chicago, Illinois, USA.

Stytz, M.R. & Banks, S.B. 2008, Toward Intelligent Agents For Detecting Cyberattacks

Thawonmas, R. Kashifuji, Y. & Chen, K. 2008. Detection of MMORPG Bots Based on Behavior Analysis. Proceedings of the 2008 International Conference on Advances in Computer Entertainment Technology. Yokohama, Japan.

Villamarín-Salomón, R. & Brustoloni, JC. 2009. Bayesian Bot Detection Based on DNS Traffic Similarity. Proceedings of the 2009 ACM symposium on Applied Computing, SAC'09, March 8-12, 2009, Honolulu, Hawaii, U.S.A.

Wang, Y., Gu, D., Xu, J. & Du, H. 2009. Hacking Risk Analysis of Web Trojan in Electric Power System. In: Proceedings of the International Conference on Web Information Systems and Mining. Shanghai, China.

Williams, C.W. 2008,, Carpet bombing in cyberspace - May 2008 - Armed Forces Journal - Military Strategy, Global Defense Strategy. Available: http://www.armedforcesjournal.com/2008/05/3375884 [2010, 7/20/2010].

Yampolskiy, RV. & Govindaraju, V. 2008. Embedded Non-interactive Continuous Bot Detection. ACM Computers in Entertainment, Vol. 5, No. 4, Article 7. Publication Date: March 2008.

Xie, Y., Yu, F., Achan, K., Panigrahy, R., Hulten, G. & Osipkov, I. 2008. Spamming Botnets: Signatures and Characteristics. Proceedings of th 2008 Conference on

Applications, Technologies, Architectures and Protocols for Computer Communications,SIGCOMM'08, August 17–22, 2008, Seattle, Washington.

Operational Aspects of Cyberwarfare or Cyber-Terrorist Attacks: What a Truly Devastating Attack Could do

Eric Filiol
ESIEA Operational Virology and Cryptology Laboratory
Laval, France

Editorial Commentary

Having explored the infrastructure and various challenges associated with the geopolitical landscape, this paper brings the reader to what perhaps is the principle issue: what could happen. Obviously it hasn't happened yet, but one often hears the ominous phrase "electronic Pearl Harbor" invoked to reference the potential for disaster in cyberspace. Here Eric Filiol, a deeply thoughtful and imaginative researcher, spells out exactly what could go wrong and how it might be executed. His scenario is simple and infective, building upon other similar examples, such as that published by John Arquilla in Wired in 1998 (The Great Cyberwar of 2002, Issue 6.02, February 1998). The great benefit of Filiol's scenario and analysis is that it challenges the modern concepts of computer security practice, the transcendant nature of cyberspace, and the inability of modern governing structures to address challenges in this space. In what some readers may find controversial, Filiol strongly implies that a defense oriented posture is the wrong way to think about the problem and will lead to cascading problems. In acknowledging that "a war purely restricted to the digital world (networks, systems, communication infrastructures…) is an aberration and does not make sense from a military or terrorist point of view", Filiol describes how such an attack might well occur and with what consequences. A particularly intriguing element to his scenario is the use of social networks in the attack. But in the end, the challenge of attribution is the key problem. This is something which vexes nation-states today and which will continue to be a problem in the future.

Abstract: Cyberwarfare and cyber-terrorism (mainly e-jihad) are nowadays a fashion topic. Since the Estonian attack in May 2007 and some intents of computer attacks by Al-Qaida, many papers have addressed, discussed not so say disputed about this. But those papers, for the most interesting ones, have just explained the effects of those attacks, drawn some conclusion and give only a very few technical details. But no paper has ever presented and pro-actively addressed the problem of operational and planning aspects of such cyber-attacks. In other words, how a terrorist group or a nation state could plan, organize, launch and conduct a real, large scale attacks? In this paper we present an in-depth reflection of how an attacker could plan such a wide-scale attack against a country, its infrastructure and its population, simply with a few clicks of a mouse. Based on real-cases analysis, military planning techniques and technical proactive research, we present a multi-step attack with the operational planning in mind (e.g. the attacker's view) without forgetting to explain how to technically execute each of the different phases of the attack. We will restrict to the case of attacks against a nation state conducted by a terrorist group or another country.

Keywords: IPSec tunnel, malware, encryption, eavesdropping, IPSec security

1. Introduction

Cyberwarfare has nowadays become a fashion topic and it is quite impossible nowadays to count them. However most of them share quite the same misleading idea: cyberwarfare is a war on the cyberworld (i.e. the set of all of the computers systems, communication system, networks infrastructure...) only and against that cyberworld only. While there is no real clear and widely accepted definition of what cyberwarfare really is, quite almost everybody seems to agree on the fact that this kind of war is naturally disconnected from any other reality and to begin with, with the real world at first. There is no such thing as a digital only war as we will try to explain in this paper. As a consequence of this misleading idea comes the fact that the real targets of computer attacks are largely underestimated thus making our countries far from being protected. Moreover, while there is a beginning of consensus about a few tools that could be technically exploited to conduct computer warfare – malware, software flaws, network attacks ...- there is no deep reflection on how such an organized attack against a nation state could be planned and conducted. What NATO calls

CNOs (*Computer Network Operations*) [NATO], still remain vague, fuzzy, imprecise and rather restricted.

In this paper, we first aim at identifying the different possible targets and methods of cyber warfare. In this respect, the analysis has been clearly inspired by the Chinese doctrine (Qiao,) which seems to have been applied in computer attacks during the recent months, as far as facts and reports enable to have a precise idea. But at the present time, know digital attacks are just digital skirmishes against a few yet critical networks (mainly defence networks from USA or Western countries for espionage or Denial of Service purposes). It is very likely that those skirmishes should be considered just as local technical repetitions of chunks of a bigger, wider attack, whose overall complexity can be neither perceived nor analysed.

Here comes the second critical point with respect to cyberwarfare: operational and planning aspects of such a war from the attackers' perspective. In other words, how a terrorist group or a nation state could plan, organize, launch and conduct a real, mid scale or large scale attack? What does he need for that? In this paper we present an in-depth reflection of how an attacker could plan such a wide-scale attack against a country, its infrastructure and its population, simply with a few clicks of a mouse. Our study is based on real-cases analysis (forensics analysis of legal cases, targeted attacks analysis) military planning techniques and technical proactive research, we present a multi-step attack with the operational planning in mind (e.g. the attacker's view) without forgetting to explain how to technically execute each of the different phases of the attack. We will restrict to the specific case of attacks conducted against a nation state, by a terrorist group or another country, for internal destabilization purpose. The case of cyber-attacks conducted in the context of military operations will not be addressed but the reader may refer to (Filiol, 2008).

The paper is organized as follows. Section 2 will shortly present the different concepts behind the notion of war and to what extent cyber attacks can interfere with those concepts. We will in particular explain why a war in the cyberspace only, is a nonsense. Section 3 then presents a "simple" tactical scenario to illustrate our approach. First the theme itself will be given and then we will detail the course of events as any newspaper reader could observe them: as a sequence of apparently uncoordinated, unrelated events. Finally, in section 4 we go behind the curtain to explain what really happened and present the previous sequence of events as the steps of a planned, organized computer attack with a true conduct of manoeuvre as military use to do.

2. Basic concepts of war and computer warfare

2.1. Introductory concepts in computer warfare

The general prevailing security concept considers that a critical system must be "bunkerized" to withstand attacks. But this is a very bad interpretation of the main existing security models. Furthermore it is never possible to ascertain the actual optimality of this approach, it is conceptually wrong. Indeed, it implies to subscribe to the belief that security is to prevent attacks - which is nonsense - while its true role is to be able to identify as quickly as possible such attacks, to move in conditions, time to restore the system and especially to leave the priority at the heart of business (industrial world) or the operational mission (military). In other words, security must consider a risk management approach and an in depth rather than a sanctuary policy.

But if this vision of defence in depth is becoming - particularly in the world of Defence and of governmental offices in the face of attacks whose number is increasing month after month - it is still very limited in scope. The perspective of the depth limit remains compartmentalized to the walls of the sanctuary: it makes more interior walls in the hope that if the wall falls outside the sanctuary is still preserved. This is an unfortunately narrow vision of security (Filiol, 2009). In a context of cyberwar, it would be a fatal, misleading sense of security. While in a conventional conflict, the enemy must eventually deal directly with a target (final phase of the battle ground after the air raids, for example) and bring down a sanctuary, in the context of cyberwarfare, it is no longer true. The target is in one way or another interconnected with other components according to a mapping and an interdependence that is often impossible to specify .except for the enemy.

The digitization of our space, it is "battle" or social causes, to our security, the abolition of time and space. In a conventional conflict, the target is located in a space and time not only different from that of the attacker, but also from "friendly components (allies)" of the target. This means at the operational management level a graduated conduct of the manoeuvre for the enemy and protective measures and / or responses for the intended target.

An excellent recent example - but unfortunately not only because this type of attack has struck the U.S. Air Force a few months ago - comes from the attack by the worm W32.Conflicker[16], attack that hit the French Defence and the British Navy. On 15 and 16 January (Blog Secret Défense, 2009) Rafale aircrafts from the French Navy Air Force have been nailed to the ground. The attack has not affected their onboard computers – they are a priori highly protected - but the air traffic control system which, under Windows, was attacked and put out of service. He never delivered the flight parameters[17]. The dependence of system did the rest. But this case is exceptional and limited in scope because the dependence is direct and supposedly easily identifiable - at least it would have been expected, and above all it is limited to a purely technical scope. Precisely it is where security still considers a too narrow a vision of the reality of the systems it is supposed to protect. Considering only the purely technical aspect, in identifying the dependencies of a system, is illusory. This is often what one finds in most security and risk analysis methodologies. Moreover, only the immediate area is generally taken into account.

The main reason is that since (too) long security based solely on the vision of the defender. Still anathema struck, the vision of the attacker is neglected and as such everything that can be implemented by the latter is ignored. The vision developed by China military experts, from this point of view, especially in advance (Qiao & Wang, 1999). The key element is to have this vision and way of thinking the military in the conduct of the operation: be the approach of infantry and cavalry based on a doctrine of warfare, strongly supported by intelligence. There is no doubt in this approach - and analysis of actual attacks is clear - that intelligence is vital to the cyber attacker. The gathering is to identify these dependencies and to establish their precise mapping. But never in our time, it has been easier to collect information, compiled and cross-gain operational scope. Blogs of military personnel or engineers working on military systems to social net-

[16] The code analysis reveals that the attack apparently originated from Russia or The Ukraine.

[17] The same case very recently (January 2009) struck a Chinese battle tank squadron.

works, through the analysis of tenders for public procurement, the critical mass of information that can easily be collected is staggering and unbelievable. This makes our central intelligence, tools suddenly obsolete and ridiculously vain. One wonders what is the role of internal security agencies (MI5 in UK, FBI in USA, DST/DPSD in France...- working very effectively, however - if the authorities and decision-makers do not take into account the risks and threats that those agencies identify every day.

This information, once collected, must be processed to establish the mapping of dependencies to determine the point of weakness and build an operational scenario. This is the central element of genuine thought and doctrine for cyberwar. In the present paper, we are going to expose how a cyber attack could be launched in a more directed towards the safety of territory and civil security, by applying the previous introductory concepts. A similar case in the context of a military operation is presented in (Filiol, 2009).

We must beforehand clarify what the term "cyber attack" means since it is still unclear to many. A commonly accepted definition is (Knowlkedgerush, 2009):

a strategy for undermining an enemy's data and information systems, while defending and leveraging one's own information edge. This type of war has no front line; potential battlefields are anywhere networked systems can be accessed --oil and gas pipelines, electric power grids, telephone switching networks, etc. Information warfare can take countless forms: trains and planes can be misrouted and caused to collide, stock exchanges can be sabotaged by electronic "sniffers" which disrupt international fund-transfer networks, and the signals of television and radio stations can be jammed and taken over and used for a misinformation campaign". However this definition still ticks too much to the technical aspects of computer attacks. That is why in our recent analysis and case studies, we rather favour the following short definition inspired by the French definition of cybercrime: "part of an attack using conventional means and/or the networks, computer systems or communications infrastructure to act in a dematerialized way so that to get rid off the limits of time and space". Thus in our definition – as in the case of cyber crime – computer/network attacks are not a goal in itself but just a tools – among many others, possibly conventional – to control or destroy a given target.

It is essential, in our opinion, to keep in mind that a war purely restricted to the digital world (networks, systems, communication infrastructures...) is an aberration and does not make sense from a military or terrorist point of view. In addition, the specificity of the attack is to operate without the constraints not only of space but also and above all of time. The attacker can act in advance of phase (put its pieces in place in advance like in chess) and especially not to leave any incriminating evidence. Finally, a cyber attack is the optimal combination of Information Operation techniques, as formalized by NATO (Nato, 2006), conventional attacks ... and a total lack of ethics (Qiao & Wang, 1999).

Before illustrating this vision with a tactical scenario, let us first explore the key approach components that a cyber attack could consider.

2.2. Key targets in a cyber attacks

Let us recall the main characteristics a cyber attack must have according to our definition:

Dematerialization. In particular, not only the true origin of the attack must remain hidden, but also it must be possible to wrongly frame an innocent party (another country or group) as the perpetrator of the attack (fooling the digital evidence). From a military perspective, the main interest is to avoid or to delay the target reaction by misleading it.

Cancelling time and space limits. Both factors are generally a strong barrier to bypass for the attacker. Network connections will just make it possible to have immediate access from anywhere and at any time.

Gaining control over time and space, and besides all over physical resources. The aim of war is precisely to gain such a control over the physical world (including people). Attacking a server with no effect over the physical resources has no sense. In other words, cyberwar is not war into the cyberspace, unless the enemy "Nation state" is Second Life! Even defacing a server directly targets the human minds and not just the server.

Exploit the complexity, interdependencies of modern system. Never attack directly the target which is generally (and hopefully) secure. Attack instead some secondary, ternary... targets whose target is depending and which are not protected, most of the time because the target dependence has not been identified yet. Among those indirect targets, you can consider anything: people or group of people including leaders and decision makers (military or police chiefs, union leader, influence leader...), transportation facilities (train, road, planes...), resources distribution (electricity, water, air conditioning...), communication facilities (telephone, internet, fax...), media... The list is quite infinite when considering the possible chain of interdependencies. As for the attacks against influent people – by wrongly framing them in criminal acts – may be dramatically efficient.

Exploit generalized intelligence. The efficiency of intelligence – contrary to what most espionage films show – directly lies on the capacity to openly collect a large amount of possibly useless or common data and to compile them in order to have a significant and deep knowledge of a given target. In our modern world of communication, the work has never been so easy: blogs, data centres, relocation of software industry[18] or critical services in low salary countries (as an example, western countries are relocating their telephone call centres and their network supervision centres in north Africa countries where the security conception is far from being the same as our), professional trade shows, analysis of public contract offers, newspapers, professional directories... This list is potentially infinite. Most of those data gathered will be very useful to draw a complete and accurate view of the interdependencies of the final target with some unprotected, unidentified systems, which are less or not protected and therefore which will become secondary targets.

Let us now detail a totally fictitious tactical scenario but in which all elements, all data, all events ... are for the most part inspired by recent events and cases. For obvious reasons of ethics, all of them have been anonymised. Moreover, we will not detail the actual procedure and technical

[18] In 2007 – 2008, a large scale espionage case based on a Trojan horse hidden in professional software has been discovered in Israel. The software was also sold in Europe. Let us recall that one of the first critical flaws found in Windows XP in 2001, had been suspected to have been introduced by an Al-Qaida programmer who managed to infiltrate the Microsoft Indian development teams. While no clear evidence has ever been officially given, the doubt still remains. Whatever the truth, this alleged case poses the problem of software development in countries where the sense of security is not comparable to ours

means used by the attackers, directed below. This does not harm the general understanding.

3. A "simple" scenario

3.1. The tactic theme (extracts)

The bidding process for the 2016 Summer Olympic Games was officially launched on May 2007. The first step for each country was to submit an initial application to the International Olympic Committee (IOC) confirming their intention to bid. Completed official bid files, containing answers to a 25-question IOC form, were to be submitted. Four candidate countries (a city) were chosen for the shortlist on June: BLUE City, YELLOW City, GREEN City, and WHITE City. Two other countries failed to make the cut (RED and PURPLE cities) officially for insufficient preparation and economic problems. But according to unofficial sources, many countries threaten to boycott the event for political reasons. Sir John Doe of RAINBOW country will head the Evaluation Commission. The commission will make on-site inspections in the second quarter of June 2009. They will issue a comprehensive technical appraisal for IOC members one month before elections; the final selection will be made by the full IOC membership around mid October 2009.

In a very uncertain economic environment, and for various reasons linked to the international situation, hosting the Summer Olympic Games represents a strategic interest for the four finalists. The objective of each of these four finalist countries is therefore to discredit the proposals of the other three during the inspections in June 2009. Moreover, RED and PURPLE countries intend in retaliation to discredit the commission and thus prove that their application was rejected because of political pressures and that the selected countries did not offer the suitable environment for the Summer Olympic Games. All the analysis as well as a few indiscretions in the entourage of the committee strongly and recurrently suggest that only the GREEN and BLUE countries have a genuine chance of being selected. Competition between these two nations, as well as the increase of respective biddings, becomes more and more intense with the approach in June 2009.

3.1.1. Environment and intelligence situation

GREEN and RED countries, as well as RED country, have a significant capacity in the field of CNOS (Computer Network Operation):

- In the GREEN country, many organized groups of pirates (hackers), strongly active e-groups of virus writers working actively for the benefit of the nationalist militia, known to be supported by the former right wing party and a large part of the army.
- In the RED country, state structures, known to drive other groups of hackers are known to have strong activity in terms of attacks; in addition, reports have established that the country handles and manipulates certain groups of hackers of the GREEN.
- The BLUE country has a huge activity in computer warfare both at the national level and at the population level (universities, militia). Moreover, the BLUE country has gained a world monopolistic position in the software industry (95 %) and the chip manufacturing industry (100 %), thus selling its products all around the world.

RED and BLUE countries are known to have a very strong capability in Intelligence. While this capability relates more to HUMINT for the RED country, the BLUE country is more has concentrated its capability on SIGINT, ELINT and COMINT.

The main telephone operator of the GREEN country is owned by the main BLUE operator which manages the supervision of the GREEN communication network (including Internet access and cell phone network). Commercial agreements have resulted in large policy of wide installation of BLUE equipments (in particular network active components and servers). A BLUE consortium is owning and managing most of the GREEN data centers. Finally, governmental GREEN encryption systems have been sold by the RED country[19].

3.2. The course of events

Let us give first the sequence of events that led to the final selection of the BLUE country by the IOC, without explanation. The core idea is to present

---

[19] As surprising as it may be, even in the field of very sensitive systems like national cryptographic equipments, many countries are not independent and consequently buy them to other nation. The Hans Bühler case in 1995 shed a particular shadow on that very specific trade.

this course of events as the reader is bound to perceive them: as the man in the street or the viewer of the prime time news would. In other words, we will present them as a sequence of events without any apparent correlation or any apparent connection. We will then analyze in the next section what really happened.

3.2.1. Initial phase: until June 2009

At the very beginning of April, recurrent strikes are triggered in the central province of GREEN city according to a phenomenon of slow spreading. Most of the industries, located in the main economic area suffer from a slowdown of their activity. Confidential documents stolen from the main companies were sent on March 26th to a major daily newspaper, which refer to a plan of massive layoffs, motivated by heavy losses of the company, due, according to these documents, to misappropriation of funds for the nationalist and extreme right militia by the different directors of the factories in the area. Forensics investigation on different computer of some companies, which has been ordered by the financial investigation court on March 27th, has confirmed the veracity of those documents and of the allegation published by the journalists. The activity of the factories progressively stops, including intermittently the production and delivery of electricity in the central province.

On March 31st, two company directors are arrested while two others are fleeing overseas. Investigation are conducted which reveals – through leaks in the press – that a generalized system of corruption for political purposes has been organized. Strikes are becoming harder.

On April 2nd, ethnical clashes erupt between gangs in northern part of GREEN city. They are relatively common in those city districts. Cars are burning, many injured with knives and an explosive situation monopolizes the attention of law enforcement. The origin of these conflicts seems related to threats and insults towards ethnic communities that have been posted on *youtube dailymotion* websites. Exchange of provocative videos cause a slow rise of tension and street confrontation between gangs until May 25th.

On April 16th, Mr Alonzo Boïs living in GREEN city is arrested under suspicion of involvement in child pornography. Three days later, after his computer at home has been analysed, the Police has collected a large amount of evidences that he was indeed guilty and he had organized a whole network in the central province of GREEN. A number of people, including some notables from the capital, have been indicted due to their belonging to that network, newspapers said.

The GREEN authorities try to minimize the case and on May 2nd a series of documents are sent to international press association which proves that some members of the GREEN government would be involved in this network of child pornography.

3.2.2. Phase 2: June 2009

As a result of new videos, on June 1st, new clashes in the northern districts of GREEN city and several deaths by firearms are recorded. The situation is tough, the police intervene. The situation is blocked: recurrent demonstrations take place in GREEN city in memory of the victims. Economic activity is disrupted. The authorities fear an escalation of violence.

On June 3rd, further investigation by the police, at the request of the financial investigation office of the High Court established that a few union leaders have been involved somehow in the misappropriation of funds that have been discovered. Those leaders would have covered the fact in exchange to personal advantages. Those facts would have been established by analyzing the home computers of those union leaders. The affair has now gained a world attention as a major event. The basis of union is disgusted and decides as retaliations a massive strike to bar the route to the "extremism and the attempts to crush democracy for the people". The strikes crush the economic activity of the province, including transportation and electricity supply (both economic sectors are key components of the union).

Between June 24th and 27th, frequent breakdowns in the telephone network disturb certain areas including the capital and major cities. Those disturbances affect intermittently the mobile telephone network and Internet communications until June 29th, electricity supply, transportation facilities (railway signalling) are intermittently recorded. Several journalists evoke an attack by a worm. The operators speak of a failure of some network equipment, being replaced.

3.2.3. Phase 3: from June 2009 to October 2009

On July 12th, Sir Allistair Been, from the UK department for culture media and sport is forced to resign since the press said that he was involved in a sexual harassment affair. Investigation is under way said the journalists since they send to the police testimony of a victim which repeatedly received emails and suggestive phone calls from Sir Been. Journalists later evoked that digital evidences have confirmed the allegation. Sir Been also resigned from his position in the IOC.

On September 3rd, Mambaza Doueki, from Western Africa, a former marathon gold medallist is arrested in London under the charges of illegal drug traffic between Africa and England. No drug has been found until now but customs officers received evidences that the traffic has been organized by Mr Doueki. Investigations in his computer, customs spokesman said, confirm the traffic. Mr Doueki has resigned from all his official positions, mainly in Culture and sport organizations. Mrs Doueki which is suspected to have taken part to the traffic has decided to stay in Africa for the moment.

October 10th, riots and mass protestations have dramatically increased in GREEN city, requiring for the Police to deploy important forces in the city. Four wounded protestors have been killed. New audio files have been released on youtube, in which a leader of one of the largest gang of GREEN city is insulting the other gang leaders and promising punitive actions against them.

October 11th, in BLUE country the world biggest company of soft drinks stopped its production for one week and decided a product recall for its production in some cities. The company's shares dramatically falled as a consequence. The company's spokesman officially spoke about "malfunction of the production chain due to failure of automated manufacturing. The products were recalled as a precautionary measure to avoid minor stomach disorders". Unconfirmed rumours told spoke about computer attacks and money extortion attempts against the company.
In October 20th, the IOC makes its decision public: the BLUE city will organize the 20xx Olympic Summer Games Summer.

4. Course of events analysis

Before presenting what really happened, it is essential to keep in mind that in any conflict, the attacker has a depth in time and not other "players". Any operational planning considers options for the forces in front, possibly by weighting them by the time factor. In the case of our tactical scenario, it was easily predictable that only the GREEN and BLUE cities had a significant chance of being selected by the IOC. While the GREEN was the victim of different attacks whose purposes aimed at undermining his candidacy with the IOC, both RED and BLUE countries could anticipate this decision in advance of phase, to include in their strategic and tactical preparation then the conduct of their respective maneuver. From there, it is easy to study and identify areas of weaknesses for local action at the operational level, through computer attacks only.

This explains the fact that operations against the country GREEN city central province began several weeks before June, far ahead before the official date of candidacy reviews by the IOC members in June and the final selection in October. Who was behind those attacks, no matter! What really matters is the nature and conduct of operations: only attacks, without a trace, leaving afterwards analysts with the opportunity of endless epilogue on real responsibilities.

A first series of attacks had targeted several companies and their leaders. False documents, imitated from information processed offshore, were placed in personal and office computers of the main company's CEOs, and later personal computers of GREEN Nationalist Party leaders and extreme right-wing militia leaders and finally those of union leaders to strengthen the movement of strikes and make it uncontrollable. Then it was enough to send these documents to the press according to an appropriate timing, consistent with the conduct of other operations. Among those targeted companies are the centers of power supply, whose production is vital for economic activity in the province. Additional information (indiscretions on engineer blogs, politicians, union leaders...) make easy to suppose that tensions existed between unions and employers. By triggering those strikes, the goal was:

- To create a deplorable economic and social climate with rampant and recurrent movements of strikes;
- To block in short term, the economic activity in the province.

Finally, social movements created intended to provide a general picture of social and economic instability, incompatible with the Olympic Games organization in GREEN city.

The second series of attacks deals with the filing of provocative videos on two sites used by young people to exacerbate their rivalries and then trigger and feed riots over a rather long period of time[20]. The idea, based on classical coverage techniques used in infantry or cavalry, is to trigger a second zone of instability and an image of unstable country where rivalries between gangs and between ethnic groups undermine social stability.

Faced with those problems, the GREEN power GREEN strives to organize. This implies an increase in communications between the various decision-making centers. A third series of attacks aimed at greatly hinder those communications and to extend the deadlines in the decision-making. Knowledge of the architecture of the telephone network has helped to see that the Research and Development network is connected to the operational network. An attack by viruses targeted against the personal laptops of several engineers and scientists of the operator (gathering information via blogs, social networks…) was used to attack the network by exploiting the fact that those engineers used to connect their laptop directly to the internal network (thus bypassing the DMZ), thus causing an indirect cause of infection. Similar attacks were launched against the main services and supplies of resources (public transport, electricity, rail and road signals management…) whose aim is to give a bad image with respect of the organization, stability and quality of public infrastructures.

Several destabilization operations against people subsequently conducted through attacks on their computers and mobile phones:

- The attack against members of the GREEN government aimed to falsely incriminate them in a case of child pornography network, aimed at discrediting the morality of the leaders of the GREEN country and thus indirectly at manipulating the world public opinion. Mr Alonzo Boïs was known to be very close to the official GREEN government members.

[20] This is based on real facts of the same nature which concerned France, fortunately in a very localized way and area, in November 2008 (*VinceNail* Case).

- In the same way, attacks against Sir Allistair Been, a member of the IOC who supported the GREEN candidacy (intelligence gained by spying his emails by means of computer Trojan) and Mr. Mambaza Douek, whose wife, also a member of the IOC who supported the GREEN candidacy, sought to shift the balance of votes in favour of the BLUE country.

Finally the attack against computer systems managing the production of the world biggest company of soft drinks was targeting in fact the major sponsor of the Olympic Games. This attack was made by manipulating RFID tags used to automatically select and mix drinks ingredients within the production chain. The analysis of the attack later showed that these attacks seemed to come from servers located in the GREEN country. The sponsor threatens to withdraw its financial support to the IOC GREEN if the GREEN country is selected.

5. Conclusion

What can we say about the origin of these operations against the GREEN country: have they been launched by the BLUE country or by the RED? It is impossible to say, even by applying the principle of "Who benefits from crime?". This is the main interest of cyberwar operations. While in a conventional war, the notion of objective evidence is a tangible one (satellite imagery, human testimony cut, outside observers...), it is no longer valid when dealing with cyber warfare operations. The concept of evidence disappears completely with the concepts of time and space. But more serious, is that it not only disappears but it can be easily manipulated. It is possible to build any picture of reality and thus framing innocent parties.

The main results of our analysis show that

- planning and conducting such attacks is unfortunately dramatically easy, both on the technical and operational (conduct of manoeuvre) level,
- our modern nation who relies too much on Internet and the Information (media) itself are currently totally unprotected and therefore totally vulnerable,
- the scope of such attacks is currently dangerously underestimated by our decision-makers and the possible targets are far more numerous than expected. We must think global as would attackers do.

This scenario is far from being hypothetical and it shows a possible aspect of what a true, generalized cyberwar can be. Far from the fantastic ideas of the concept of virtual war, which would run on the networks only, the war, may it be real or "cyber", has the sole purpose to intervene in the real: control of resources, territories, power ... as such, the targets of a cyber war are also very real, but much more difficult to identify because of mapping very difficult to establish.

In our scenario, the IOC have secure networks (defence bunker-type), indirect attacks can cause so much havoc. To do this, simply hit the physical or logic resources (including people) on which they more or less indirectly depend. This non-exhaustively includes:

- attacks against persons (deception, disinformation, wrong criminalization...);
- attacks against lines of communication and transportation (demonstrations, riots, movements of crowds ...);
- attacks against any possible vital resources (telephony, industry, services, goods, water, electricity ...);
- influence (InfoOps) or manipulation of the media (Black InfoOps) or public opinion through the media…;

The type of attack scenario we presented in this article may seem easy to achieve for the attacker. This is only in appearance. This type of approach, in addition to a phase of long and tedious intelligence gathering, is a complicated design, plan and lead. The timing must be accurate, but must allow some flexibility at the same time. Several options should be considered to switch from one to another depending on the actual effects on the ground (the "battlefield") and the reactions of opponents or "human pions" on which the situation and or the target indirectly depends.

Finally, it is necessary to situate the concept of computer war in the broader context of war (Qiao & Wang, 1999) and emphasize the concepts of intelligence, taking into account the real by the policies and policy makers and protect professional (professional discretion) and personal information (privacy).

References

Blog Secret Défense (2009), « Les armées attaquées par un virus informatique » (French Defence attacked by a computer virus), [online] Last retrieved February 5th 2009, http://secretdefense.blogs.liberation.fr/defense/2009/02/les-armes-attaq.html

Col. Qiao, L. and Wang X. (1999) "Unrestricted Warfare". People Liberation Army Litterature and Arts Publishing House, Beijing. [online] http://www.terrorism.com/documents/TRC-Analysis/unrestricted.pdf

Filiol, E and Raynal, F. (2009) « Cyberguerre : de l'attaque du bunker à l'attaque dans la profondeur » (Cyber war : the attack on the bunker to attack in depth). Revue de Défense Nationale (National Defence Journal), to appear March 2009.

Knowledgerush. Information Warfare [online], http://knowledgerush.com/kr/encyclopedia/Information_warfare/ .Last retrieved January 26th, 2009.

NATO (2006) "Information Operations – Analysis Support and Capability Requirements". Research and Technology Organization, TR-SAS-057. [online] http://ftp.rta.nato.int/public//PubFullText/RTO/TR/RTO-TR-SAS-057/$$TR-SAS-057-ALL.pdf

Cyber Antagonism Between Hacker Groups Develops new Challenges

Roland Heickerö
Swedish Defence Research Agency (FOI)
Stockholm, Sweden

Editorial Commentary

In this paper, Roland Heickero addresses the challenge of what is normally referred to as criminal behavior in cyberspace and how those kinds of activities can escalate into intra-criminal conflicts, which spill over into and affect other parts of society. The spill-over may take the form of mob mentality, with volunteers cyber-flocking to the cause, or even cause physical conflicts. The examples given are sober reminders of the power of words, music, and ideas, which impact the human imagination forcefully. A nation intent on security in cyberspace might well be concerned with this type of activity because it is so very contagious and spreads easily across national borders. In fact, we do see evidence that nations are concerned with this: the attempts of the Egyptian government to shut down internet access during the protests of January 2011 were directly related to trying to control the spread of ideas and calls to action. See "Egypt Shut Down Its Net With a Series of Phone Calls"
By Ryan Singel January 28, 2011, Wired Magazine,
http://www.wired.com/threatlevel/2011/01/egypt-isp-shutdown/
for more information.

This paper is important because it speaks to the non-economic aspects of competition as well as to the criminally motivated conflicts. When idea-driven motivation becomes the raison d'etre for conflict and the conflicts are waged in a medium that is global in nature, the conflicts by definition are global in nature, at the very least in impact. Ideas have power and the truth does not always immediately present itself. Hacker groups, terrorists, governments, and corporations are all dependent upon the cyber ecosystem. Each can use the ecosystem to have spats and contests, with some damage done, but none dare ruin the entire ecosystem. In reality, the situation now is one of mutually assured destruction: the dependency is so deep that only limited damage, such as defacements, have been seen to date. What about the future, though? If one group should become sufficiently annoyed at another group, it is indeed possible that the cyberspace equivalent of a nuclear bomb might be deployed. In real space, nuclear weapons are the subject of conventions and controls. In cyberspace, how would such a weapon even be detected prior to execution? This paper illustrates that non-state actors are already using the networks as a place for competition. What the future may bring is a cause for both concern and for consideration.

Abstract: The rapid development of information technology does not only change the way to interact, communicate and distribute information between people and organisations. It also creates new possibilities for conducting antagonistic, criminal and hazardous activities by using the Internet. A qualified cyber attack against an opponent's critical information infrastructure can within a very short period of time effect a country's security policy. One area of great concern is malicious hacking and hacktivism. This paper discusses the escalation of conflict on the Internet between different kinds of hacker groups fuelled by political, religious and national manifestations that tend to increase over time. The level and intensity of the activities are governed by recent incidents, whereas conflicts are spreading from the physical sphere into cyber space. Symbols of different kinds are often used as tools for escalating conflicts. Whenever a cyber conflict is initiated a situation develops where different parties are willing to help either side. Unhealthy alliances form between disparate groups of people that could come from all over the world. The conflicts burst on various internet forums with everything from rumours and accusations from one party to another to directed cyber attacks on a large scale. Misleading information is continuously disseminated with the purpose or creating antagonism. In the text several examples are given on cyber antagonism with malicious hackings and defacement attacks that have developed from the physical sphere. For instance the infected debate of the Mohamed Cartoons as well as the publishing of the Swedish painter Lars Vilks "Roundabout dog", the second Intifada between Israelis and Palestinians and the ongoing quarrel between Pakistani and Indian hacker groups, all have implications on a security policy level. The paper ends with a short discussion on the risk for cyber escalation and the need to improve both information security and international cooperation in order to hinder or reduce the negative effects of antagonistic cyber operations.

Keywords: cyber conflicts, hacker groups, defacement attacks, hacktivism, Indian-Pakistan hacker conflict, cyber escalation

1. Introduction

The rapid development of information technology does not only change the way to interact, to communicate and to distribute information between people and organisations. It also creates new possibilities for conducting antagonistic, criminal and hazardous activities by using the Internet. A qualified cyber attack against an opponent's critical information infrastructure such as the command and control functions in financial system, the energy sector and flight and communication networks, can within a very short period of time affect a country's security policy.

The first officially and publicly described cyber assault against one singular country was aimed at Estonia during the spring of 2007. The incident was initialized by the removal of a Soviet military statue from the centre of Tallinn into a nearby graveyard in the city. The war monument is considered by many Estonians as a symbol of the Soviet occupying force and the annexation of the Baltic States. The removal caused a lot of anger to exiled Russians in the country and riots started in the streets of the capital. In conjunction with that, feverish activities arose on the Internet. An operation was initiated with the objective of attacking Estonian computer systems and various national web sites. Within a few days, servers and networks were overloaded with information which led to reduced functionality. Some websites had to be shut down. It has not yet been fully established whom or what groups and organisations lay behind the operation. It still remains to be seen. The cyber attack ceased as fast as it started.

The Estonian cyber incident shows the risks of cyber antagonism that has to be understood and studied. It creates new challenges to be dealt with.

1.1. Objectives

The objective of this paper is to describe the escalation of conflict on the internet between different kinds of hacker groups fuelled by political, religious and national manifestations that tend to increase over time. In the text several examples are given on cyber antagonism with malicious hackings and defacement attacks that has developed from the physical sphere, for instance the conflicts between Indian and Pakistani hacker groups. The paper ends with a discussion on the risk for cyber escalation and consequences for security policy as well as the need for regulation of malicious cyber behaviours. A short conclusion is made.

2. Development of cyber conflicts

2.1. General

Many digital conflicts on the Internet originate from the physical sphere. For example, the American bombing 1999 by mistake of the Chinese embassy in Belgrade, lead to massive cyber attacks between Chinese hacker groups and American ditto. In a similar way, incidents between opponents in the Kashmir region, Chechnya and Gaza strip continue on the Internet. Symbols of various kinds could be used to ignite and to fuel an escalation of conflicts.

One present case is the quarrel about the published Mohamed cartoons which in some countries in the Middle East lead to a banning of dairy products from Denmark, assaults on consulate and embassies as well as a burning of the flag of Denmark and other countries. Through the dissemination of the controversial cartoons, conflicts break out on the Internet. Groups of Islamic hackers for example; "Gangs of pro-Muslim hackers" attacked Danish web sites with the suffix .dk not less than six hundred times during one week period (Cochran 2009). Danish hackers and groupings connected to them, on their side tried with different means and methods both to protect their domains and to conduct counter attacks against its adversaries. The publishing of the Swedish painter Lars Vilks "Roundabout dog" depicting Mohamed brought with it in a similar way to consequences on the net where Swedish web pages were attacked by hackers from Turkey among others.

Whenever a cyber conflict is initiated a situation develops where different parties are willing to help either side. Unholy alliances form between disparate groups of people that could come from all over the world. The conflicts burst on various internet forums with everything from rumours and accusations from one part towards another to directed cyber attacks on a large scale.

Misleading information is continuously disseminated with the purpose to create antagonism. There are signs showing that Islamic hacker movements from different countries and regions are organised actively against servers and web pages in the West. Israel is one important target. In similar way individuals and hacker groups from Europe and USA and others, form connections in order to attack Islamic web pages and hackers.
In connection with the second Intifada started in September 28, 2000, pro-Palestinian hackers succeeded for instance in their mission to attack web pages hosted by Bank of Israel, the stock exchange in Tel Aviv as well as the Israeli army. The economy in Israel is very dependent on well functioned electronic commerce. The consequence of the attacks was that trade went down by eight percent (Attwan 2006). During the Intifada period, the pro-Palestinian groupings managed to attack more than five times the number of sites than the Israelis did. The Israeli invasion in Gaza strip December 2008 caused new tensions on the Internet. Several thousands of web sites were attacked among them the American army. Also the NATO web page is said to have been compromised by Turkish hackers (Raza 2009).

A couple of weeks before the September 11 terrorist attack, the pro-Taliban web site *Taleban.com* hacked by a western activist according to the Web site Hack-in-the-box. The reason for doing that was the Taliban proclamation to shut down Internet in Afghanistan and their threats to punish every eventual user of the Internet. The web site was the Taliban movements' official page. Moreover, the activist also wrote various obscenities against the Taliban's and the leader of al Qaeda, Osama bin Laden. The web page *afghan-ie.com* was also compromised and forced to shut down. The September 11 attack brought a strong feeling of indignation by many hacker groups in the West (Marturion 2009). Six days after the event, the German group *Chaos Computer Club* published on their web site a proclamation to hackers to revenge the infamous outrage by initiating denial of service attacks (DOS) against targets in Afghanistan and Pakistan. Another proclaimed purpose was to steal vital information and data from different systems.

Shortly after, the European hacker group *Yihat* (Young Intelligent Hackers Against Terror) announced that they managed to break into computers that belonged to the Al Shamel Bank in Sudan and penetrate accounts said to be owned by al Qaeda. The correctness of the statement could be discussed. In Yihats program proclamation, referred at the Information Warfare Site (IWS), on the Internet says that the objective with their tasks is to find terrorists, identify them and hack their system in order to get information so they could be caught and jailed, for instance by organisations such as FBI. Through their own sources Yihat says that the number of members in 2001 was approximately 800 persons. The number is probably exaggerated; perhaps not more than 15-20 are more or less active.

Yihats goal to point out potential terrorists on the Internet has raised a lot of anger in some part of the hacker community. Some individuals and groups have felt that they have wrongly been pointed out as being cyber antagonists. This in turn has led to counter reactions especially from hackers in Pakistan according to the website Attribute. A web page under Yihat's domain, www.kill.net, has been attacked by the hacker *Fluffi Bunni* and forced to shut down. After that incident, Yihat acts more carefully on the Internet and try to avoid exposing themselves.

2.2. Antagonism between Pakistani and Indian hacker groups

One of the most serious and dangerous conflicts on the Internet is between Pakistani and Indian hacker groups. Since 1998 conflicts are ongoing in cyber space among groupings from both countries. The Indian nuclear blast is said to be the starting point. Shortly after the official announcement from India of the testing of Pokhran II missile, the hacker group *Milworm* attacked Bhabha Atomic Research Centre web page. They made a so called defacement-attack and changed the web site information into anti-Indian messages. The grouping also succeeded to hijack e-mail messages on the research centre network (Jamshed 2009), (Chowdhuri 2002). The identity of the hacker group is somewhat unclear. Some persons say that the members are based in USA and Australia, others that they come from Pakistan.

A period later another group of Pakistani hackers made an operation against the Indian army web page. This time they used *social engineering* (Chowdhuri *ibid*). Responsible persons for the web site were contacted by telephone and asked to move the web sites IP-address to another address. After the removal the hacker group changed the information to anti-Indian slogans. One reason why they succeed is because the server that controlled the site was not under physical control by Indian authorities, instead it was located abroad. This shows the danger not to have a proper control function for servers with sensitive information.

During the period 1998-2001 the number of Pakistani defacement-attacks against Indian web sites increased from four in 1999 to more than 150 in springtime 2001 according to the Indian Computer Emergency Response Team (CERT India). The number of Indian attacks against its adversaries was seven in 2000 and grew the year after to 18. Between the years 2002-2004 the situation stabilised and the conflict faded.
The first "real cyber war" between hackers from both countries ended with a cease fire when members from the Pakistani groups *Pakistan Hackers Club* (PHC) and *G-Force*, respectively and the Indian group *NEO* agreed not to continue the fight. During the five year conflict hundreds of sites on both sides had been attacked. More than 150 hacker groups and hackers from the Pakistani side were involved and at least 10 from the Indian side.

In November 2008 a new cyber conflict flourished. The reason was the terror attack in Bombay initiated from Pakistani soil. In conjunction to that, the Indian group *HMG* attacked the Ministry of Oil and Gas web page in Pakistan (OGRAS) which went down for several minutes. As an answer to the insult, one of the now leading hacker groups in Pakistan, the *Pakistan Cyber Army* (PCA), defaced at least five Indian web sites such as Indian Oil and Natural Gas. The PCA also addressed a warning on the Internet to HMG and the Indian hacker community to stop their activities.

In just a few days a large number of pages were compromised on both sides. The Pakistani group *KSA*, based on their own information says that they managed to penetrate several of the largest banks in India such as Bank of Barroda. The Indians on their side threatened to attack the Internet system in Pakistan. The conflict continued some weeks and ended in late November. An agreement was signed between the Pakistani groups PCA and KSA together with *Indian Cyber Warriors* (ICW) and HMG. In December 2008 a small incident occurred when the Pakistani side accused the Indians of having tried to compromise a forum discussing the Pakistan Armed Forces. Automatically the incident caused a chain reaction of increments from both sides and the cease fire was broken.

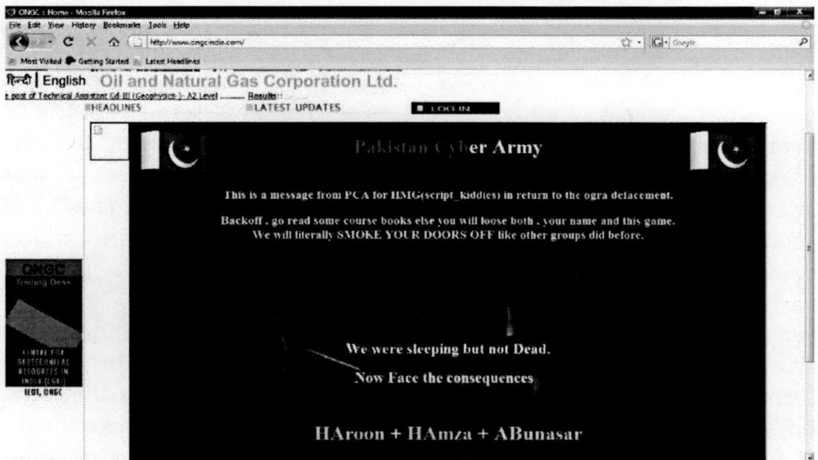

Figure 1: A warning from the Pakistan Cyber Army towards Indian hacker groups

The defacement attacks are by no means sanctioned by authorities either in Pakistan or India. On governmental level both countries try the best they can to prevent hacking.

Responsible organisations for network security such as the National Informatics Centre, NIC, in India and the Federal Investigation Authority, FIA, in Pakistan work actively to hinder an escalation and reduce effects of cyber antagonism.

3. Discussion

The development of a global hacking is fuelled by political, religious and national manifestations and tends to increase over time. The level and intensity of the activities are governed by recent incidents whereas conflicts are spreading from the physical sphere into cyber space. Symbols are used as tools for escalating conflicts. Most attacks between cyber groupings, so far, have been quite harmless with defacement of the opponents' web pages, to address negative messages and alternatively to overload web sites with information so they have to shut down. Such activities are pretty annoying for the concerned parties which are often third persons that by no means have anything to do with conflict.

But, there is a possibility that the contracting parties believe that defacement attacks are not enough anymore, instead they increase gradually the stakes and by that also the level of risks. The development could in a short period of time lead to an unpleasant direction that is hard to control or manage. An escalation could appear, more or less unintentionally. In reference to the cyber attacks against Estonia in 2007 and on Georgia a year after, there is a growing concern that activists of different kinds will and could carry out large and coordinated cyber operations towards critical objects.

Such operations could lead to security policy consequences and by that also spread to other areas. A snowball effect could occur with national security implications and also diffuse rapidly over borders. At the same time it is very difficult to know whom or what groups that initiate the attack and for what purpose. There is an obvious risk of the wrong perpetrator being pinpointed and of the responses to an attack being disproportionate.

Moreover, cyber aggression has jurisdictional and legal aspects. Common criteria and agreements have to be defined between all major nations on how to behave in cyberspace and the level of response if an attack occurs. There is a need for regulations and operating procedures providing guidance on how to act in order to limit consequences. The problem is what should be regulated, how it should be regulated and in what form this should be done.

Is it a task for the law enforcement authorities or a matter for the military or some other organization to deal with? Should it be carried out and resolved on a national level or internationally? How should phenomena such as cyber terrorism, cyber crime and cyber espionage be handled? One tricky issue is how to deal with non-state hackers engaging in every aspect of cyber aggression while providing plausible deniability to the host governments. For instance, the activities of 'black hat' hackers are not limited to any one specific area; they cover a wide range over the whole scale of malicious behaviours, from hacktivism, cyber crime to cyber warfare.

4. Conclusions

The emerging cyber threats from hacktivism and other types of malicious behaviours show the need to improve both information security and international cooperation in order to hinder or reduce the negative effects of antagonistic cyber operations. The issue of cyber threats must be resolved on a worldwide scale, involving all major parties and the law enforcement agencies of all nations. Conventions have to be rewritten because cyber antagonism confounds principles such as proportionality, neutrality and distinction. By cooperating to make cyberspace more secure against criminal intrusion, the work will also lead to improved security for military information operations. The conclusion is that cyber rules of engagement need to be discussed further. But, in order to design viable forms of guidelines how to behave on the Internet, it is most important to understand the modus operandi of different actors, the culture as well as the logic behind their acting as well as motives and driving forces.

References

Atwan, Abdel Bari (2006). The secret History of al Qaeda. University of California Press. Berkley. USA

CERT India. http://www.cert-in.org.in/knowledgebase/whitepapers/analysis_defacewebsites.htm

Chowdhuri, Satybrata Rai. Subversive activities through cyber space. The Tribune May 20, 2002. http://www.tribuneindia.com72002/20020520/login/main5.htm

Cochran, A. Muslim Hackers Assaulting Websites Since Cartoon Controversy Began. October 12, 2009. http://counterterrorismblog.org/2006/02/muslim_hackers_assaulting_webs.php.

IWS, The Information Warfare Site. Cyber Protests Related to the War on Terrorism: The Current Threat . September 12, 2009. http://www.iwar.org.uk/cip/resources/nipc/cyberprotestupdate.htm

Jamshed, Arsalan. Cyberwars between India and Pakistan. October 5, 2009 http://www.Goarticles.com/cgi-bin/showa.cgi?C=859977.

Marturion, Damon. Will hackers keep the cyber peace? New Business News. September 10, 2009. http://www.newbusinessnews.com/.

Raza, Muhammed Ali. Thousands of Websites Hacked by Muslims Hackers to Protest Gaza Attacks. January 16, 2009. http://propakistani.com.

Afghan Taliban website hacked as Internet outlawed. August 27, 2001. http://www.hackinthebox.org/modules.php?

http://attribute.org/news/content/01-10-22001.html

http://www.pakistanidefenceforum.com/

Changing Security Speech and Environment: From Nation States to Corporation Security

Aki-Mauri Huhtinen[1] and Kari Laitinen[2]
[1]National Defence University, Helsinki, Finland
[2]Police College of Finland, Tampere, Finland

Editorial Commentary

This paper introduces and addresses an extremely problematic element in the arena of information warfare: that of who decides what "security" consists of, how that security is instantiated, and what repercussions exist for lapses of security. The paper is a difficult one to read for those who are not well versed in the language of sociology but the reward for reading it is great, in that the paper addresses some extremely thorny issues associated with the information warfare debate. Those issues include whether or not strict attribution should be required, which would by definition eliminate both anonymity and pseudo-anonymity, both incredibly important aspects of dissident speech in repressive regimes. A related issue raised and discussed is the tension between being free from fear and being free to think. These thorny issues are discussed in the context of government desires for closer cooperation with industry for security purposes. This is presented as a recipe for making internal security a critical element of state goals, to the detriment of a free society. So the question is raised: who is responsible for security and how do we, as a polity, manage the tension between security and freedom?

Abstract: Security in organizations is embedded in texts and speech that influence our understanding on it. Furthermore, texts dealing with security and threats influence our security environment, like organizations, and the way security is man-

aged. All in all, the concept of security is very problematic. The faith in and search for security are evident in nearly all sectors of society and also in organizations. Security is something we can swear to. By definition, security is a good thing – who would want to promote insecurity? Due to the problematic conceptual foundation, security should be seen as a process. At the level of politics, this would lead to the question of which direction the process is to be steered towards and which goals are to be set for the process, knowing that complete security can never be achieved. Consequently, our notions of security vary constantly. This article addresses the concept and speech of security and its consequences to society and security organisations. The main focus of the article is on security organisations that are run by governments, but the increase of private security sector is also noted. This context brings up the concept of securitisation. In brief, securitisation means seeing various matters and phenomena, as well as social problems, as security issues, which alters the political take on them and the means used to resolve them[21]. Security operators, or organisations, at the national and international levels[22] compete regarding data, knowledge, information, resources and power of speech in the social discussion. These "gatekeepers" of security – security authorities and the political elite – also determine what constitutes a threat, while simultaneously deciding on resource allocation and means to be deployed. This speech of security is neither innocent nor free of consequences, which is why it should be taken into consideration.
Keywords: security, securitization, terrorism, organization, information, discourse

1. Introduction: The security concept and changing security environment

The purpose of this article is to explicate the force of language, particular focus is on security speech, and how it both influences the way we conceive the world, but it also changes real structures and their functions and objectives. Theoretical context and framework of the article could be understood locating in social sciences and particularly in the tradition of Critical Theory (The Frankfurt School). It follows that texts and documents matter and there can be seen certain hegemonic discourses that greatly influence the way we understand the world surrounding us. Security speech has strong effect on the content of general politics, and therefore will in-

[21] De-securitisation, on the other hand, refers to the opposite tendency.
[22] Security operators comprise the traditional authorities: the police, army and various state security services, but to an increasing extent also private-sector operators and even civil organisations that contribute to the generation of security or influence the content of security, for example, by raising issues related to different threats.

fluence how we "feel" about security, the concept of security, and thus what kind of threat images we "create" and maintain. The way security is understood affects the manner how security organisations and actors are organised and how they function.

The current security environment starts from an individual's personal circle of life and extends all the way to the global security environment in which pandemics, nuclear weapons, environmental and economic changes have a direct, quick influence on an individual's life. Globalisation has significantly increased the number of factors that affect our security environment, as well as our perceptions of the security environment.

Globalisation has linked all security actors and organisations, both state-owned and private security corporations, more closely to each other. The expansion of our security environment has affected our understanding of security and even our security-related practices but, on the other hand, the deep-rooted traditional security mindsets also still remain. However, it seems obvious that traditional ways of managing security issues are not up to date anymore.

One of the reasons for the problem in defining precisely the concept of "security" is probably due the diversity of the players involved: governments, political blocks, corporations, organizations, institutions, commercial actors, media, citizens, the police forces and the military. This problem of finding a definition is revealed by the different approaches taken by the broad range of sources which, each with their point of view and specific interests, adopt the one that is most appropriate at the time. The different departments of security organizations, like UN, EU, and NATO, have their own definitions that evolve through doctrines formulated over time. Also myths come in play. Western doctrine of global and international security is a clean and smooth automatic and technologies process guaranteeing the end of physical and kinetic violence.

According to Clegg & co. Courpasson, & Phillips[23], we have been moving from the model of 'risk society' of Ulrich Beck to a model of 'state of insecurity' within the changing face of modern forms of identity. Still the main question is how far organisations can be truly democratic and allow differ-

---

[23] Clegg, Courpasson, & Phillips 2006, 364, 371–374

ent kinds of identity to remain alive alongside the necessity of hierarchy of power. If we lose the traditional hierarchies of authority, what new possibilities do we have for managing the power of organisations? One answer is to use available surveillance technologies to seek a new kind of 'soft' human authority. We are transforming human power into electronic power. The electronic Panopticon is going global in an increasingly insecure world. Also, bio-psychological screening is becoming ever more closely intertwined with genetic and security screening. The global egoistic and narcissistic subjectivity become celebrated as post-modern identity and are tied to consumption rather than production. This means fragmentation and ambiguity of identities, along with immaterial labour producing immaterial goods such as a service or a cultural or symbolic product. Thus, the traditional security context and environment where a nation-state produces security to her subjects is seriously tottering.

2. The political nature of security speech

For us, the core of security lies in the fear of the unknown and the desire for surety, which, when combined, provide us with a familiar, controlled life with causality and rationality as the key signs of sovereignty and the best protection against the forces of randomness. In other words, a secure life requires secure truths. Security requires faith. Security is a group of illusions, visions, and because we want to believe in them, they become real.[24] A written agreement or a security strategy starts to resemble a castle wall that carries and protects our lives. The terrorist attacks in September 2001 shattered the security illusion and raised terrorism as a threat to a whole new level, particularly in the United States[25]. The attacks also created a 'dictatorship of threats'[26]. It is a valid thought that these events contributed to the emergence of a dictatorship of security or fear – the world and societies in it are being governed by means of security deficit and fear. In whose interest is this?

In this light, security approaches the issues of propaganda, as well as the role of politics and the media as the shapers of our security reality, which is

---

[24] Der Derian 1995, 34.

[25] A similar shattering of the illusion of security took place in the United States during the cold war era, when the Soviet Union successfully detonated a nuclear blast and developed missile technology capable of reaching over the oceans.

[26] Ollila 2006, 10.

problematic in itself. The connection between propaganda and security relates to the generation of the above-mentioned “atmosphere of fear” and, on a more extensive scale, the international development and its impact on security thinking and threat formation in Finland. The freedom-seeking world becomes security-seeking – when will the war on terrorism, for example, reach the point of maturity? “If you control your life extensively, you'll end up with little to control”[27]. This shift in thinking is further emphasised as the media increasingly focuses on the world of crime and risks. The shifts in the media and political discourse are also significant factors in the communication between individuals and institutions. We can see a transition from the pursuit of the good life towards a political language that is increasingly connected to individualised insecurities and fears.[28]

Our preconception of the structure of (security) reality is significant. Our understanding of the nature of reality is reflected in our understanding of threats and security and, consequently, also in the means we have to influence them. In other words, the way we speak about security generates security in reality and in speech, and ultimately certain kind of security organisations and structures both in state- and private sector-level. The meanings of words and contents of concepts shift in keeping with social changes. Historically, there are no timeless concepts that would prevail over all others; there are concepts that are perceived in a certain manner depending on the time and surrounding society[29]. The concept of security is an instrument of politics. For example, it is difficult to oppose anything that has been declared important for national security by the holders of political power.

The term 'securitisation' [30] is used, above all, to describe an event of speech in which a matter and/or phenomenon is named or interpreted as a security issue[31]. This means that security can be understood as speech – as is also the case with politics, and therefore security cannot be seen as a

[27] Ollila 2006, 24.
[28] Mythen & Walklate 2006, 124.
[29] Skinner 1988, 31–58.
[30] See. Buzan, Wæver & De Wilde 1998.
[31] The conceptual idea of securitisation relies on the speech act theory, see Austin 1981; Searle 1995.

one-and-only, defined and constant status, an unchanged reality, but as something that is in a state of constant change. The reality relating to security is created through and by language. According to this interpretation, reality is created in the process of understanding. Securitisation can, above all, be understood as a deed with political consequences. The starting point and basic idea of securitisation thinking is that a certain matter presents itself as a sudden or dramatic threat to the sovereignty of a state, for example, and this calls for emergency measures. Securitisation calls on the impression of a threat against the preconditions of existence of a certain political community that will be realised in the future. Securitisation is used to generate a certain order. It is used to create borders of security – or, more accurately, insecurity – between different operators: who is with us and who is with them?

The way we talk about security is an essential factor, for example in security management. For example, issues deviating from the prevailing rhetoric of so-called extensive security and the practices embedded therein – some of which function quite well – are seen as increasing threats and the solution to these threats is sought through conventional means: monitoring, control, even violence. This, in turn, leads to difficulties if the aim is to resolve security problems and in this way remove the burden of threats. The use of military force, the emphasised role of security organisations, actions covered by secrecy and rhetoric labelled by juxtapositioning result in a security-political setting from which it is difficult to see the way out. Hence, traditional security models mainly reproduce the existing practices and maintain threats – this is the conventional security mindset. The use of military force in anti-terrorism activities is an illustrative example. Security policies are politics, i.e. it is a matter of choices to be made. Security as a state of mind refers to a strong, comprehensive perception in which new, rising threats are placed into the traditional equation of security politics without being able to perceive new approaches. A policy involving a departure from the existing security practices would impose desecuritisation, which, in turn, entails that "all things" should not be seen as threats that must be securitised.

3. Emergence of new security environment and structures

The academic research into security has considered the impossibility of distinguishing the internal security from the external to be a fact for a long time. A key factor explaining this is the change in international relations so that a complex "force" called globalisation impacts on the structures and parties of international relations, as well as on the internal structures of the parties. The concurrent change in the creation of threats and the diversification of these threats has led to a situation in which the traditional ways of understanding security or insecurity, not to mention those of responding to threats, are no longer sufficient. Responding to threats calls for multidisciplinary, increasingly in-depth international co-operation[32]. Current development seems ambiguous - on the one hand, and particularly after 9/11 governments have made some serious moves the regain their dominance in the field of security. On the other, we are witnessing significant growth of private sector in various fields of security. Hence there are two contradictory tendencies taking place both privatising (corporations of security) of security and increase of state-centred security practices.

In addition, the production of security seems to become increasingly dispersed. In addition to the actual security authorities, the third sector with civil organisations and private security companies is increasingly involved in security production[33].Our security environment has changed and, therefore, also our mindsets and practices should change. Environmental issues, on the one hand, and the threat of terrorism on the other are forcing changes on different sides of the field of security production, desired or not.

The certain infinity, as well as the disintegration of the field of security has imposed a new kind of situation on security operators. The European Union reflects the development labelled by disintegration, but its active politics also contribute to the disappearing of the borderlines of external and internal security that stood strong in the cold war era. Membership in the European Union has influenced the relations between governmental bodies, not to mention legislation.

---

[32] See Loader 2002; De Boer 2006; Booth 2005, Roberts 2008, 12-30.

[33] See Button 2008, 3-24; CEPOL report 2007.

In the context of security, social development has been labelled by fear and insecurity in the past few years. This entails more than just the fear of terrorism. The culture of fear has penetrated our social thinking and activity. It can be stated that the dimension of risks and fear is, in a way, embedded in our society. Evidently, in terms of politics, the problem is not the risk as such but the way this risk is observed and understood. It seems that risks and fear create a reality of their own. The notions of what is and what could be are coming closer to each other – the worlds of the possible, likely and impossible are nearing each other.[34] The securitisation of matters and aiming towards control of security by authorities as well as the private-sector security operators has been seen as one solution.

Internal security has become a key issue in governmental security planning; this phenomenon is also visible in Finland. Furthermore, the new situation has forced operators, states in particular, into closer co-operation in the field of internal security. Especially in the European Union, security in general and internal security in particular, has been a key issue. Hence it can be noted that security in its different forms has "descended" from the field of international politics into societies. Extensive security and changes in international politics have brought about a genuine horizontal and vertical shift in security. The producers of security have adopted new operational models that are based on alleviating, controlling and predicting security threats instead of completely eliminating them[35]. The significance of security politics and the ability to influence society and political guidelines have increased in importance.

Consequently, the agenda of internal security has been clearly visible in the national security strategies of EU member states recently. As the external threat of war has subsided, states have allocated resources, aimed their security planning and directed various crisis readiness resources towards internal security.[36] This, in turn, has led to a situation in which internal se-

[34] See Furedi, 2002 and 2005; Beck 1992 and 2002 a&b; Laitinen 2006.
[35] See Virta 2009, whose article describes the shift in security thinking towards the predictive direction within the EU due to the threat of terrorism.
[36] See, e.g. Ministry of the Interior and Kingdom relations, 2008; Sisäasiainministerio (Finnish Ministry of the Interior) 2008.

curity is at the top of the international security agenda[37]. The circumstances have changed a lot since the cold war era, even though no changes of a similar scale have taken place in the underlying basic security practices. Armed, military confrontations between states have not disappeared from world politics, even though the possibility of such a war is no longer considered to be likely in Europe – this mindset is confirmed, for example, by the fact that Sweden recently decided to dissolve its conscription army.

Looking at the field of European security operators, one notices how the international and national security operators and organisations are coming closer to one another on the one hand, yet competing with each other at the same time. As the result of this security culture, the logic of securitisation penetrates the different sectors of society. The change in our operating environment, as understood in terms of security, features several similar development trends that influence our understanding of security, as well as the practices of security generation and our states of mind.[38]

In other words, the point is that security is spreading nearly everywhere inside societies. This security dynamic produces practices that influence our everyday security, legislation and growing markets for security technology products. All these factors combine to strengthen the presence of security, both in public administration and in citizens' lives. Such development, aiming at positive security, can easily generate elements that lead towards a society of monitoring and control, in which the state distances itself from the citizens but yet at the same time increases its power and control over them through security management[39]. Security management can be seen in the growth of the private security business and the consequent increasing presence of private security operators in our circles of life. This results in a comprehensive security culture[40] that, while not planned (as in conspiracy), is nevertheless dominating and produces new

---

[37] International crime and terrorism have been given significantly more attention on the agendas of states (the EU) and various international organisations. After 2001, terrorism quickly became a convenient enemy.

[38] See Virta 2009; Laitinen 2008; Bigo & Tsoukala 2008; Laitinen 2005, 50–51; Buzan & al. 1998, 23–26.

[39] Security and surveillance technology enable such development.

[40] See Case 2006, citing Bigo, Guittet & Smith 2004, 5-34; also see Andreas & Nadelmann 2006, 189; Wood & Shearing 2007, 74–77.

kinds of security technologies, security bureaucracy and overlapping and parallel security practices that are not (necessarily) covered by democratic control.[41] Therefore, some of the risks of the extended concept of security that have been discussed in the post-cold war era seem to have been realised. Another problem is the prevalence of the traditional security thinking that will also lead to a dead end, as has been proven by the politics of the great powers.

4. Conclusion

Security-related practices and studies indicate how the international dimension is reflected in national security politics and practices in an increasingly fast and versatile manner.[42] Security in its current format and content bears links to war, immigration, terrorism and organised crime, for example, but not to humane dimensions such as unemployment, health, and the environment or car accidents which, nevertheless, are key sources of insecurity in people's everyday lives. Hence, security has returned to control, information and coercive action in cases that threaten the sanctity of a state and community. In other words, elements of violence and control seem to form the core of security instead of seeing security as a process that offers a framework for abandoning problematic practices.

When analysing the current development of security, we can see ongoing processes concerning its dynamics that feature security routines, iterative and overlapping actions of the modern society generating the current reality of security. These entail numerous activities and practices carried out by different operators in the field of security, some of which are coordinated and planned. On the other hand, the various operators also pursue their own goals, which lead to a complex reality of security actions

---

[41] Due to the threat of terrorism, the United States and Great Britain have interfered in citizens' basic rights in an exceptional manner. With regard to the security-related development, there would be the need for a more extensive discussion on the legislative development taking place in the EU and in Finland – for example, how the multinational dimension reflects in Finnish society and our public administration practices.

[42] See e.g. Bigo & Tsoukala 2008.

without anyone owning, let alone controlling, and the big picture[43]. This leads to increased interaction between security operators, but there is also some evident non-compliance in the goals, interests, norms and practices of different parties. These so-called everyday security routines and overlapping activities are problematic because they are covered under administrative bureaucracy and do not present themselves as actual additional security practices (e.g. monitoring, faster and increased information exchange and legislative development). Due to their routine-like nature, these "securitisation moves" are lost in the mass and never make it to the public discussion (security bureaucracy is traditionally secretive and non-transparent). If publicly featured at all, the new securitisation moves are presented by the politicians and the media as standard actions.

References

Anderson, Craig A.; Gentile, Douglas A.; & Buckley, Katherina E. 2007. *Violent Video Game Effects on Children and Adolescents: Theory, Research, and Public Policy.* Oxford University Press.

Andreas, Peter & Ethan, Nadelmann (2006): *Policing the Globe: Criminalization and Crime Control in International Relations.* Oxford: Oxford University Press.

Austin, J.L. (1980): "How to do things with words". In: J, O, Urmson, J.O & Sbisá, M (ed.) *How to do things with words: the William James lectures delivered at Harvard University in 1955.* Oxford: Oxford University Press.

Beck, Ulrich (1992): *Risk Society: Towards a New Modernity.* London: SAGE Publications.

Beck, Ulrich (2002a): "The Terrorist Threat: World Risk Society Revisited". *Theory, Culture & Society* 19(4), 39–55.

Beck, Ulrich (2002b): "The Silence of Words and the Political Dynamics in the World". *Logos* 1(4), 1–18.

Bigo, Didier & Anastassia, Tsoukala (ed.) (2008): *Terror, Insecurity and Liberty: Illiberal practices of liberal regimes after 911.* UK: Routledge.

Bigo, Didier & Guittet, Emmanuel-Pierre & Andy, Smith (2004): "La participation des militaires à la sécurité intérieure: RU, Irlande du Nord". *Cultures & Conflits,* 56: 11-34.

Booth, Ken (ed.) (2005): *Critical Security Studies and World Pol*itics. Boulder: Lynne Rienner.

[43] The intent to compile a national strategy on security research was partly provoked by the detection of this problem. See Proposal for national strategy on safety and security research 2009.

Braun, Abdalbarr. 2002. Warrior, Waldgaenger, Anarch. (http://www.fluxeuropa.com/juenger-anarch.htm, last accessed on 20.7.2008).

Bousquet, Antoine. 2009. *The Scientific Way of Warfare: Order and Chaos on the Battlefields of Modernity*. London: Hurst & Company.

Button Mark (2008): *Doing Security: Critical Reflections and an Agenda for Change*. UK: Palgrave MacMillan.

Buzan, Barry, Wæver, Ole & Jaap, de Wilde (1998): *Security: A Framework for Analysis*. Boulder: Lynne Rienner.

CASE (2006): *Critical Approaches to Security in Europe*. Draft programme for research seminar, TAPRI Tampere 28-30.6.2006.

Carter, Chris; Clegg, Stewart R.; & Kronberger, Martin. 2008. 'Strategy As Practice?' *Strategic Organization* Vol. 6, No. I, 83–99.

Ceaser, James. 2004. 'The Philosophical Origins of Anti-Americanism in Europe', *Understanding Anti-Americanism, Its Origins and Impact at Home and Abroad*, ed. Paul Hollander, Ivan R. Dee, Chicago.

CEPOL-report (2007): *Perspectives of Police Science in Europe. Project Group on a European Approach to Police Science*. European Police College, April 2007.

Chia, Robert & MacKay, Brad. 2007. 'Post-processual Challenges for the Emerging Strategy-As-Practice Perspective: Discovering Strategy in the Logic of Practice', Human Relations *Vol. 60, No. I, 217–242.*

Clegg, Stewart R.; Courpasson, David; & Phillips, Nelson. 2006. Power and Organizations. Sage.

Dalby, Simon (1997):"Contesting an Essential Concept: Reading the Dilemmas in Contemporary Security Discourse". In: Krause, K & Williams, M. C. (ed.) *Critical Security Studies*. Minneapolis: University of Minnesota Press, 3–31.

De Boer Monica (2006): "Fusing the Fragments: Challenges for EU Internal Security Governance on Terrorism". In: Mahncke, D & Monar, J (ed.) *International Terrorism. A European Response to a Global Threat?* College of Europe Studies No. 3, Brussels, Peter Lang Publishers, 83-111.

Der Derian, James (1995): "The Value of Security: Hobbes, Marx, Nietzsche and Baudrillard". In: Lipschutz, R. D (ed.) *On Security*. New York: Columbia University Press, 24–45.

Furedi, Frank (2002): *Culture of Fear: Risk Taking and the Morality of Low Expectation*. London: Continuum.

Furedi, Frank (2005): "Terrorism and the Politics of Fear". In: Hale, C, Hayward, Wahidin, A & E, Wincup (ed.) *Criminology*. Oxford: Oxford University Press, 307–22.

Joenniemi, Pertti (2005): Myötä- vai vastakarvaan? Turvallisuus muuttuvien uhkien maailmassa. *Kosmopolis.* 3/2005.

Gray, Colin S. 2005. *Another Bloody Century: Future Warfare*. London: Weidenfeld & Nicolson.

Jackson, Richard. 2005. *Writing the War on Terrorism: Language, Politics and Counter-Terrorism*. Manchester University Press.

Krause, Keith & Williams, Michael C. (1997): "From Strategy to Security: Foundations of Critical Security Studies." In: Krause, K & M. C., Williams (ed.) *Critical Security Studies*. USA: UCL Press, 33–59.

Laitinen Kari (2006): "Sirpaloitunut turvallisuus – turvallista hallintaa vai pelon hysteriaa?" In: Huhtinen, A & J, Rantapelkonen (ed.) *Sirpaleita sotilaskulttuurin raja-alueilta: Suomen puolustusjärjestelmä globaalin muutoksen kourissa*. Maanpuolustuskorkeakoulu: Johtamisen laitos.

Laitinen, Kari (1999): *Turvallisuuden todellisuus ja problematiikka. Tulkintoja uusista turvallisuuksista kylmän sodan jälkeen*. Tampereen yliopiston politiikan tutkimuksen laitoksen sarja: Studia Politica Tamperensis No. 7.

Laitinen, Kari (2005): "Emansipaatio synnyttää turvallisuutta – turvallisuus on emansipaatiota", *Kosmopolis*. 3/2005.

Laitinen, Kari (2008): "New(?) terrorism and a question of radicalisation: contemporary challenges for security organisations and policing". In: Virta, S (toim.) *Policing Meets New Challenges: Preventing Radicalization and Recruitment*. CEPOL reports, published by University of Tampere, CEPOL, and Police College of Finland, 2008.

Laitinen, Kari (ed.) (2002): *Valtapolitiikan ajattomuus — Maailmanpolitiikan tulkintoja 9.11. jälkeen.* Studia Politica Tamperensis No.10, 2002, Tampereen yliopisto.

Laitinen, Kari (ed.) (2007): *Tuhat ja yksi uhkaa – tulkintoja terrorismista*. Poliisiammattikorkeakoulun tiedotteita 66/2007. Tampere: Cityoffset.

Loader, Ian (2002): "Governing European Policing: some problems and prospects", *Policing and Society* 12(4) 291-306.

Medby, Jamison Jo & Glenn, Russell W. 2002. *Street Smart: Intelligence Preparation of the Battlefield for Urban Operations*. Santa Monica, California: RAND.

Ministry of the Interior and Kingdom Relations (2008), *The Netherlands' National Security Strategy*. http://www.minbzk.nl, 26.6.2009.

Mythen, Gabe & Sandra, Walklate (2006): "Communicating the terrorist risk: Harnessing a culture of fear?". *Crime, Media & Culture* 2(2), 123–142.

Mäkipää, Leena (2004): *Henkirikos Ilta-Sanomissa: Journalistisen kulttuurin murros ja rikosjournalismi.* Poliisiammattikorkeakoulun tiedotteita 37.Helsinki: Edita Prima Oy.

Ollila, Marja-Riitta (2006): Tulevaisuuden turvallisuus: pirstaleista kokonaisuuteen". In: Rantala, K & S, Virta (ed.) *Tieto – mahdollisuus, uhka vai turva?* Poliisiammattikorkeakoulun tiedotteita 47. Helsinki: Edita Prima Oy, 8-25.

Rasmussen, Mikkel Vedby. 2006. *The Risk Society at War: Terror, Technology and Strategy in the Twnety-First Century*. Cambridge University Press.

Roberts, David (2008): *Human Insecurity*. EU: Zed Books Ltd.

Sheehan, Michael A. 2008. *Crush the Cell: How to Defeat Terrorism Without Terrorizing Ourselves*. New York: Crown Publishers.

Skinner Quentin (1988): Quentin Skinner on Interpretation. Teoksessa Skinner, Q & and His Critics (toim.) *Context and Meaning*. UK: Polity Press.

Sloan, Stephen. 2007. *Terrorism: The Present Threat in Context*. Oxford: Berg.

Smith, Rupert*. 2007. The Utility of Force: The Art of War in the Modern World. New York: Alfred A. Knopf.*

*Statewatch http://www. statewatch.org, 26.6.200*9.

Syrjälä, Hanna (2007): *Väkivalta lööppijulkisuudessa.* Journalismin tutkimusyksikkö, Tiedotusopin laitos, Tampereen yliopisto, julkaisuja sarja A 101/2007.

The National Coordinator for Counterterrorism, NCTb (2006): *Counterterrorism at Local* Level: A guide. http://english.nctb.nl/current_topics/reports/index.aspx?q=o&p5=rapport&p7=2000-06-21&select=3, 26.6.2009.

Thornton, Rod. 2007. *Asymmetric Warfare: Threat and Response in the Twenty-first Century*. USA: Polity Press.

Van Creveld, Martin. 2006. *The Changing Face of War: Lessons of Combat, from the Marne to Iraq*. New York: Ballantine Books.

Ventre, Daniel. 2007. *Information Warfare*. USA: Wiley.

Virta, Sirpa (2009): "Re/Building the EU: governing through counter terrorism". In: Bajc, V. & W, de Lint (ed.) *Security in Everyday Life*. Routledge, 2009 (forthcoming).

Wood, Jennifer & Clifford, Shearing (2007): *Imagining security*. UK: Willan Publishing.

Williams, John Allen. 2008. *The Military and Society Beyond the Postmodern Era*. Foreign Policy Institute, Elsevier Limited: 199–215.

Zur, Ofer (1987):"The Psychohistory of Warfare: The Co-Evolution of Culture, Psyche and Enemy". *Journal of Peace Research.* 24;125.

Intelligence-Driven Computer Network Defense Informed by Analysis of Adversary Campaigns and Intrusion Kill Chains

Eric Hutchins, Michael Cloppert and Rohan Amin
Lockheed Martin, USA

Editorial Commentary

This paper presents an in-depth look at one avenue of attack that can be used for various purposes. The problems it describes, that of advanced persistent threats and targeted malicious emails, are serious and significant. They are extremely difficult to detect and defend against, making them extremely high payoff weapons. They also require quite a detail of investment on the part of the attacker: developing both the knowledge and the approach to launching such an attack is not easy and takes a lot of time. The fact that these attacks exist in surprising numbers indicates that the payoff for that investment is positive. This deep look into the challenges of one corporation in detecting and eliminating these threats is instructive in how hard it is to defend against a persistent enemy attacking through information systems and networks

Abstract: Conventional network defense tools such as intrusion detection systems and anti-virus focus on the vulnerability component of risk, and traditional incident response methodology presupposes a successful intrusion. An evolution in the goals and sophistication of computer network intrusions has rendered these approaches insufficient for certain actors. A new class of threats, appropriately dubbed the "Advanced Persistent Threat" (APT), represents well-resourced and trained adversaries that conduct multi-year intrusion campaigns targeting highly sensitive economic, proprietary, or national security information. These adversaries accomplish their goals using advanced tools and techniques designed to defeat most conventional computer network defense mechanisms. Network defense techniques which leverage knowledge about these adversaries can create an intelligence feedback loop, enabling defenders to establish a state of information superiority which decreases the adversary's likelihood of success with each subsequent intrusion attempt. Using a kill chain model to describe phases of intrusions, mapping adversary kill chain indicators to defender courses of action, identifying patterns that link individual intrusions into broader campaigns, and understanding the iterative nature of intelligence gathering form the basis of intelligence-driven computer network defense (CND). Institutionalization of this approach reduces the likelihood of adversary success, informs network defense investment and resource prioritization, and yields relevant metrics of performance and effectiveness. The evolution of advanced persistent threats necessitates an intelligence-based model because in this model the defenders mitigate not just vulnerability, but the threat component of risk, too.

Keywords: incident response, intrusion detection, intelligence, threat, APT, computer network defense

1. Introduction

As long as global computer networks have existed, so have malicious users intent on exploiting vulnerabilities. Early evolutions of threats to computer networks involved self-propagating code. Advancements over time in antivirus technology significantly reduced this automated risk. More recently, a new class of threats, intent on the compromise of data for economic or military advancement, emerged as the largest element of risk facing some industries. This class of threat has been given the moniker "Advanced Persistent Threat," or APT. To date, most organizations have relied on the technologies and processes implemented to mitigate risks associated with automated viruses and worms which do not sufficiently address focused, manually operated APT intrusions. Conventional incident response methods fail to mitigate the risk posed by APTs because they make two flawed assumptions: response should happen after the point of compromise, and the compromise was the result of a fixable flaw (Mitropoulos et al., 2006; National Institute of Standards and Technology, 2008).

APTs have recently been observed and characterized by both industry and the U.S. government. In June and July 2005, the U.K. National Infrastructure Security Co-ordination Centre (UK-NISCC) and the U.S. Computer Emergency Response Team (US-CERT) issued technical alert bulletins describing targeted, socially-engineered emails dropping trojans to exfiltrate sensitive information. These intrusions were over a significant period of time, evaded conventional firewall and anti-virus capabilities, and enabled adversaries to harvest sensitive information (UK-NISCC, 2005; US-CERT, 2005). Epstein and Elgin (2008) of Business Week described numerous intrusions into NASA and other government networks where APT actors were undetected and successful in removing sensitive high-performance rocket design information. In February 2010, iSec Partners noted that current approaches such as anti-virus and patching are not sufficient, end users are directly targeted, and threat actors are after sensitive intellectual property (Stamos, 2010).

Before the U.S. House Armed Services Committee Subcommittee on Terrorism, Unconventional Threats and Capabilities, James Andrew Lewis of the Center for Strategic and International Studies testified that intrusions occurred at various government agencies in 2007, including the Department of Defense, State Department and Commerce Department, with the intention of information collection (Lewis, 2008). With specificity about the nature of computer network operations reportedly emanating from China, the 2008 and 2009 reports to Congress of the U.S.-China Economic and Security Review Commission summarized reporting of targeted intrusions against U.S. military, government and contractor systems. Again, adversaries were motivated by a desire to collect sensitive information (U.S.-China Economic and Security Review Commission, 2008, 2009). Finally, a report prepared for the U.S.-China Economic and Security Review Commission, Krekel (2009) profiles an advanced intrusion with extensive detail demonstrating the patience and calculated nature of APT.

Advances in infrastructure management tools have enabled best practices of enterprise-wide patching and hardening, reducing the most easily accessible vulnerabilities in networked services. Yet APT actors continually demonstrate the capability to compromise systems by using advanced tools, customized malware, and "zero-day" exploits that anti-virus and patching cannot detect or mitigate. Responses to APT intrusions require an evolution in analysis, process, and technology; it is possible to anticipate and mitigate future intrusions based on knowledge of the threat. This paper describes an intelligence-driven, threat-focused approach to study intrusions from the adversaries' perspective. Each discrete phase of the intrusion is mapped to courses of action for detection, mitigation and response. The phrase "kill chain" describes the structure of the intrusion, and the corresponding model guides analysis to inform actionable security intelligence. Through this model, defenders can develop resilient mitigations against intruders and intelligently prioritize investments in new technology or processes. Kill chain analysis illustrates that the adversary must progress successfully through each stage of the chain before it can achieve its desired objective; just one mitigation disrupts the chain and the adversary. Through intelligence-driven response, the defender can achieve an advantage over the aggressor for APT caliber adversaries.

This paper is organized as follows: section two of this paper documents related work on phase based models of defense and countermeasure strategy. Section three introduces an intelligence-driven computer network defense model (CND) that incorporates threat-specific intrusion analysis and defensive mitigations. Section four presents an application of this new model to a real case study, and section five summarizes the paper and presents some thoughts on future study.

2. Related work

While the modeling of APTs and corresponding response using kill chains is unique, other phase based models to defensive and countermeasure strategies exist.

A United States Department of Defense Joint Staff publication describes a kill chain with stages find, fix, track, target, engage, and assess (U.S. Department of Defense, 2007). The United States Air Force (USAF) has used this framework to identify gaps in Intelligence, Surveillance and Reconnaissance (ISR) capability and to prioritize the development of needed systems (Tirpak, 2000). Threat chains have also been used to model Improvised Explosive Device (IED) attacks (National Research Council, 2007). The IED delivery chain models everything from adversary funding to attack execution. Coordinated intelligence and defensive efforts focused on each stage of the IED threat chain as the ideal way to counter these attacks. This approach also provides a model for identification of basic research needs by mapping existing capability to the chain. Phase based models have also been used for antiterrorism planning. The United States Army describes the terrorist operational planning cycle as a seven step process that serves as a baseline to assess the intent and capability of terrorist organizations (United States Army Training and Doctrine Command, 2007). Hayes (2008) applies this model to the antiterrorism planning process for military installations and identifies principles to help commanders determine the best ways to protect themselves.

Outside of military context, phase based models have also been used in the information security field. Sakuraba et al. (2008) describe the Attack-Based Sequential Analysis of Countermeasures (ABSAC) framework that aligns types of countermeasures along the time phase of an attack. The ABSAC approach includes more reactive post-compromise countermeasures than early detection capability to uncover persistent adversary campaigns. In an application of phase based models to insider threats, Duran et al. (2009) describe a tiered detection and countermeasure strategy based on the progress of malicious insiders. Willison and Siponen (2009) also address insider threat by adapting a phase based model called Situational Crime Prevention (SCP). SCP models crime from the offender's perspective and then maps controls to various phases of the crime. Finally, the security company Mandiant proposes an "exploitation life cycle". The Mandiant model, however, does not map courses of defensive action and is based on post-compromise actions (Mandiant, 2010). Moving detections and mitigations to earlier phases of the intrusion kill chain is essential for CND against APT actors.

3. Intelligence-driven computer network defense

Intelligence-driven computer network defense is a risk management strategy that addresses the threat component of risk, incorporating analysis of adversaries, their capabilities, objectives, doctrine and limitations. This is necessarily a continuous process, leveraging indicators to discover new activity with yet more indicators to leverage. It requires a new understanding of the intrusions themselves, not as singular events, but rather as phased progressions. This paper presents a new intrusion kill chain model to analyze intrusions and drive defensive courses of action.

The effect of intelligence-driven CND is a more resilient security posture. APT actors, by their nature, attempt intrusion after intrusion, adjusting their operations based on the success or failure of each attempt. In a kill chain model, just one mitigation breaks the chain and thwarts the adversary, therefore any repetition by the adversary is a liability that defenders must recognize and leverage. If defenders implement countermeasures faster than adversaries evolve, it raises the costs an adversary must expend to achieve their objectives. This model shows, contrary to conventional wisdom, such aggressors have no inherent advantage over defenders.

3.1. Indicators and the indicator life cycle

The fundamental element of intelligence in this model is the indicator. For the purposes of this paper, an indicator is any piece of information that objectively describes an intrusion. Indicators can be subdivided into three types:

- Atomic – Atomic indicators are those which cannot be broken down into smaller parts and retain their meaning in the context of an intrusion. Typical examples here are IP addresses, email addresses, and vulnerability identifiers.
- Computed – Computed indicators are those which are derived from data involved in an incident. Common computed indicators include hash values and regular expressions.
- Behavioral – Behavioral indicators are collections of computed and atomic indicators, often subject to qualification by quantity and possibly combinatorial logic. An example would be a statement such as "the intruder would initially used a backdoor which generated network traffic matching [regular expression] at the rate of [some frequency] to [some IP address], and then replace it with one matching the MD5 hash [value] once access was established."

Using the concepts in this paper, analysts will reveal indicators through analysis or collaboration, mature these indicators by leveraging them in their tools, and then utilize them when matching activity is discovered. This activity, when investigated, will often lead to additional indicators that will be subject to the same set of actions and states. This cycle of actions, and the corresponding indicator states, form the indicator life cycle illustrated in Figure 1.

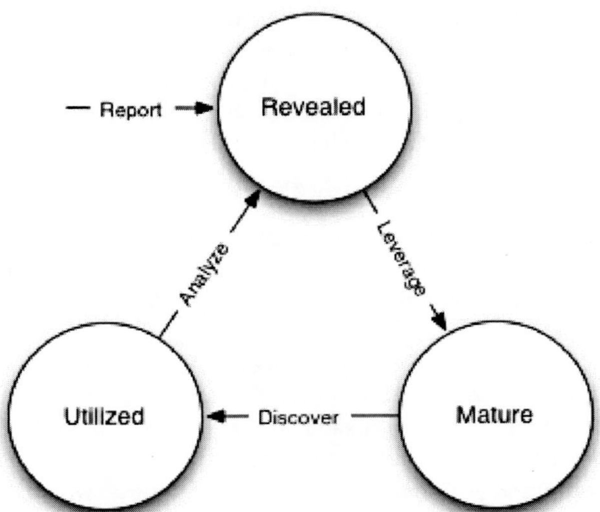

Figure 1: Indicator life cycle states and transitions

This applies to all indicators indiscriminately, regardless of their accuracy or applicability. Tracking the derivation of a given indicator from its predecessors can be time-consuming and problematic if sufficient tracking isn't in place, thus it is imperative that indicators subject to these processes are valid and applicable to the problem set in question. If attention is not paid to this point, analysts may find themselves applying these techniques to threat actors for which they were not designed, or to benign activity altogether.

3.2. Intrusion kill chain

A kill chain is a systematic process to target and engage an adversary to create desired effects. U.S. military targeting doctrine defines the steps of this process as find, fix, track, target, engage, assess (F2T2EA): find adversary targets suitable for engagement; fix their location; track and observe; target with suitable weapon or asset to create desired effects; engage adversary; assess effects (U.S. Department of Defense, 2007). This is an integrated, end-to-end process described as a "chain" because any one deficiency will interrupt the entire process.

Expanding on this concept, this paper presents a new kill chain model, one specifically for intrusions. The essence of an intrusion is that the aggressor must develop a payload to breach a trusted boundary, establish a presence inside a trusted environment, and from that presence, take actions towards their objectives, be they moving laterally inside the environment or violating the confidentiality, integrity, or availability of a system in the environment. The intrusion kill chain is defined as reconnaissance, weaponization, delivery, exploitation, installation, command and control (C2), and actions on objectives.

With respect to computer network attack (CNA) or computer network espionage (CNE), the definitions for these kill chain phases are as follows:

- Reconnaissance - Research, identification and selection of targets, often represented as crawling Internet websites such as conference proceedings and mailing lists for email addresses, social relationships, or information on specific technologies.
- Weaponization - Coupling a remote access trojan with an exploit into a deliverable payload, typically by means of an automated tool (weaponizer). Increasingly, client application data files such as Adobe Portable Document Format (PDF) or Microsoft Office documents serve as the weaponized deliverable.
- Delivery - Transmission of the weapon to the targeted environment. The three most prevalent delivery vectors for weaponized payloads by APT actors, as observed by the Lockheed Martin Computer Incident Response Team (LM-CIRT) for the years 2004-2010, are email attachments, websites, and USB removable media.
- Exploitation - After the weapon is delivered to victim host, exploitation triggers intruders' code. Most often, exploitation targets an application or operating system vulnerability, but it could also more simply exploit the users themselves or leverage an operating system feature that auto-executes code.
- Installation - Installation of a remote access trojan or backdoor on the victim system allows the adversary to maintain persistence inside the environment.
- Command and Control (C2) - Typically, compromised hosts must beacon outbound to an Internet controller server to establish a C2 channel. APT malware especially requires manual interaction

rather than conduct activity automatically. Once the C2 channel establishes, intruders have "hands on the keyboard" access inside the target environment.

- Actions on Objectives - Only now, after progressing through the first six phases, can intruders take actions to achieve their original objectives. Typically, this objective is data exfiltration which involves collecting, encrypting and extracting information from the victim environment; violations of data integrity or availability are potential objectives as well. Alternatively, the intruders may only desire access to the initial victim box for use as a hop point to compromise additional systems and move laterally inside the network.

3.3. Courses of action

The intrusion kill chain becomes a model for actionable intelligence when defenders align enterprise defensive capabilities to the specific processes an adversary undertakes to target that enterprise. Defenders can measure the performance as well as the effectiveness of these actions, and plan investment roadmaps to rectify any capability gaps. Fundamentally, this approach is the essence of intelligence-driven CND: basing security decisions and measurements on a keen understanding of the adversary.

Table 1 depicts a course of action matrix using the actions of detect, deny, disrupt, degrade, deceive, and destroy from DoD information operations (IO) doctrine (U.S. Department of Defense, 2006). This matrix depicts in the exploitation phase, for example, that host intrusion detection systems (HIDS) can passively detect exploits, patching denies exploitation altogether, and data execution prevention (DEP) can disrupt the exploit once it initiates. Illustrating the spectrum of capabilities defenders can employ, the matrix includes traditional systems like network intrusion detection systems (NIDS) and firewall access control lists (ACL), system hardening best practices like audit logging, but also vigilant users themselves who can detect suspicious activity.

Table 1: Courses of action matrix

Phase	Detect	Deny	Disrupt	Degrade	Deceive	Destroy
Reconnaissance	Web analytics	Firewall ACL				
Weaponization	NIDS	NIPS				
Delivery	Vigilant user	Proxy filter	In-line AV	Queuing		
Exploitation	HIDS	Patch	DEP			
Installation	HIDS	"chroot" jail	AV			
C2	NIDS	Firewall ACL	NIPS	Tarpit	DNS redirect	
Actions on Objectives	Audit log			Quality of Service	Honeypot	

Here, completeness equates to resiliency, which is the defender's primary goal when faced with persistent adversaries that continually adapt their operations over time. The most notable adaptations are exploits, particularly previously undisclosed "zero-day" exploits. Security vendors call these "zero-day attacks," and tout "zero day protection". This myopic focus fails to appreciate that the exploit is but one change in a broader process. If intruders deploy a zero-day exploit but reuse observable tools or infrastructure in other phases, that major improvement is fruitless if the defenders have mitigations for the repeated indicators. This repetition demonstrates a defensive strategy of complete indicator utilization achieves resiliency and forces the adversary to make more difficult and comprehensive adjustments to achieve their objectives. In this way, the defender increases the adversary's cost of executing successful intrusions.

Defenders can generate metrics of this resiliency by measuring the performance and effectiveness of defensive actions against the intruders. Consider an example series of intrusion attempts from a single APT campaign that occur over a seven month timeframe, shown in Figure 2. For each phase of the kill chain, a white diamond indicates relevant, but passive, detections were in place at the time of that month's intrusion attempt, a black diamond indicates relevant mitigations were in place, and an empty cell indicates no relevant capabilities were available. After each intrusion, analysts leverage newly revealed indicators to update their defenses, as shown by the gray arrows. The illustration shows, foremost, that at last one mitigation was in place for all three intrusion attempts, thus mitigations were successful. However, it also clearly shows significant differences in each month. In December, defenders detect the weaponization and block the delivery but uncover a brand new, unmitigated, zero-day exploit in the process. In March, the adversary re-uses the same exploit, but evolves the weaponization technique and delivery infrastructure, circumventing detection and rendering those defensive systems ineffective. By June, the defenders updated their capabilities sufficiently to have detections and mitigations layered from weaponization to C2. By framing metrics in the context of the kill chain, defenders had the proper perspective of the relative effect of their defenses against the intrusion attempts and where there were gaps to prioritize remediation.

	December	March	June
Reconnaissance			
Weaponization	◇		→ ◇
Delivery	◆		→ ◆
Exploitation		→ ◆	→ ◆
Installation	◆	→ ◆	→ ◆
C2	◆	→ ◆	→ ◆
Actions on Objectives			

Legend ◇ *Detection* ◆ *Mitigation* → *Leverage new indicators*

Figure 2: Illustration of the relative effectiveness of defenses against subsequent intrusion attempts

3.4. Intrusion reconstruction

Kill chain analysis is a guide for analysts to understand what information is, and may be, available for defensive courses of action. It is a model to analyze the intrusions in a new way. Most detected intrusions will provide a limited set of attributes about a single phase of an intrusion. Analysts must still discover many other attributes for each phase to enumerate the maximum set of options for courses of action. Further, based on detection in a given phase, analysts can assume that prior phases of the intrusion have already executed successfully.

Only through complete analysis of prior phases, as shown in Figure 3, can actions be taken at those phases to mitigate future intrusions. If one cannot reproduce the delivery phase of an intrusion, one cannot hope to act on the delivery phase of subsequent intrusions from the same adversary. The conventional incident response process initiates after our exploit phase, illustrating the self-fulfilling prophecy that defenders are inherently disadvantaged and inevitably too late. The inability to fully reconstruct all intrusion phases prioritizes tools, technologies, and processes to fill this gap.

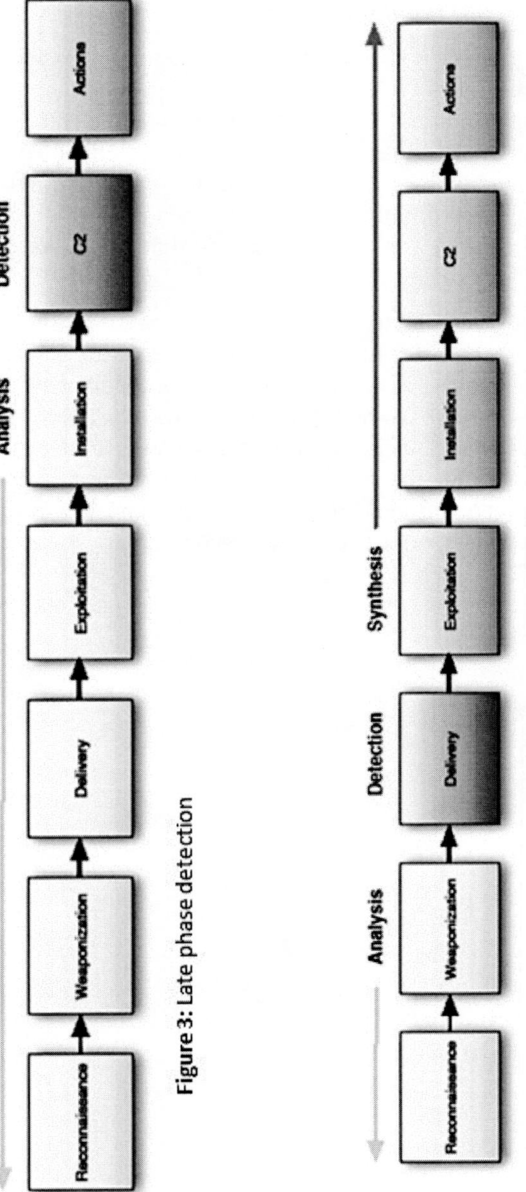

Figure 3: Late phase detection

Figure 4: Earlier phase detection

Defenders must be able to move their detection and analysis up the kill chain and more importantly to implement courses of actions across the kill chain. In order for an intrusion to be economical, adversaries must re-use tools and infrastructure. By completely understanding an intrusion, and leveraging intelligence on these tools and infrastructure, defenders force an adversary to change every phase of their intrusion in order to successfully achieve their goals in subsequent intrusions. In this way, network defenders use the persistence of adversaries' intrusions against them to achieve a level of resilience.

Equally as important as thorough analysis of successful compromises is synthesis of unsuccessful intrusions. As defenders collect data on adversaries, they will push detection from the latter phases of the kill chain into earlier ones. Detection and prevention at pre-compromise phases also necessitates a response. Defenders must collect as much information on the mitigated intrusion as possible, so that they may synthesize what might have happened should future intrusions circumvent the currently effective protections and detections (see Figure 4). For example, if a targeted malicious email is blocked due to re-use of a known indicator, synthesis of the remaining kill chain might reveal a new exploit or backdoor contained therein. Without this knowledge, future intrusions, delivered by different means, may go undetected. If defenders implement countermeasures faster than their known adversaries evolve, they maintain a tactical advantage.

3.5. Campaign analysis

At a strategic level, analyzing multiple intrusion kill chains over time will identify commonalities and overlapping indicators. Figure 5 illustrates how highly-dimensional correlation between two intrusions through multiple kill chain phases can be identified. Through this process, defenders will recognize and define intrusion campaigns, linking together perhaps years of activity from a particular persistent threat. The most consistent indicators, the campaigns key indicators, provide centers of gravity for defenders to prioritize development and use of courses of action. Figure 6 shows how intrusions may have varying degrees of correlation, but the inflection points where indicators most frequently align identify these key indicators. These less volatile indicators can be expected to remain consistent, predicting the characteristics of future intrusions with greater confidence the more frequently they are observed. In this way, an adversary's persistence becomes a liability which the defender can leverage to strengthen its posture.

The principle goal of campaign analysis is to determine the patterns and behaviors of the intruders, their tactics, techniques, and procedures (TTP), to detect "how" they operate rather than specifically "what" they do. The defender's objective is less to positively attribute the identity of the intruders than to evaluate their capabilities, doctrine, objectives and limitations; intruder attribution, however, may well be a side product of this level of analysis. As defenders study new intrusion activity, they will either link it to existing campaigns or perhaps identify a brand new set of behaviors of a theretofore unknown threat and track it as a new campaign. Defenders can assess their relative defensive posture on a campaign-by-campaign basis, and based on the assessed risk of each, develop strategic courses of action to cover any gaps.
Another core objective of campaign analysis is to understand the intruders' intent. To the extent that defenders can determine technologies or individuals of interest, they can begin to understand the adversary's mission objectives. This necessitates trending intrusions over time to evaluate targeting patterns and closely examining any data exfiltrated by the intruders. Once again this analysis results in a roadmap to prioritize highly focused security measures to defend these individuals, networks or technologies.

4. Case study

To illustrate the benefit of these techniques, a case study observed by the Lockheed Martin Computer Incident Response Team (LM-CIRT) in March 2009 of three intrusion attempts by an adversary is considered. Through analysis of the intrusion kill chains and robust indicator maturity, network defenders successfully detected and mitigated an intrusion leveraging a "zero-day" vulnerability. All three intrusions leveraged a common APT tactic: targeted malicious email (TME) delivered to a limited set of individuals, containing a weaponized attachment that installs a backdoor which initiates outbound communications to a C2 server.

4.1. Intrusion attempt 1

On March 3, 2009, LM-CIRT detected a suspicious attachment within an email discussing an upcoming American Institute of Aeronautics and Astronautics (AIAA) conference. The email claimed to be from an individual who legitimately worked for AIAA, and was directed to only 5 users, each of whom had received similar TME in the past. Analysts determined the malicious attachment, tcnom.pdf, would exploit a known, but unpatched, vulnerability in Adobe Acrobat Portable Document Format (PDF): CVE-2009-0658, documented by Adobe on February 19, 2009 (Adobe, 2009) but not patched until March 10, 2009. A copy of the email headers and body follow.

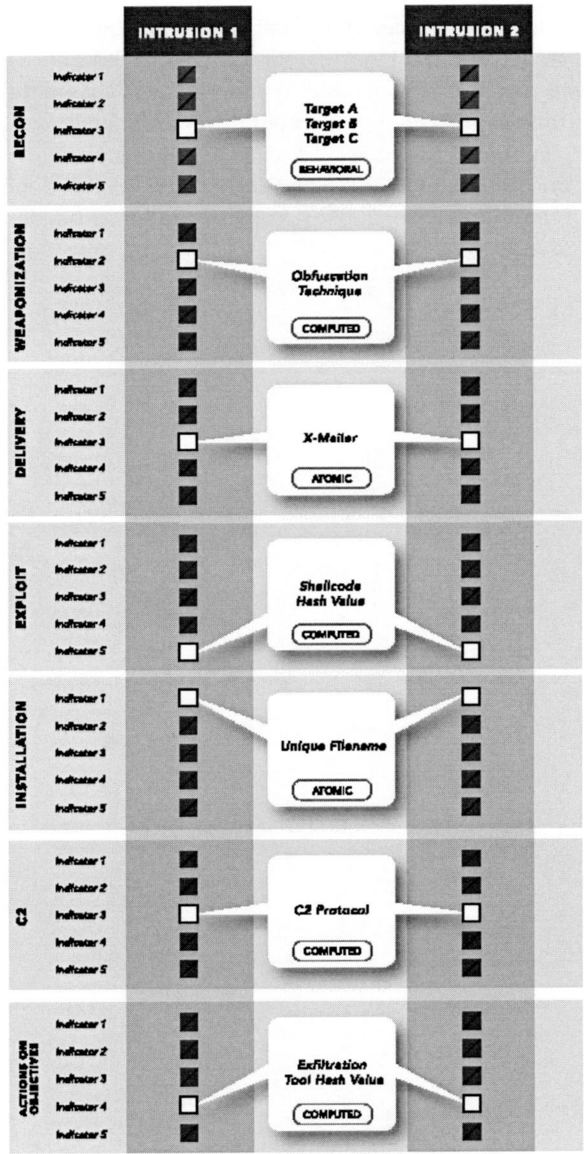

Figure 5: Common Indicators between intrusions

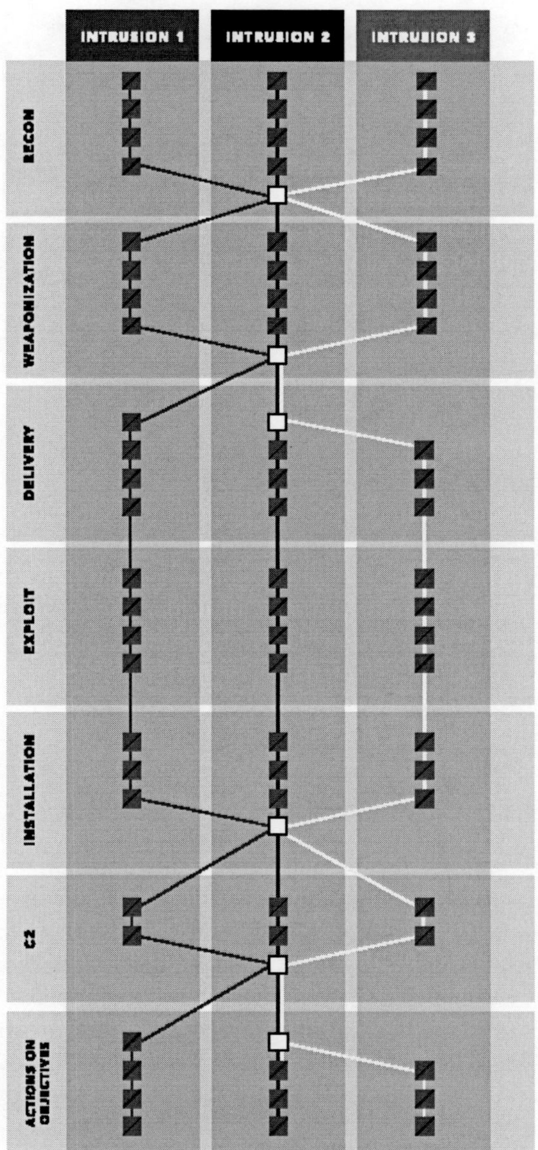

Figure 6: Campaingn key indicators

```
Received: (qmail 71864 invoked by uid 60001); Tue,
03 Mar 2009 15:01:19 +0000
Received:        from        [60.abc.xyz.215]        by
web53402.mail.re2.yahoo.com via HTTP; Tue,
03 Mar 2009 07:01:18 -0800 (PST)
Date: Tue, 03 Mar 2009 07:01:18 -0800 (PST)
From: Anne E...<dn...etto@yahoo.com>
Subject: AIAA Technical Committees
To: [REDACTED]
Reply-to: dn...etto@yahoo.com
Message-id:
<107017.64068.qm@web53402.mail.re2.yahoo.com>
MIME-version: 1.0
X-Mailer: YahooMailWebService/0.7.289.1
Content-type:      multipart/mixed;      bound-
ary="Boundary_(ID_Hq9CkDZSoSvBMukCRm7rsg)"    X-
YMail-OSG:
Please  submit  one  copy  (photocopies  are
acceptable) of this form, and one copy of
nominee's resume to: AIAA Technical Com-
mittee Nominations,
1801 Alexander Bell Drive, Reston, VA 20191. Fax
number is 703/264-
7551. Form can also be submitted via our web site at
www.aiaa.org, Inside
AIAA, Technical Committees
```

Within the weaponized PDF were two other files, a benign PDF and a Portable Executable (PE) backdoor installation file. These files, in the process of weaponization, were encrypted using a trivial algorithm with an 8-bit key stored in the exploit shellcode. Upon opening the PDF, shellcode exploiting CVE-2009-0658 would decrypt the installation binary, place it on disk as C:\Documents and Settings\[username]\Local Settings\fssm32.exe, and invoke it. The shellcode would also extract the benign PDF and display it to the user. Analysts discovered that the benign PDF was an identical copy of one published on the AIAA website at:
http://www.aiaa.org/pdf/inside/tcnom.pdf, revealing adversary reconnaissance actions.

The installer fssm32.exe would extract the backdoor components embedded within itself, saving EXE and HLP files as C:\Program Files\Internet Explorer\IEUpd.exe and IEXPLORE.hlp. Once active, the backdoor would send heartbeat data to the C2 server 202.abc.xyz.7 via valid HTTP requests. Table 2 articulates the identified, relevant indicators per phase. Due to successful mitigations, the adversary never took actions on objectives, therefore that phase is marked "N/A."

Table 2: Intrusion attempt 1 indicators

Phase	Indicators
Reconnaissance	[Recipient List] Benign File: tcnom.pdf
Weaponization	Trivial encryption algorithm: Key 1
Delivery	dn...etto@yahoo.com Downstream IP: 60.abc.xyz.215 Subject: AIAA Technical Committees [Email body]
Exploitation	CVE-2009-0658 [shellcode]
Installation	C:\...\fssm32.exe C:\...\IEUpd.exe C:\...\IEXPLORE.hlp
C2	202.abc.xyz.7 [HTTP request]
Actions on Objectives	N/A

4.2. Intrusion attempt 2

One day later, another TME intrusion attempt was executed. Analysts would identify substantially similar characteristics and link this and the previous day's attempt to a common campaign, but analysts also noted a number of differences. The repeated characteristics enabled defenders to block this activity, while the new characteristics provided analysts additional intelligence to build resiliency with further detection and mitigation courses of action.

```
Received: (qmail 97721 invoked by uid 60001); 4 Mar
2009 14:35:22 -0000
Message-ID:
```

```
<552620.97248.qm@web53411.mail.re2.yahoo.com>
Received: from [216.abc.xyz.76] by
web53411.mail.re2.yahoo.com via HTTP; Wed,
04 Mar 2009 06:35:20 PST
X-Mailer: YahooMailWebService/0.7.289.1
Date: Wed, 4 Mar 2009 06:35:20 -0800 (PST)
From: Anne E... <dn...etto@yahoo.com>
Reply-To: dn...etto@yahoo.com
Subject: 7th Annual U.S. Missile Defense Confer-
ence
To: [RE-
DACTED]
MIME-Version:
1.0
Content-Type: multipart/mixed; boundary="0-
760892832-1236177320=:97248"
Welcome to the 7th Annual U.S. Missile Defense Con-
ference
```

The sending email address was common to the March 3 and March 4 activity, but the subject matter, recipient list, attachment name, and most importantly, the downstream IP address (216.abc.xyz.76) differed. Analysis of the attached PDF, MDA_Prelim_2.pdf, revealed an identical weaponization encryption algorithm and key, as well as identical shellcode to exploit the same vulnerability. The PE installer in the PDF was identical to that used the previous day, and the benign PDF was once again an identical copy of a file on AIAA's website
(http://www.aiaa.org/events/missiledefense/MDA_Prelim_09.pdf).

The adversary never took actions towards its objectives, therefore that phase is again marked "N/A." A summary of indicators from the first two intrusion attempts is provided in Table 3.

Table 3: Intrusion attempts 1 and 2 indicators

Phase	Intrusion 1	Intrusion 2
Reconnaissance	[Recipient List] Benign File: tcnom.pdf	[Recipient List] Benign File: MDA_Prelim_09.pdf
Weaponization	Trivial encryption algorithm: Key 1	
Delivery	Downstream IP: 60.abc.xyz.215 Subject: AIAA Technical Committees [Email body]	Downstream IP: 216.abc.xyz.76 Subject: 7th Annual U.S. Missile Defense Conference [Email body]
	dn...etto@yahoo.com	
Exploitation	CVE-2009-0658 [shellcode]	
Installation	C:\...\fssm32.exe C:\...\IEUpd.exe C:\...\IEXPLORE.hlp	
C2	202.abc.xyz.7 [HTTP request]	
Actions on Objectives	N/A	N/A

4.3. Intrusion attempt 3

Over two weeks later, on March 23, 2009, a significantly different intrusion was identified due to indicator overlap, though minimal, with Intrusions 1 and 2. This email contained a PowerPoint file which exploited a vulnerability that was not, until that moment, known to the vendor or network defenders. The vulnerability was publicly acknowledged 10 days later by Microsoft as security advisory 969136 and identified as CVE-2009-0556 (Microsoft, 2009b). Microsoft issued a patch on May 12, 2009 (Microsoft, 2009a). In this campaign, the adversary made a significant shift in using a brand new, "zero-day" exploits. Details of the email follow.

```
Received: (qmail 62698 invoked by uid 1000); Mon, 23 Mar 2009 17:14:22 +0000
Received: (qmail 82085 invoked by uid 60001); Mon, 23 Mar 2009 17:14:21 +0000
Received: from [216.abc.xyz.76] by
```

```
web43406.mail.sp1.yahoo.com via HTTP; Mon,
23 Mar 2009 10:14:21 -0700 (PDT)
Date: Mon, 23 Mar 2009 10:14:21 -0700 (PDT)
From: Ginette C... <ginette.c...@yahoo.com>
Subject: Celebrities Without Makeup
To: [REDACTED]
Message-id:
<297350.78665.qm@web43406.mail.sp1.yahoo.com>
MIME-version: 1.0
X-Mailer: YahooMailClassic/5.1.20 YahooMailWebSer-
vice/0.7.289.1
Content-type: multipart/mixed; bound-
ary="Boundary_(ID_DpBDtBoPTQ1DnYXw29L2Ng)"
<email body blank>
```

This email contained a new sending address, new recipient list, markedly different benign content displayed to the user (from "missile defense" to "celebrity makeup"), and the malicious PowerPoint attachment contained a completely new exploit. However, the adversaries used the same downstream IP address, 216.abc.xyz.76, to connect to the webmail service as they used in Intrusion 2. The PowerPoint file was weaponized using the same algorithm as the previous two intrusions, but with a different 8-bit key. The PE installer and backdoor were found to be identical to the previous two intrusions. A summary of indicators from all three intrusions is provided in Table 4.

Table 4: Intrusion attempts 1, 2, and 3 indicators

Phase	Intrusion 1	Intrusion 2	Intrusion 3
Reconnaissance	[Recipient List] Benign PDF	[Recipient List] Benign PDF	[Recipient List] Benign PPT
Weaponization	Trivial encryption algorithm		
	Key 1		Key 2
Delivery	[Email subject] [Email body]	[Email subject] [Email body]	[Email subject] [Email body]
	dn...etto@yahoo.com		ginette.c...@yahoo.com
	60.abc.xyz.215	216.abc.xyz.76	
Exploitation	CVE-2009-0658 [shellcode]		[PPT 0-day] [shellcode]
Installation	C:\...\fssm32.exe C:\...\IEUpd.exe C:\...\IEXPLORE.hlp		
C2	202.abc.xyz.7 [HTTP request]		
Actions on Objectives	N/A	N/A	N/A

Leveraging intelligence on adversaries at the first intrusion attempt enabled network defenders to prevent a known zero-day exploit. With each consecutive intrusion attempt, through complete analysis, more indicators were discovered. A robust set of courses of action enabled defenders to mitigate subsequent intrusions upon delivery, even when adversaries deployed a previously-unseen exploit. Further, through this diligent approach, defenders forced the adversary to avoid all mature indicators to successfully launch an intrusion from that point forward.

Following conventional incident response methodology may have been effective in managing systems compromised by these intrusions in environments completely under the control of network defenders. However, this would not have mitigated the damage done by a compromised mobile asset that moved out of the protected environment. Additionally, by only focusing on post-compromise effects (those after the Exploit phase), fewer indicators are available. Simply using a different backdoor and installer would circumvent available detections and mitigations, enabling adversary success. By preventing compromise in the first place, the resultant risk is reduced in a way unachievable through the conventional incident response process.

5. Summary

Intelligence-driven computer network defense is a necessity in light of advanced persistent threats. As conventional, vulnerability-focused processes are insufficient, understanding the threat itself, its intent, capability, doctrine, and patterns of operation is required to establish resilience. The intrusion kill chain provides a structure to analyze intrusions, extract indicators and drive defensive courses of actions. Furthermore, this model prioritizes investment for capability gaps, and serves as a framework to measure the effectiveness of the defenders' actions. When defenders consider the threat component of risk to build resilience against APTs, they can turn the persistence of these actors into a liability, decreasing the adversary's likelihood of success with each intrusion attempt.

The kill chain shows an asymmetry between aggressor and defender, any one repeated component by the aggressor is a liability. Understanding the nature of repetition for given adversaries, be it out of convenience, personal preference, or ignorance, is an analysis of cost. Modeling the cost-benefit ratio to intruders is an area for additional research. When that cost-benefit is decidedly imbalanced, it is perhaps an indicator of information superiority of one group over the other. Models of information superiority may be valuable for computer network attack and exploitation doctrine development. Finally, this paper presents an intrusions kill chain model in the context of computer espionage. Intrusions may represent a broader problem class. This research may strongly overlap with other disciplines, such as IED countermeasures.

References

Adobe. APSA09-01: Security Updates available for Adobe Reader and Acrobat versions 9 and earlier, February 2009. URL http://www.adobe.com/support/security/advisories/apsa09-01.html.

Duran F, Conrad, S. H, Conrad, G. N, Duggan, D. P and Held E. B. Building A System For Insider Security. IEEE Security & Privacy, 7(6):30–38, 2009. doi: 10.1109/MSP.2009.111.

Epstein, Keith, and Elgin, Ben. Network Security Breaches Plague NASA, November 2008. URL http://www.businessweek.com/print/magazine/content/08_48/b4110072404167.htm.

LTC Ashton Hayes. Defending Against the Unknown: Antiterrorism and the Terrorist Planning Cycle. The Guardian, 10(1):32–36, 2008. URL http://www.jcs.mil/content/files/2009-04/041309155243_ spring2008.pdf.

Krekel, Bryan. Capability of the People's Republic of China to Conduct Cyber Warfare and Computer Network Exploitation, October 2009. URL http://www.uscc.gov/researchpapers/2009/NorthropGrumman_ PRC_Cyber_Paper_FINAL_Approved%20Report_16Oct2009.pdf.

Lewis, James Andrew Holistic Approaches to Cybersecurity to Enable Network Centric Operations, April 2008. URL http://armedservices.house.gov/pdfs/TUTC040108/Lewis_Testimony040108.pdf.

Mandiant. M-Trends: The Advanced Persistent Threat, January 2010. URL http://www.mandiant.com/products/services/m-trends.

Microsoft. Microsoft Security Bulletin MS09-017: Vulnerabilities in Microsoft Office PowerPoint Could Allow Remote Code Execution (967340), May 2009a. URL http://www.microsoft.com/technet/security/ bulletin/ms09-017.mspx.

Microsoft. Microsoft Security Advisory (969136): Vulnerability in Microsoft Office PowerPoint Could Allow Remote Code Execution, April 2009b. URL http://www.microsoft.com/technet/security/advisory/969136.mspx.

Sarandis Mitropoulos, Dimitrios Patsosa, and Christos Douligeris. On Incident Handling and Response: A state-of-the-art approach. Computers & Security, 5:351–370, July 2006. URL http://dx.doi.org/10.1016/j.cose.2005.09.006.

National Institute of Standards and Technology. Special Publication 800-61: Computer Security Incident Handling Guide, March 2008. URL http://csrc.nist.gov/publications/PubsSPs.html.

National Research Council. Countering the Threat of Improvised Explosive Devices: Basic Research Opportunities (Abbreviated Version), 2007. URL http://books.nap.edu/catalog.php?record_id=11953.

Sakuraba, T. Domyo, S, Chou Bin-Hui and Sakurai, K. Exploring Security Countermeasures along the Attack Sequence. In Proc. Int. Conf. Information Security and Assurance ISA 2008, pages 427–432, 2008. doi:10.1109/ISA.2008.112.

Stamos, Alex. "Aurora" Response Recommendations, February 2010. URL https://www.isecpartners. com/files/iSEC_Aurora_Response_Recommendations.pdf.

Tirpak, John A.. Find, Fix, Track, Target, Engage, Assess. Air Force Magazine, 83:24–29, 2000. URL http://www.airforce-magazine.com/MagazineArchive/Pages/2000/July%202000/0700find.aspx.

UK-NISCC. National Infrastructure Security Co-ordination Centre: Targeted Trojan Email Attacks, June 2005. URL https://www.cpni.gov.uk/docs/ttea.pdf.

United States Army Training and Doctrine Command. A Military Guide to Terrorism in the Twenty-First Century, August 2007. URL http://www.dtic.mil/srch/doc?collection=t3&id=ADA472623.

US-CERT. Technical Cyber Security Alert TA05-189A: Targeted Trojan Email Attacks, July 2005. URL http://www.us-cert.gov/cas/techalerts/TA05-189A.html.

U.S.-China Economic and Security Review Commission. 2008 Report to Congress of the U.S. China Economic and Security Review Commission, November 2008. URL http://www.uscc.gov/annual_report/2008/ annual_report_full_08.pdf.

U.S.-China Economic and Security Review Commission. 2009 Report to Congress of the U.S.-China Economic and Security Review Commission, November 2009. URL http://www.uscc.gov/annual_report/2009/ annual_report_full_09.pdf.

U.S. Department of Defense. Joint Publication 3-13 Information Operations, February 2006. URL http://www.dtic.mil/doctrine/new_pubs/jp3_13.pdf.

U.S. Department of Defense. Joint Publication 3-60 Joint Targeting, April 2007. URL http://www.dtic. mil/doctrine/new_pubs/jp3_60.pdf.

Willison, Robert and Siponen. Mikko Overcoming the insider: reducing employee computer crime through Situational Crime Prevention. Communications of the ACM, 52(9):133–137, 2009. doi: http://doi.acm. org/10.1145/1562164.1562198.

Information Warfare – A European Perspective of Recent Developments?

Andy Jones
Technical Group Leader
Edith Cowan University
Perth, Australia

Editorial Commentary

Andy Jones, who at the time of writing was the Technical Group Leader at Edith Cowan University in Perth, Australia, brings us "Information Warfare - a European Perspective of Recent Developments." Professor Jones claims allegiances to both Australia and to Europe, and more recently to the Middle East, having accepted a position in the United Arab Emirates. He is currently resident at the University of Science, Technology and Research (KUSTAR), in Sharjah, United Arab Emirates. In this paper, Andy Jones reviews the recent history of thought regarding information warfare, beginning in the 1990s when we all thought this was more about competitive hacking than it was about serious geopolitical strife. He then takes the reader through the changes that occurred, both in the political and technical landscapes. He reviews the reported incidents of activities that could be classified variously as hactivism, cyber-activism, of cyber-warfare, and explores the common factors of each instance. The clear derivation in the development of cyber-weapons for various efforts is a genie that is out of the bottle. Further, he concludes that since most of the reported "incidents took place during periods of increased tension between the countries involved", it is likely that the use of cyber-activities of one sort or another are likely to be a more common aspect of geopolitical strife in the future and, in fact, of any strife in the future.

This review and analysis is useful from many perspectives. First, it is useful as a history lesson. The mantra, "those who do not read history are doomed to repeat it" is the favorite refrain of history teachers and politicians and yet it is startling how often many of us do not read history. This short history is illustrative of the types of challenges we can easily expect to face in the future: they are not science fiction, they are science fact. The second perspective from whence this review is useful is in an exploration of what may be in terms of management of strife. Knowing what may be is the first ingredient to proactively managing what is or should be allowable. Finally, the unheralded but intriguingly important part of this analysis is the underlying theme of connectedness. The intertwining of critical and non-critical information assets creates a web in which we are all trapped and in which we are all intimate. This then becomes the persistent vulnerability which creates the environment in which cyber-weapons become useful and employable.

Abstract: This paper looks at the developments that have taken place in the way in which Information Warfare and Information Operations are perceived both in the West and in the East. It will examine the effect a number of major influences that have affected the understanding of the subject and will look at a chronology of significant activities that have been reported and undertake an interpretation of the probable impact of these activities. Finally the paper will examine the likely future development and implementation of the concepts of information warfare and information operations and the integration of these concepts into conventional military and political activities.

Keywords: IW, IO, information warfare, operations, political, military

1. Introduction

Since the early 1990s concept of Information Warfare has been discussed in the public arena. Prior to that it had, in the main, only been discussed in Government and the military. This open discussion of the concept was largely about the potential impact on computing and the then young Internet and World Wide Web. By the second half of the decade, it had become clear that a number of the major Western nations, led by the USA and the UK, had taken the subject seriously and countries were increasingly developing policies, procedures and techniques for the use of both defensive and offensive Information Warfare (IW). In addition to the major Western nations, there were also indications that countries such as India and China had recognised the potential benefits and problems of this new concept and had started to teach Information Warfare to their military staffs in the defence colleges. From China, reports indicated that not only had the Peoples Liberation Army (PLA) developed policy and techniques, but that they had also created a number of military units of battalion strength to address what was considered to be the new battlespace. These new PLA Information Warfare units were reported to have carried out a number of large-scale exercises to practice their new skills and tactics.

At the same time there was considerable discussion regarding a range of other, new, potential weapons, ranging from High Energy Radio Frequency (HERF) and Electro Magnetic Pulse (EMP) weapons to embedded hardware and firmware, viruses, worms and Trojan horses. Particularly in the USA, there was the development of what was to be a new breed of soldier, the cyber warrior, who would take the battle into the new domain of cyberspace. These soldiers were highly computer literate and would take the battle, both offensive and defensive, into the fourth dimension (the others being land, sea and air), where their skills were seen as being able to provide a 'force enhancement' to conventional operations.

2. History of the terms used

Towards the end of the 1990s, a new term - Information Operations (IO) was also coined. This was used to define the battlefield implementation of the generic term of Information Warfare, which had, until that point, covered all aspects. By 2003, the US Department of Defense (DoD), in its Information Operations Roadmap, had refined the definition of IO to be *"The integrated employment of the core capabilities of electronic warfare [EW], computer network operations [CNO], psychological operations [PSYOP], military deception, and operations security [OPSEC], with specified supporting and related capabilities to influence, disrupt, corrupt, or usurp adversarial human and automated decision making while protecting our own.'*

The creation of a separate definition for the battlefield implementation was understandable as it became clear that the scope of any future use of the Internet and the Global Information Infrastructure (GII) as a dimension of warfare could take place outside the timeframes and the battle space that are the normal area of operations and responsibility of the military.

2.1. The effects of 9/11

So what developments have there been in the last few years? In reality, in the West, the attention on Information Warfare and Information Operations was overtaken by the events in the USA of 9/11. In the period after the terrorist attacks, emphasis was on dealing with the new, physical, threat and to fight back and wage the war on the new fundamentalist terrorism. As a result, the effort and a considerable proportion of the available funding and resources were directed to fighting this new threat.

The visibility of developments in IW or IO has also been obscures by what appears to have been a change in emphasis and the introduction of new terminology such as Network Enabled Capability (NEC) in the UK and Network Centric Warfare (NCW), which appears to have come from the USA. The use of the term NEC, as it is defined by the UK MoD in Joint Service Publication (JSP) 777 is '*Network Enabled Capability offers decisive advantage through the timely provision and exploitation of information and intelligence to enable effective decision-making and agile actions. NEC will be implemented through the coherent and progressive development of Defence Equipment, software, processes, structures, and individual and collective training, underpinned by the development of a secure, robust and extensive network or networks*'. What this definition broadly seems to mean is the use of currently available high technology equipment to give UK forces 'force multiplier' as a result of them being better informed and more agile than the opposition (getting inside the enemy's Observe, Orient, Decide, Act (OODA) loop). If friendly forces are able to react more rapidly to an incident or available information than their opponent, the friendly forces are more agile and, as a result, will be more effective. The term that appears to have originated in the USA, NCW, describes an approach to gain power for the war fighting elements through the effective use of computer networking. At the core of the concept is providing all elements of the friendly forces (land, sea, air, forward and rear), which may be geographically dispersed, with a high level of shared battle space awareness that can be exploited to achieve commanders' aims. This would provide all of the disparate elements that may be involved in the campaign with access to the same information picture, as close as possible to at the same time, which should enable them to be more effective.

The question must be asked as to whether the apparent reduction in the apparent level of reporting of Information Warfare and Information Operations and reduced level of interest means that the concept and its implementation have failed or run into difficulties. It is clear that this is not the case. Early views that cyber warriors would be deployed with the front line forces and have a significant new role in the conduct of a military operation have certainly matured. They have, in the maturing process, been modified to more realistically mirror what is likely to be achievable, and is capable of being integrated into the accepted, tried and tested conventional military operations. This is a significant issue, as the lives of members of the fighting forces will potentially be lost if the tools and techniques fail. The use of this new concept also has to be understandable and trusted by the fighting forces if it is to be use able. In reality, what this means is, how will you be able to convince a soldier on the ground or the pilot of an aircraft that a cyber attack to destroy an enemy capability has been effective.

In a scenario of a pilot flying an aggressive mission that will take him into enemy controlled airspace, and being told that the enemy air defence system that covers part of his flight path has been destroyed by the 'cyber warriors' and that it is safe for him to over-fly the area, how will it be possible to reassure them? There is no history of the use of this type of capability and the air defence installation, which would previously have been destroyed by kinetic weapons, still exists and has no apparent damage. It takes a great deal of faith for a man who is expecting to come under hostile fire and who is probably carrying a payload of explosives, to believe that a 'cyber warrior' working from a safe location far from the front line has neutralised a target that would normally have been destroyed by high explosives. When kinetic weapons destroy a target, then it is normally possible to carry out a 'battle damage assessment (BDA)' through the use of imagery and human intelligence, to determine whether the target has been either partially or totally destroyed. Once they have confirmation of the degree of visible damage that has been caused to a target, experience of previous conflicts allows the military staffs to be able to calculate, with some accuracy, how long it will take before the enemy are likely to be able to repair or replace it. In the event of the attack being conducted with cyber weapons or HERF or EMP weapons, there will, in many cases be no visible damage and the conventional BDA techniques will be ineffective. With the lack of experience of the conventional military forces in the use of this new 'weapon', the confidence that the cyber weapon will have been effective will take time to gain.

The potential credibility that information operations would have on the battlefield is compounded by the fact that to date, the tools and techniques remain largely untested and unproven as a war fighting capability. If the concept of information warfare will have trouble being accepted in its battlefield implementation, how viable is it? If you take an early version of the concept, which was provided by Miller in 1995 as, *"Information Warfare embraces several related, but distinct sets of ideas which are not always clearly distinguished. For many defense analysts, it refers primarily the military application of' computers and other information technologies, and the organizational, operational and doctrinal changes this implies for the US and other military establishments. For other writers, however, Information Warfare is a much broader idea, relating to the emergence of "Information Age" civilization and the development of associated modes of political and social conflict which point toward the gradual erosion of nation-states and their monopoly of organized violence."*, it was clear that information warfare would have an impact that extended far beyond any potential battlefield implementation and will be based on political requirements.

Given this wider potential use of this type of tools and techniques to achieve political ends, which is also normally considered to be the function of armed forces, is there any indication that information warfare tools and techniques have been used?

The likelihood that there will ever be a declaration of 'cyber war' by a nation state is extremely remote. We have seen several 'cyber wars' or 'cyber jihads' declared by individuals and groups of Internet users who have a grievance against another group or a nation state, but declarations of war are properly the preserve of governments. In modern society it is unusual that there is a declaration of war, even for the large number of conventional armed conflicts that have taken place. During this period however, there have been a number of incidents reported. Given the percentage of information security incidents that are reported, there have undoubtedly been many more that have not. The incidents that have been reported give an indication that 'Information Warfare' techniques have been used. One of the major problems that is faced is the attribution of blame for these incidents, which can probably best be described as 'antisocial' activity on the networks. While individuals, small groups and possibly a terrorist group would probably claim credit for their actions, it is unlikely that a nation state or an organised crime group would. One of the problems with warfare in cyberspace is that the entry level for individuals and groups to take part has been lowered to a point where nearly everyone, potentially has the capability. This reduction in the level of knowledge, equipment and resources have created what Dr. Jamie Mackintosh of the UK Defence Academy has called the 'empowered small agent' to describe individuals and groups that can have been enabled by the Internet and high technology to have a disproportionate impact on others. This has resulted in the ability to accurately identify the cause of significant attacks on systems being made much more difficult.

3. Recent events

In the following paragraphs a number of incidents, most of which were reported as Information Warfare attacks are detailed.

In 1982, according to reports (Hoffman 2004), a Trojan horse that has been inserted into software that they had stolen from the USA was the cause of an explosion is a Russian gas pipeline. While this is well before the concept of 'Information Warfare' was coined and came into use in the military, it is characteristic of the techniques that the term subsequently came to describe.

In 1998, it was reported that an Indian Army website (Gera 2001) had been hacked by Pakistani intelligence agents in advance of talks that were due to take place in Islamabad in October 1998. The website had been launched by the Indian Army in August 1998 to provide what they claimed was *'factual information about daily events in Kashmir'*. Attempts access the site were redirected to a server that contained anti-India propaganda as a result of the hacking.

In March 2000, it was reported that members of the Aum Shinryko cult had developed a software system that they had procured to track 150 police fleet vehicles, including a number of unmarked cars, by the Japanese Metropolitan Police Department. This was the group that was blamed for the release of Sarin gas in the Tokyo subway in 1995, which resulted in the deaths of 12 people and injury to approximately 6,000 more. By the time that the connection to the cult was discovered, classified tracking data on 115 vehicles had already been handed over to the developers. The group were subsequently reported to have also developed software for at least 10 other government agencies and 80 Japanese companies. The report (Denning 2000) speculated that the cult members may have installed Trojan horses to enable them to launch or facilitate cyber attacks in the future.

According to a report in October 2000, Israel came under a cyber attack and several of the official Israeli web sites were taken off line as a result of a concerted jamming campaign by Islamic groups around the world (BBC News 2000). The websites affected included the Israeli parliament that was penetrated by hackers believed to be based in Saudi Arabia, the foreign ministry website, the Office of the Prime Minister's and that of the website of the Israeli Defence Forces (IDF). The attacks on the Israeli websites were reported to have been caused by attacks by a group of Israeli teenagers who had sabotaged a Hezbollah organisation website and an Israeli teenager who claimed to have destroyed an Iraqi Government internet site the previous year.

Following the collision between a Chinese fighter and a U.S. spy plane that was gathering intelligence off the Chinese mainland in April 2001, a 'hacking war' (Gregory 2001) broke out between hackers in China and the U.S.A. It was reported that nearly 40 Chinese and U.S. websites were attacked in a single day and it was also estimated that hundreds were attacked over a period of about one month. Reports suggested that the attacks on the websites in the U.S.A. had been "state-sponsored" by China. This claim was based on the level of control that the Chinese Government was thought to have over Internet access. The controls had been implemented in an attempt to filter out Western influences and as a considered in the West that, if the attacks were not directly sponsored by the government, then they must have been carried out with at least their knowledge and tacit agreement.

According to a statement (Hess 2002) from the U.S. Pentagon in May 2002, a series of cyber attacks on the Department of Defense that were anticipated from hackers that were based in China, did not occur. This was reported to be after the Chinese government had apparently told private hackers not to repeat the defacements of U.S. government Websites that had taken place the previous year.

In a September 2003 report (Shu-ling 2003), the Taiwanese Cabinet spokesman Lin Chia-lung was quoted as stating that "National intelligence has indicated that an army of hackers based in China's Hubei and Fujian provinces has successfully spread 23 different Trojan horse programs to the networks [of] 10 private high-tech companies here to use them as a springboard to break into at least 30 different government agencies and 50 private companies." The report stated that the networks that had been affected in the attack included the Ministry of National Defense, the National Police Administration, the Central Election Commission and the Central Bank of China. The attacks were thought to be aimed at paralyzing a number of the nation's significant computer systems, the theft of large quantities of sensitive government information (similar to attacks on systems in the USA or in an intelligence gathering operation in preparation for future information warfare attacks.

In another report (The Marmot Blog 2004) in 2004, the Institute for Traditional Korean Studies Movement and a number of other civic groups threatened to carry out cyber attacks on Chinese websites. The groups threatened to attack and disrupt the services of the websites belonging to the Chinese Foreign Ministry, the Beijing Municipal Government, the Xinhua News and the People's Daily newspaper.

In April 2004 the Peoples Liberation Army (PLA) daily newspaper reported (Jinlin and Zhenjiang 2004) that an Info-warfare Group Army that was attached to the Beijing Military Area Command had just finished a number of Information Warfare combat exercises. During these exercises the "Red Army" had launched a number of attacks utilising a range of different offensive tactics. These included precision strikes, which were said to have been launched against both soft and hard targets of the "Blue Army" and resulted in the communication systems of the Blue Army being quickly disabled. The report also indicated that the military forces had joined their efforts with a number of research institutes to develop a computer network, multimedia and virtual technology training system to simulate a 'communications battlelab'.

The following year, in April 2005, at a time of increased international tension between China and Japan, Japan's police and defence agencies came under a cyber attack which reduced access to those systems (The Australian Tokyo Correspondent 2005), apparently as a result of a Chinese website calling for the jamming of Japanese servers. The increased tension had arisen as a result of the Japanese announcement that it had authorised a number of its companies to drill for oil and gas in an area of the East China Sea and also following the Japanese approval of a history textbook that China claimed would whitewash Japan's wartime record.

In the same month, Japanese hackers were reported (Tae-Gyu 2005) to have stepped up cyber attacks on Korean Web sites during a dispute between the two nations over sovereignty of the Dokdo islets in the East Sea. According to the report, Japanese based hackers accounted for more than 15 percent of the April 2005 foreign network attacks, with attacks that originated in China leading the table with 45 percent.

The following month, a number of reports (Dickinson 2005) (Blackhurst 2005) were published about a case of industrial espionage that involved a number of significant Israeli companies. The companies involved included the YES satellite TV Company, Cellcom and Pelephone Communications. According to the reports, a total of 21 people were arrested and 11 of them worked as private detectives from three of the top Israeli investigation agencies. The industrial espionage, which was thought to have taken place over a period of more than 18 months, was carried out using Trojan horses inserted into their competitor's computer systems.

Also in 2005 (June), the UK's National Infrastructure Security Co-ordination Centre (NISCC) issued a report (NISCC Briefing 2005) that stated that approximately 300 UK government departments and businesses critical to the country's infrastructure had been targeted by hackers using a series of specially crafted Trojan horse attacks. The report stated that the Trojan horse attacks, of which many originated in the Far East, were delivered using email attachments or by exploiting links to malicious websites. The attacks appeared to an attempt to covertly obtain commercial or economic information and the attacks had been going on for some time, but have recently become more sophisticated.

In August 2005, a report from the USA (Tiboni 2005) stated that over the preceding five years, Chinese hackers had successfully probed and penetrated a number of U.S. Department of Defense (DoD) networks. It was reported that in at least one of the attacks, malicious Trojan horse software was used to obtain data from a future Army command and control system. The report quoted a Pentagon spokesman as saying that '*Beijing has focused on building the infrastructure to develop advanced space-based command, control, communications, computers, intelligence, surveillance and reconnaissance and targeting capabilities.*'

4. Conclusions

This catalogue of individual incidents, over a number of years, may seem to be unconnected, however, there are a number of common factors that occur throughout. To date there has been no clear evidence of the use of IW tactics by terrorists, but there are indications of the use of the techniques to gather information and demonstrates that there is the potential for them to cause significant disruption. While no nation state has admitted that it has sponsored this type of activity, many of the incidents have characteristics that may make them 'Information Warfare' attacks.

Indications of this can be derived from the fact that that the majority of the incidents took place during period of increased tension between the countries involved. The second is that a large proportion of the incidents involve China in one-way or another (China-Japan, China- Korea, China-Taiwan, China-UK, China-USA). Also of interest is the fact that as early as 2002, the Chinese Government appeared to have sufficient control over access to the Internet and the WWW from systems within China to be able to prevent cyber attacks on the USA when they chose to do so. Also, in 2004, the Chinese were seen to exercise their Military Information Warfare Units in conjunction with academic institutes.

Most of the conventional definitions of IW state that the aim of its use is to gain advantage over the enemy and to affect their decision-making processes. The battlefield implementation (IO) is, realistically, constrained to the period of the conflict, but the wider use of the techniques during periods of increased tension can achieve the purpose of IW in influencing the decision makers to satisfy the aims of the aggressor by affecting the economy or the feeling of wellbeing of the populace of the opposition

As there have been no claims for the incidents, determining whether any of the incidents detailed above were initiated or sponsored by the nation states in order to exert pressure on the opposition is not possible, but it is also clear that while coincidence cannot be discounted, it is difficult to see how the detected pattern of incidents could all be attributed to it.

None of the reports that have been used above indicate any use of the techniques by the major Western nations, where the concepts were first aired. In reality, the rise of the new, fundamentalist terrorist threat has overshadowed and perhaps displaced the reporting of subtler and less destructive attacks. However, even with the changes of focus and the diversion of effort to fight the 'War on terrorism', there is evidence that development and investment in IW and IO has continued. Evidence of this is in the investment plans for a US Joint Integrated Information Operations Range (JIIOR) that is to come into effect from 2006. More evidence can be found in the January 2005 publication of US Air Force doctrine document 2-5 on Information Operations and the number of US military units that openly claim Information Warfare as part, or all, of their role. In the UK, the House of Commons Defence Committee report on the Lessons of Iraq, produced in March 2004, gave indications of the use of IW techniques during Operation Telic in Iraq.

It is clear that Information Warfare is continuing to be developed and tested in a large number of countries in the developed world. Both the battlefield implementations and the wider political use of the techniques appear to have been 'field tested' and the results of these tests have undoubtedly been analysed, both in the East and the West. It is apparent that, for the present and the foreseeable future, the use of these tools and techniques is likely to occur between countries during periods of increased tension and that it will be the civil and government infrastructures that are targeted. It is also clear that, given the current level of technology, it will continue to be very difficult to conclusively identify the source of an attack. In addition, it would appear that China is either prepared to condone IW style attacks by its citizens or is actually sponsoring this type of attack in order to further its aims and to create political pressure or gain economic advantage through the theft of valuable intellectual property.

To date there has been no evidence of the use of cyber weapons by terrorists, but there is reasonable evidence of their use by organised crime, commercial organisations and nation states.

References

BBC News,(2000) Israel Under Cyber Attack, Thursday, Oct 26, 2000.

Blackhurst C (2005) Keeping (secrets), European Business, May 2005.

Denning DE. (2000) CYBERTERRORISM, Testimony before the Special Oversight Panel on Terrorism Committee on Armed Services U.S. House of Representatives, May 23, 2000.

Dickinson P. (2005) Israeli Police Charge 18 With Industrial Espiage, Information Week, May 31, 2005.

Gera YK. (2001) Asian Journal of International Terrorism and Conflicts, Article 5,Vol 2, no 3.

Gregory M, (2001) US under Chinese hack attack, BBC, Apr 30, 2001.

Hess P. (2002) China prevented repeat cyber attack on US, United Press International, Oct 29, 2002.

Hoffman D E. (2004) CIA slipped bugs to Soviets, Memoir recounts Cold War technological sabotage, Washington Post, Feb. 27, 2004

Jinlin f and Zhenjiang C (2004) Group army improves its IT fighting power, PLA Daily, Apr. 27, 2004

Knight A. The Conduct of American Foreign Policy: Ronald Reagan's Watershed Year?, Foreign Affairs.

NISCC Briefing Id: 20050616-00494 (2005) Targeted Trojan E-mail Attacks, NISCC, 16 June 2005.

Shu-ling K. (2003) Cabinet says computers under attack, Taipei Times, Sep 04, 2003.

Tae-Gyu K (2005) Japan Heightens Cyber Attack on Korea, Korea Times, May 10, 2005.

The Marmot Blog, (2004) Hack the dragon?, The Marmot's Hole, Jul 28, 2004.

Tiboni F. (2005) The new Trojan war: Defense Department finds its networks under attack from China, FCW.com, Aug. 22, 2005.

Tokyo Correspondent, (2005) Japan suspects Chinese cyber attack, The Australian, Apr 14, 2005.

War and Ethics in Cyberspace: Cyber-Conflict and Just War Theory

Andrew Liaropoulos
University of Piraeus,
Greece

Editorial Commentary

How information warfare might be conducted is just one problem to be dealt with. Whether and under what conditions it might occur are two other problems that need to be considered. In this paper, Liaropoulos leads the reader through an analysis of 'just war' theory in order to address these considerations. The challenges of defining the context of a just war in cyberspace include and transcend the normal questions. Certainly one must consider the questions of collateral damage, legitimacy of targets, legitimacy of weapons, and concepts of neutrality: all normal questions for all forms of warfare. But one must also consider more difficult questions, such as that of attributability of attacks and what level of action rises to the level of armed attack in cyberspace. One example provided for consideration is that of "a cyber-attack that shuts down a power grid." Liaropoulos states emphatically that this type of attack would in fact rise to the level of an armed attack and provides a convincing rationale for making such an assertion. However, what if the attack was launched by a single person with no governmental authority? Would it still rise to the level of armed attack? Or would it simply be a criminal act? The attribution becomes a critical part of this analysis, which makes the area of legal analysis of information warfare so extremely tricky. Readers who are interested in delving deeper into the topic are referred to the on-going analyses sponsored by and published on the website of the Cooperative Cyber Defence Centre of Excellence (http://www.ccdcoe.org).

Abstract: Over the last two decades there is a growing body of literature over exploiting cyberspace for offensive and defensive purposes. Cyber-conflict is after all the newest mode of warfare and cyber-weapons have been described as weapons of mass disruption. Although the attention on the technical and military dimensions of cyberspace is justifiable, one needs also to look into the legal and ethical aspects of cyber-conflict, in order to comprehend the complex nature of cyberspace. Conflict in cyberspace raises many ethical questions for both theorists and practitioners of warfare. In particular, the lack of an international legal framework that defines the use of force in cyberspace, operational difficulties in deterring and identifying cyber-attacks as well as the asymmetric dimension of cyber-conflicts pose without a doubt, great pressure on the just war tradition. This paper applies just war theory (jus ad bellum, jus in bello and jus post bellum) in cyberspace and explores when and how states may justly resort to cyber-conflict, operate during such a conflict and terminate it. Cyberspace is accessible to all and there are no rules or norms providing guidelines for the use of force. In addition to that, cyber-conflict appears to be less lethal and has a global reach. As a result, cyberspace makes conflict more thinkable, but that does not mean that it must also be unjust.

Keywords: war, ethics, cyberspace, cyber-conflict, just war theory, law

1. Introduction

The Information Revolution has transformed not only the way society functions, but also the way war is conducted and a new type of conflict that takes place in cyberspace has emerged (Toffler 1993). Cyber-conflict is one of the greatest threats to international security and has become a part of modern warfare. Cyber-attacks are rapid; they cross borders and can serve both strategic and tactical goals (Liaropoulos 2009). Militaries and terrorist groups now have the capability to launch cyber-attacks not only against military networks, but also against critical infrastructures that depend on computer networks. Critical infrastructures consist of the physical and cyber assets of public and private institutions in sectors like water, public health, emergency services, government, defense industrial base, information and telecommunications, energy, transportation, banking and finance. Cyberspace is the nervous system of all these infrastructures.Therefore, securing cyberspace is essential to national security.

Recent cases of cyber-attacks in Estonia in April-May 2007 and Georgia in August 2008 certify that the conflict spectrum has expanded and includes cyberspace as well (Blank 2008). The Georgia cyber-attack defaced the presidential website and made other government websites unavailable.

The Estonia cyber-attack, which primarily targeted commercial financial networks, shut down the heavily online Estonian banking system for several days. Cyber-conflict is primarily disruptive, rather than destructive; and its low entry cost makes it possible for states, terrorist groups (Bunker 2000) and even individuals to acquire cyber-conflict capabilities with relative ease. The less lethal appearance of cyber-conflict and the possibility of concealing the attacker's true identity (plausible deniability) put serious pressure on every war-related aspect and just war theory in particular.

The paper will first define the terms cyberspace and cyber-conflict, in order to describe the context under which cyber-attacks take place. In the next section, after analysing the just war theory (jus ad bellum, jus in bello and jus post bellum), the research will apply this concept in the cyber-conflict context. Based on the way just war theory has been applied and redefined in relations to past types of warfare (aerial bombardment, nuclear weapons etc), the research will use the historical evidence to provide some guidelines about conducting cyber-conflict in a just manner.

2. War and ethics in cyberspace

Cyberspace refers to the fusion of all communication networks, databases and information sources into a global virtual system and cyber-conflict is defined as cyberspace-based attacks on the civilian and military infrastructures (transportation, power, communications and financial infrastructures) upon which societies and armed forces increasingly depend. Echoing James Mulvenon, cyber-conflict is defined as "the conduct of large scale, politically motivated conflict based on the use of offensive and defensive capabilities to disrupt digital systems, networks and infrastructures" (Mulvenon 2005). Cyber-related terms are hard to define and due to the nature of cyberspace (anonymity and plausible deniability), it is very often difficult to discern between cyber-conflict, cyber-war (cyber-based confrontation between states) and cyber-terrorism.

By definition, cyberspace is transnational, thus cyber-conflict raises several issues related to sovereignty and security in the international realm. Furthermore, due to the potentially strategic impact of an attack, cyber-conflict must be treated as a subset of the larger literature about war and security (Mulvenon 2005). As a new realm that encompasses fast-moving new technologies for both states and non-state actors, legal and ethical aspects of cyber-conflict need to be further explored. The most important set of issues relates to the legal definitions of cyber-conflict and the implications of conflict in cyberspace for civilian, military and economic networks. In particular, when does a cyber-conflict constitute a use of armed force or an actual act of war? What actions would constitute a war crime? Furthermore, it is important to explore the possibilities for international cooperation and arms control in the cyberspace realm. In addition, governments need to consider whether pledges for a no first-strike use of cyber-weapons is of any use, and if so in what context (Mulvenon 2005)?

3. Cyber-conflict and just war theory

Throughout history, the just war tradition has provided us with one of the most perpetual frameworks for the question of when it is right to go to war, and how war ought to be conducted. In general, just war theories attempt to conceive of how the use of arms might be restrained, made more humane, and ultimately directed towards the aim of establishing lasting peace and justice. Just war theory is probably the most influential perspective on the ethics of war and peace and drives its inspiration from the writings of Augustine, Aquinas, Grotius, Suarez, Vattel, Grotius and Waltzer. The reason that we need a just war theory is that we live in a non-ideal world, where war might be ethically inescapable. Therefore, the purpose is to give some wars legal and moral justification, to condemn those that do not comply with the criteria and impose restrictions on the actual conduct of war. Just war theorists have traditionally concerned themselves with the grounds for going to war in the first place and with questions about ethical conduct in warfare (Waltzer 2000, Evans 2005). A third stage of war that of just peace, has gained the attention of just war theorists over the last years (Orend 2002, 2004).

The just war theory can be divided into three areas. The first one, jus ad bellum, refers to the transition from peace to war and basically lays out when states may lawfully resort to armed conflict. The second one, jus in bello, also known as the law of armed conflict, refers to the actual use of force during war. The third one, jus post bellum, which is the least developed part of just war theory, concerns the justice of peace agreements and the termination phase of war. Therefore, the key concepts of just war theory fall into the categories of criteria for going to war (jus ad bellum), of fighting justly during war (jus in bello) and for terminating war in a just manner (jus post bellum).

The jus ad bellum criteria are: *Right Purpose.* Reasons for going to war revolve around the concept of self-defence, which Article 51 of the United Nations Charter deems an "inherent right". Notions of right purpose generally also include ideas like pre-emption, but are less open to the idea of preventive war. *Duly constituted authority.* A necessary condition for having a just war is that the decision to fight must come from a government, or a coalition of states, not from an individual. *Last resort.* War cannot be considered just unless it follows exhaustive pursuit of negotiations and other means of conflict resolution (Arquilla 1999).

The jus in bello criteria are: *Noncombatant immunity.* According to just war theory, those waging the war must strive to avoid harming civilians or enemy troops that have surrendered. *Proportionality.* When waging war, force must be applied in a manner that avoids excessive use. *More good than harm.* When force is used, the ethical conduct requires calculation of the net good to be achieved by a particular use of force (Arquilla 1999).

The jus post bellum criteria differ, depending on the way war is ended. Wars might end with surrender, with an armistice, with regime change or even with the commitment of international organizations to build peace (Williams and Caldwell 2006). Nevertheless, the most common criteria are the following: *Proportionality.* The peace settlement should be measured and reasonable. *Rights Vindication*. The settlement should secure those basic human rights whose violation triggered the justified war in the first place. *Discrimination.* Distinction needs to be made between the leaders, the soldiers, and the civilians in the defeated country one is negotiating with. *Punishment.* The ones responsible for the harm caused should be held responsible. *Compensation.* The reimbursement should be subject to both proportionality and discrimination (Orend 2002, 2004).

The absence of international rules that define the use of force in cyberspace (Delibasis 2002), and technical difficulties in identifying cyber-attacks challenge every aspect of just war theory. Uncertainty and confusion have always been part of the battlefield and the same applies for the cyberspace. The implications of uncertainty are most pronounced for deterrence. Deterrence depends on the threat of retaliation to change the opponent's calculus of the benefits and costs of an attack. But it is hard to convincingly threaten an unknown cyber-attacker. Likewise, uncertainty about collateral damage will affect decisions by political leaders, who may be unwilling to incur the risk of a cyber attack that could widen or escalate a conflict (Lewis 2009). This uncertainty also affects the ethics of conducting cyber-attacks. Over the past years, the just war-fighting issues have gained the attention of political scientists (Schmitt 2002, Pretorius 2003, Rowe 2008). Recent doctrinal developments and governmental initiatives for the protection of critical infrastructure necessitate a thorough analysis of the way just war theory can be applied in cyber-conflict. Following the 2007 cyber-attack on Estonia, NATO began to invest in the defense of cyberspace, and Allied nations have acknowledged the need to secure networks.

The range of operations that might make use of cyberspace extends broadly, from the battlefield to the enemy home front. Cyber-conflict scenarios include attacks on both the software (logic bombs, computer viruses, etc) and hardware (electromagnetic weapons). Cyber-conflict may serve as a form of close support for military forces during active operations. It may also be employed in strategic campaigns designed to strike directly at the will and logistical support of an opponent. This last notion, in which it may be pursued without a prior need to defeat an adversary's armed forces, is an area of particular interest and in many respects; it resembles notions of the strategic use of airpower that emerged in the 1920s and 1930s (Rattray 2001).

Nevertheless, although airpower can generally perform much destruction on fixed points, cyber-attacks will inflict far less destruction. Their effects are disruptive in nature, and may occur over wide areas. Another difference is that, whereas strategic aerial bombardment inevitably causes civilian losses, even with today's guided weapons, attacks in the critical infrastructure will lead to far lower levels of loss of life - despite their widespread disruptive effects. This lower lethality and destructiveness might make cyber-conflict a more 'attractive' form of conflict. In addition, it may make the damage done by cyber-attacks somewhat harder to assess accurately - and may complicate calculations to design a proportional response.

In addition, it is important to note the inherent blurriness with regard to defining combatants and acts of war. Whereas in other types of warfare, it is quite clear who is making the attacks, in cyber-conflict, almost anyone can fight. Thus, it is important, from an ethical perspective, to make a distinction between those with access to advanced information technology and those using it for purposes of waging cyber-attacks. Further, the very nature of cyber-attacks is such that it may often be difficult to discern between criminal, terrorist, and military acts.

Potential cyber-attacks on critical infrastructure, using directed-energy weapons will pose a great threat in the near future. These high-power microwave weapons produce thousands of volts of energy that destroy electronic devices and melt semi-conductors. They render phones, computers, and anything dependent on electronic components useless, while not harming human beings. The weapons thus can be seen as much more humane than conventional bombs, and would seem to respect the immunity of innocent civilians, for instance, if used in cities. On the battlefield they would destroy control and command functions without killing soldiers - who might be persuaded to surrender. Such attacks would make possible the reduction of killing and wounding troops.

Although such cyber-attacks do not harm people directly, they still raise an ethical issue because they can destroy a country's infrastructure (from providing water and electricity, to communications and transportation). Consider any western capital city. To deprive it of electricity would be to paralyze it. Adding to that the destruction of the communications systems, the transportation system, as well as private and business computers, the city would stop functioning except on the most primitive level, and hence the effect on innocent civilians would be devastating. The infrastructure of a society can be destroyed by conventional weapons as well, and these weapons at least do not target or directly harm people (De George 2003). We should bear in mind, that certain types of cyber-attacks, might damage a wider range of the infrastructure than conventional weapons.

On the other hand, that case seems appropriate with respect to battlefield use, if such weapons are used to reduce the loss of life. The danger of cyber-weapons, of course, is greatest for those most dependent on electronics. In both cases, whether applied in the battlespace or the civilian infrastructure, the more electronically-dependent an actor is, the more vulnerable it is. Both technologically advanced armies and technologically advanced countries are more vulnerable than those that are less developed. Furthermore, in a future conflict against guerrilla fighters that use conven-

tional weapons, directed-energy bombs are useless. But they are obviously not useless against an army such as the U.S. forces.
Directed-energy bombs do not yet have the power, to affect whole cities and their present range is much smaller geographically (theatre of operations). Nonetheless, if these new bombs can be developed and used over wide areas, they will become weapons of mass disruption. They will make modern life, dependent on electricity and computers, impossible. They will lead to innumerable civilian deaths from the absence of potable water, from hospitals that are non-functional, from food distribution that becomes impossible, from communications that do not work, and so on. As such, weapons of mass disruption rival weapons of mass destruction in their effects. Developing such weapons raises the same ethical issues as the development of the atom bomb. As such they may well deserve similar conventions outlawing them.

Under existing just war theory, prevention lies on shaky ground. But cyber-conflict might prove especially useful in derailing the rise of a threatening power - particularly those forms of attack that might be necessary in slowing down a potential adversary's process of proliferation of weapons of mass destruction. Regarding duly constituted authority, the very nature of weaponry may challenge this long-established ethical concept. For the types of capabilities needed to conduct a cyber-campaign (especially in the cases of attacking software) there is little need for traditional forces.

Although there are plans about the creation of cyber-corps, almost anyone can become a cyber-warrior. Therefore, the state monopoly on war reflected in the concept of duly constituted authority will likely be shaken, as non-state actors rise in their ability to wage cyber-war (Arquilla 1999). The ease of entry into the realm of cyber-war also suggests that the convention regarding going to war only as a last resort will come under strain. Cyber-attacks may disrupt much, but they do little actual destruction and therefore can be viewed as somewhat akin to economic sanctions, as a tool of coercion.

Cyber-attacks that strike an adversary's infrastructure must be seen as a kind of war that targets non-combatants in a deliberate manner. They will suffer, inevitably and seriously, from such attacks. In common with strategic aerial bombardment, the purpose is to undermine the enemy's will to resist. Another problematic issue is proportionality. In particular, a cyber-attacker might strike at an opponent's critical infrastructures, but have few or none of his own that could be retaliated against by similar means. This prompts the question of when more traditional military measures - including some degree of lethal force - might be used in response to cyber-attacks without violating notions of proportionality. Alike, another problem arises if the defender/target that is struck by cyber-weapons has little or no means of responding with the same cyber-weapons (Arquilla 1999). Massive retaliatory threat may be the only credible deterrent that a potential victim of cyber-conflict may have. Therefore and despite its less lethal profile, cyber-conflict might trigger a potentially bloody war. Despite the widely held belief that the nature of cyber-attacks is disruptive and not destructive, and therefore cyber-conflict is less life-threatening than a kinetic weapon, the dissemination of cyber-capabilities, can actually have the opposite effect. In particular, the fact that cyber-attacks may be cheaper and easier to conduct in the near future, might actually increase the number of conflicts, both in and outside cyberspace. This will inevitably increase the number of casualties.

Aside from deliberately disproportionate responses, there is also the problem of estimating the comparability of damage done by radically differing weapons systems (exploding smart bombs *vs* computer logic bombs) is going to prove quite difficult. Finally, the problem of perpetrator ambiguity further weakens proportionate response, as one may simply not have enough data to determine just who is responsible for a particular attack.

4. Defining and responding to cyber-attacks

Cyber attacks come in many different forms, and their destructive potential is limited only by the creativity and skill of the attackers behind them. The cyber-conflict battlefield is comprised of many components that include the Internet and all things that connect from a computer to the Internet. This would include: web servers, enterprise information systems, client server systems, communication links, network equipment, and the computers in businesses and homes. The terrain also encompasses information systems like the electrical grids, telecommunication systems, and various corporate and military robotics systems.

As a result there is a broad typology of cyber-attacks. Some of the most common are cyber-espionage, web vandalism, denial of service (DOS) and attacks on critical infrastructure. Cyber-espionage is the act or practice of obtaining secrets (sensitive, proprietary or classified information) from individuals, competitors, rivals, groups, governments and enemies also for military, political, or economic advantage using illegal exploitation methods on internet, networks, software and or computers. Web vandalism involves attacks that deface web pages, or denial-of-service attacks, where a large number of computers are controller by one actor. Finally, attacks on computer networks that involve power plants, water supply stations, communications hubs, and commercial infrastructure facilities are high on the security agenda.

Although certain cyber attacks can constitute armed attacks, especially in light of their ability to injure or kill, the legal community has been reluctant to adopt this approach because cyber attacks do not resemble traditional armed attacks with conventional weapons. Technically cyber-attacks are difficult to attribute and as a result scholars and practitioners have developed analytical models to evaluate such unconventional attacks and equate cyber-attacks with armed attacks (Carr 2010). For example, a cyber-attack that shuts down a power grid is an armed attack. The reason is that shutting down a power grid requires dropping a bomb, or the use of some other form of kinetic force. Since cyber-attacks are used to achieve the same result with conventional attacks, they are therefore treated the same way as armed attacks. A cyber-attack that temporarily interrupts service of another state's local phone company and causes some hundred people to be without a phone, does not amount to an armed attack. On the contrary, a cyber-attack that compromises the control system of a chemical or biological plant, and thereby causes the release of toxic gases over a city, is equivalent of an armed attack (Joyner and Lotrionte 2001). Likewise, a cyber-attack that manipulated information across a state's banking and financial institutions to seriously disrupt commerce in the state is an armed attack. The logic is that the disruptive effects that the attack had on the state's economy is a severe enough overall consequence that it warrants treatment as an armed attack (Carr 2010).

A scholar that advocated such analytical models is Michael Schmitt. His analytical framework for evaluating cyber-attacks, discerns six criteria: severity, immediacy, directness, invasiveness, measurability, and presumptive legitimacy (Schmitt 1999). *Severity* looks at the scope and extent of an attack. So, if people are killed or there is extensive property damage, the action is considered an armed attack, the less damage, the less likely the action is a use of force. *Immediacy* examines the duration of the effects of a cyber-attack. The longer the duration and effects of an attack, the stronger the argument that it is an armed attack. *Directness* refers to the harm that is caused. If the action taken is the sole cause of the result, it is more likely to be viewed as a use of force. *Invasiveness* looks at the origin of the attack. A violated border is still an indicator of military operations; actions that are mounted from outside a target nation's borders are probably more diplomatic or economic. *Measurability* quantifies the damage. If the effect can be quantified immediately, it is more likely that it will be considered as an armed attack. Finally, *presumptive legitimacy* focuses on state practice. The less a cyber-attack looks like accepted state practice, the more possible it is that it will be regarded as an armed attack (Schmitt 1999).

Despite the fact that Schmitt's six criteria has gained wide acceptance in the legal community, technological limitations on attack detection and attack classification, make states hesitant to adopt these criteria with relative ease and characterize all cyber-attacks as armed attacks (Carr 2010). Jus ad bellum requires states to ensure that the cyber-attack originates from a sanctuary state. Only then can a state lawfully respond. The problem is that cyber-attacks are frequently conducted through intermediate computer systems to disguise the true identity of the cyber-attacker. As a result, trace programs run the risk of incorrectly identifying the true source of an attack. This creates an apparent problem because an attack could be incorrectly perceived as coming from a state that is not the actual state of origin (Carr 2010).

5. Conclusion

Information societies are build around critical information infrastructures, that are easy to access, friendly to use, but also vulnerable to cyber-attacks. Modern armies develop advanced capabilities in cyberspace. These capabilities are focused not only on collecting sensitive information, but also on achieving military effects capable of causing economic harm, damaging critical infrastructure, and influencing the outcome of conventional armed conflicts. Thus, a major challenge for national governments and global organizations is to secure cyberspace, while maintaining an open society, all carried out through lawful and just means.

The use of just war theory as a theoretical framework, for the analysis of cyber-conflict, revealed that international law must define more sharply the criteria that characterize cyber-attacks as equivalent to armed attacks. The recent cyber-attacks in Estonia and Georgia, stress the need to define what sort of responses are permissible as self-defense by a state that is targeted. International law must evolve and adapt, because cyber-warriors, have taken the threat out of the realm of the abstract and made it real.

Acknowledgements

The author would like to thank Professor Michael Sheehan, Professor Michael Evans, Dr. Ioannis Konstantopoulos, Anneli Poolakese and Kai-Helin Kaldas for their comments and research support.

References

Arquilla, J. (1999) "Can Information Warfare Ever be Just?", Ethics and Information Technology, Vol 1, pp 203-212.

Blank, S. (2008) "Web War I: Is Europe's First Information War a New Kind of War?", Comparative Strategy, Vol 27, No.3, pp 227-247.

Bunker, R. (2000) "Weapons of Mass Disruption and Terrorism", Terrorism and Political Violence, Vol 12, No.1 pp 37-46.

Carr, J. (2010) Inside Cyber Warfare, O'Reilly, Beijing.

De George, R. (2003) "Post-September 11: Computers, Ethics and War", Ethics and Information Technology, Vol 5, pp 183-190.

Delibasis, D. (2002) "The Right of States to Use Force in Cyberspace: Defining the Rules of Engagement", Information & Communication Technology Law, Vol 11, No.3, pp 255-268.

Evans, M. ed. (2005), Just War Theory. A Reappraisal, Edinburgh University Press, Edinburgh.

Joyner C. and Lotrionte C. (2001) "Information Warfare as International Coercion: Elements of Legal Framework", European Journal of International Law, Vol 12 No.5, pp 825-865.

Lewis, J. (2009) "The Fog of Cyberwar. Discouraging Deterrence", International Relations and Security Network (ISN) http://www.isn.ethz.ch/isn/layout/set/print/content/view/full/22009, last accessed 20 January 2010.

Liaropoulos, A. (2009) The Transformation of Warfare in the Information Age, Themata: Policy and Defence, No.28, Defence Analyses Institute, Athens.

Mulvenon, J. (2005) "Toward a Cyberconflict Studies Research Agenda", IEEE Security & Privacy, Vol 3 No.4 pp 52-55.

Orend, B. (2002) "Justice After War", Ethics and International Affairs, Vol 16 No.1, pp 43-56.

Orend, B. (2004) "Kant's Ethics of War and Peace", Journal of Military Ethics, Vol 3 No.2, pp 161-177.

Pretorius, J. (2003) "Ethics and International Security in the Information Age", Defense & Security Analysis, Vol 19, No.2 pp 165-175.

Rattray, G. (2001) Strategic Warfare in Cyberspace, MIT Press, Cambridge.

Rowe, N. (2008) "Ethics of Cyber War Attacks", In: Janczewski, L.J. and Colarik, A. M. eds., Cyber Warfare and Cyber Terrorism, Information Science Reference, Hershey, pp 105-111.

Schmitt, M. (1999) "Computer Network Attack and the Use of Force in International Law: Thoughts on a Normative Framework", Columbia Journal of Transnational Law, Vol 37 No.885, pp 885-937.

Schmitt, M. (2002) "Wired Warfare: Computer Network Attacks and Jus in Bello", International Review of the Red Cross, Vol 84 No.846, pp 365-399.

Toffler, A. and H. (1993) War and Anti-war: Survival at the Dawn of the 21st Century, Warner Books, New York.

Waltzer, M. (2000) Just and Unjust Wars: A Moral Argument with Historical Illustrations, Basic Books, New York.

Williams, R. Jr. and Caldwell D. (2006) "Jus Post Bellum: Just War Theory and the Principles of Just Peace", International Studies Perspectives, Vol 7 No.4, pp 309-320.

Theoretical Offensive Cyber Militia Models

Rain Ottis
Cooperative Cyber Defence Centre of Excellence
Tallinn, Estonia

Editorial Commentary

Concomitant to the legal issues associated with warfare in cyberspace are questions about defenses against cyberwarfare. The types of attacks that have been seen to date are fairly broad-based in effects, striking both official targets and civilian targets equally. In this paper, Ottis presents a concept of cooperative cyber-defense through militia type models. The concept is intriguing, as it both builds upon and leverages the way that hacker groups and terrorist organizations have developed cooperative capabilities for group behavior (see Chapter 4 for more discussion on this topic).

However, discussion of the topic also raises some thorny issues, including one of whether individuals should have the right to individual or collective self-defense. This question may seem self-evident on its face: well, the casual observer may say, of course, people should have the right to self-defense. After all, do they not already practice some aspect of self-defense, such as maintaining firewalls and anti-virus software? But when one starts to really push on the concept of what self-defense in cyberspace entails, it quickly becomes murky.

In the physical world, self-defense may include returning force for force in order to beat off an attacker. For example, if an attacker is actively trying to kill a person, it is generally held that it is perfectly acceptable for the person under attack to fight back with equal or even greater force because the threat is so great. In other cases, it is less clear how much force a person is entitled to use. For example, if a person is simply being robbed, should that person be entitled to kill the attacker to prevent the robbery? In many jurisdictions, the answer has evolved to some version of "no, the person should only use sufficient force to defend herself." This of course gets tricky when the would-be robber is quite persistent and the only way to keep the robbery from occurring is to injure the robber. Should that injury result in the permanent maiming or death of the robber, the person defending herself could find herself in trouble. In some jurisdictions, it is illegal to carry weapons for self-defense.

Given the differing levels of standards in many different physical jurisdictions, it becomes a very real question as to how these varying standards of behavior apply or translate into cyberspace. Should simple self-defense be allowed in cyberspace? The possession of firewalls and anti-virus software is considered to be common sense for individual systems: are we in any danger of these being classified as weapons? Probably not at this point in time in technology, but it is useful to consider the question. As firewall technology evolves, it is possible that part of the functionality might be aggressive attribution identification of attack packets. In order to accomplish that function, a set of techniques known as "hack back" might be included, which transcend from simply defensive to potentially offensively capable technology. At this time, in some countries, the use of "hack back" technologies is illegal, thus rendering self-defense somewhat limited in scope. If the current legal regime were to continue without modifications, such aggressive self-defense would potentially be rendered moot. But the one lesson we have all learned is that technology marches on, despite legal constraints or weapons agreements. In such cases, how will governments control whether the technologies are actually used for self-defense rather than aggression? Can they? Is it even appropriate? There are interesting and important questions that need to be addressed, and this paper starts that discussion on its way.

Abstract. Volunteer based non-state actors have played an important part in many international cyber conflicts of the past two decades. In order to better understand this threat I describe three theoretical models for volunteer based offensive cyber militias: the Forum, the Cell and the Hierarchy. The Forum is an ad-hoc cyber militia form that is organized around a central communications platform, where the members share information and tools necessary to carry out cyber attacks against their chosen adversary. The Cell model refers to hacker cells, which engage in politically motivated hacking over extended periods of time. The Hierarchy refers to the traditional hierarchical model, which may be encountered in government sponsored volunteer organizations, as well as in cohesive self-organized non-state actors. For each model, I give an example and describe the model's attributes, strengths and weaknesses using qualitative analysis. The models are based on expert opinion on different types of cyber militias that have been seen in cyber conflicts. These theoretical models provide a framework for categorizing volunteer based offensive cyber militias of non-trivial size.

Keywords: cyber conflict, cyber militia, cyber attack, patriotic hacking, on-line communities

1. Introduction

The widespread application of Internet services has given rise to a new contested space, where people with conflicting ideals or values strive to succeed, sometimes by attacking the systems and services of the other side. It is interesting to note that in most public cases of cyber conflict the offensive side is not identified as a state actor, at least not officially. Instead, it often looks like citizens take part in hactivist campaigns or patriotic hacking on their own, volunteering for the cyber front.

Cases like the 2007 cyber attacks against Estonia are a good example where an informal non-state cyber militia has become a threat to national security. In order to understand the threat posed by these volunteer cyber militias I provide three models of how such groups can be organized and analyze the strengths and weaknesses of each.

The three models considered are the Forum, the Cell and the Hierarchy. The models are applicable to groups of non-trivial size, which require internal assignment of responsibilities and authority.

1.1. Method and limitations

In this paper I use theoretical qualitative analysis in order to describe the attributes, strengths and weaknesses of three offensively oriented cyber militia models. I have chosen the three plausible models based on what can be observed in recent cyber conflicts. The term *model* refers to an abstract description of relationships between members of the cyber militia, including command, control and mentoring relationships, as well as the operating principles of the militia.

Note, however, that the description of the models is based on theoretical reasoning and expert opinion. It offers abstract theoretical models in an ideal setting. There may not be a full match to any of them in reality or in the examples provided. It is more likely to see either combinations of different models or models that do not match the description in full. On the other hand, the models should serve as useful frameworks for analyzing volunteer groups in the current and coming cyber conflicts.

In preparing this work, I communicated with and received feedback from a number of recognized experts in the field of cyber conflict research. I wish to thank them all for providing comments on my proposed models: Prof Dorothy Denning (Naval Postgraduate School), Dr Jose Nazario (Arbor Networks), Prof Samuel Liles (Purdue University Calumet), Mr Jeffrey Carr (Greylogic) and Mr Kenneth Geers (Cooperative Cyber Defence Centre of Excellence).

2. The forum

The global spread of the Internet allows people to connect easily and form "cyber tribes", which can range from benign hobby groups to antagonistic ad-hoc cyber militias. (Williams 2007, Ottis 2008, Carr 2009, Nazario 2009, Denning 2010) In the case of an ad-hoc cyber militia, the Forum unites like-minded people who are "willing and able to use cyber attacks in order to achieve a political goal." (Ottis 2010b) It serves as a command and control platform where more active members can post motivational materials, attack instructions, attack tools, etc. (Denning 2010)

This particular model, as well as the strengths and weaknesses covered in this section, are based on (Ottis 2010b). A good example of this model in recent cyber conflicts is the *stopgeorgia.ru* forum during the Russia-Georgia war in 2008 (Carr 2009).

2.1. Attributes

The Forum is an on-line meeting place for people who are interested in a particular subject. I use Forum as a conceptual term referring to the people who interact in the on-line meeting place. The technical implementation of the meeting place could take many different forms: web forum, Internet Relay Chat channel, social network subgroup, etc. It is important that the Forum is accessible over Internet and preferably easy to find. The latter condition is useful for recruiting new members and providing visibility to the agenda of the group.

The Forum mobilizes in response to an event that is important to the members. While there can be a core group of people who remain actively involved over extended periods of time, the membership can be expected to surge in size when the underlying issue becomes "hot". Basically, the Forum is like a flash mob that performs cyber attacks instead of actions on the streets. As such, the Forum is more ad-hoc than permanent, because it is likely to disband once the underlying event is settled.

The membership of the Forum forms a *loose network* centered on the communications platform, where few, if any, people know each other in real life and the entire membership is not known to any single person (Ottis 2010b). Most participate anonymously, either providing an alias or by remaining passive on the communication platform. In general, the Forum is an informal group, although specific roles can be assumed by individual members. For example, there could be trainers, malware providers, campaign planners, etc. (Ottis 2010b). Some of the Forum members may also be active in cyber crime. In that case, they can contribute resources such as malware or use of a botnet to the Forum.

The membership is diverse, in terms of skills, resources and location. While there seems to be evidence that a lot of the individuals engaged in such activities are relatively unskilled in cyber attack techniques (Carr 2009), when supplemented with a few more experienced members the group can be much more effective and dangerous (Ottis 2010a).

Since most of the membership remains anonymous and often passive on the communications platform, the leadership roles will be assumed by those who are active in communicating their intent, plans and expertise. (Denning 2010) However, this still does not allow for strong command and control, as each member can decide what, if any, action to take.

2.2. Strengths

One of the most important strengths of a loose network is that it can form very quickly. Following an escalation in the underlying issue, all it takes is a rallying cry on the Internet and within hours or even minutes the volunteers can gather around a communications platform, share attack instructions, pick targets and start performing cyber attacks.
As long as there is no need for tightly controlled operations, in terms of timing, resource use and targeting, there is very little need for management. The network is also easily scalable, as anyone can join and there is no lengthy vetting procedure.

The diversity of the membership means that it is very difficult for the defenders to analyze and counter the attacks. The source addresses are likely distributed globally (black listing will be inefficient) and the different skills and resources ensure heterogeneous attack traffic (no easy patterns). In addition, experienced attackers can use this to conceal precision strikes against critical services and systems.

While it may seem that neutralizing the communications platform (via law enforcement action, cyber attack or otherwise) is an easy way to neutralize the militia, this may not be the case. The militia can easily regroup at a different communications platform in a different jurisdiction. Attacking the Forum directly may actually increase the motivation of the member (Ottis 2010b).

Last, but not least, it is very difficult to attribute these attacks to a state, as they can (seem to) be a true (global) grass roots campaign, even if there is some form of state sponsorship. Some states may take advantage of this fact by allowing such activity to continue in their jurisdiction, blaming legal obstacles or lack of capability for their inactivity. It is also possible for government operatives to “create” a “grass roots” Forum movement in support of the government agenda (Ottis 2009).

2.3. Weaknesses

A clear weakness of this model is the difficulty to command and control the Forum. Membership is not formalized and often it is even not visible on the communication platform, because passive readers can just take ideas from there and execute the attacks on their own. This uncoordinated approach can seriously hamper the effectiveness of the group as a whole. It may also lead to uncontrolled expansion of conflict, when members unilaterally attack third parties on behalf of the Forum.

A problem with the loose network is that it is often populated with people who do not have experience with cyber attacks. Therefore, their options are limited to primitive manual attacks or preconfigured automated attacks using attack kits or malware (Ottis 2010a). They are highly reliant on instructions and tools from more experienced members of the Forum.

The Forum is also prone to infiltration, as it must rely on relatively easily accessible communication channels. If the communication point is hidden, the group will have difficulties in recruiting new members. The assumption is, therefore, that the communication point can be easily found by both potential recruits, as well as infiltrators. Since there is no easy way to vet the incoming members, infiltration should be relatively simple.

Another potential weakness of the Forum model is the presumption of anonymity. If the membership can be infiltrated and convinced that their anonymity is not guaranteed, they will be less likely to participate in the cyber militia. Options for achieving this can include "exposing" the "identities" of the infiltrators, arranging meetings in real life, offering tools that have a phone-home functionality to the members, etc. Note that some of these options may be illegal, depending on the circumstances (Ottis 2010b).

3. The cell

Another model for a volunteer cyber force that has been seen is a hacker cell. In this case, the generic term *hacker* is used to encompass all manner of people who perform cyber attacks on their own, regardless of their background, motivation and skill level. It includes the hackers, crackers and script kiddies described by Young and Aitel (2004). The hacker cell includes several hackers who commit cyber attacks on a regular basis over extended periods of time. Examples of hacker cells are Team Evil and Team Hell, as described in Carr (2009).

3.1. Attributes

Unlike the Forum, the Cell members are likely to know each other in real life, while remaining anonymous to the outside observer. Since their activities are almost certainly illegal, they need to trust each other. This limits the size of the group and requires a (lengthy) vetting procedure for any new recruits. The vetting procedure can include proof of illegal cyber attacks.

The command and control structure of the Cell can vary from a clear self-determined hierarchy to a flat organization, where members coordinate their actions, but do not give or receive orders. In theory, several Cells can coordinate their actions in a joint campaign, forming a confederation of hacker cells.

The Cells can exist for a long period of time, in response to a long-term problem, such as the Israel-Palestine conflict. The activity of such a Cell ebbs and flows in accordance with the intensity of the underlying conflict. The Cell may even disband for a period of time, only to reform once the situation intensifies again.

Since hacking is a hobby (potentially a profession) for the members, they are experienced with the use of cyber attacks. One of the more visible types of attacks that can be expected from a Cell is the website defacement. Defacement refers to the illegal modification of website content, which often includes a message from the attacker, as well as the attacker's affiliation. The Zone-H web archive lists thousands of examples of such activity, as reported by the attackers. Many of the attacks are clearly politically motivated and identify the Cell that is responsible.

Some members of the Cell may be involved with cyber crime. For example, the development, dissemination, maintenance and use of botnets for criminal purposes. These resources can be used for politically motivated cyber attacks on behalf of the Cell.

3.2. Strengths

A benefit of the Cell model is that it can mobilize very quickly, as the actors presumably already have each other's contact information. In principle, the Cell can mobilize within minutes, although it likely takes hours or days to complete the process.

A Cell is quite resistant to infiltration, because the members can be expected to establish their hacker credentials before being allowed to join. This process may include proof of illegal attacks.

Since the membership can be expected to be experienced in cyber attack techniques, the Cell can be quite effective against unhardened targets. However, hardened targets may or may not be within the reach of the Cell, depending on their specialty and experience. Prior hacking experience also allows them to cover their tracks better, should they wish to do so.

3.3. Weaknesses

While a Cell model is more resistant to countermeasures than the Forum model, it does offer potential weaknesses to exploit. The first opportunity for exploitation is the hacker's ego. Many of the more visible attacks, including defacements, leave behind the alias or affiliation of the attacker, in order to claim the bragging rights (Carr 2009). This seems to indicate that they are quite confident in their skills and proud of their achievements. As such, they are potentially vulnerable to personal attacks, such as taunting or ridiculing in public. Stripping the anonymity of the Cell may also work, as at least some members could lose their job and face law enforcement action in their jurisdiction (Carr 2009). As described by Ottis (2010b), it is probably not necessary to actually identify all the members of the Cell. Even if the identity of a few of them is revealed or if the corresponding perception can be created among the membership, the trust relationship will be broken and the effectiveness of the group will decrease.

Prior hacking experience also provides a potential weakness. It is more likely that the law enforcement know the identity of a hacker, especially if he or she continues to use the same affiliation or hacker alias. While there may not be enough evidence or damage or legal base for law enforcement action in response to their criminal attacks, the politically motivated attacks may provide a different set of rules for the local law enforcement.
The last problem with the Cell model is scalability. There are only so many skilled hackers who are willing to participate in a politically motivated cy-

ber attack. While this number may still overwhelm a small target, it is unlikely to have a strong effect on a large state.

4. The hierarchy

The third option for organizing a volunteer force is to adopt a traditional hierarchical structure. This approach is more suitable for government sponsored groups or other cohesive groups that can agree to a clear chain of command. For example, the People's Liberation Army of China is known to include militia type units in their IW battalions (Krekel 2009). The model can be divided into two generic sub-models: anonymous and identified membership.

4.1. Attributes

The Hierarchy model is similar in concept to military units, where a unit commander exercises power over a limited number of sub-units. The number of command levels depends on the overall size of the organization.

Each sub-unit can specialize on some specific task or role. For example, the list of sub-unit roles can include reconnaissance, infiltration/breaching, exploitation, malware/exploit development and training. Depending on the need, there can be multiple sub-units with the same role. Consider the analogy of an infantry battalion, which may include a number of infantry companies, anti-tank and mortar platoons, a reconnaissance platoon, as well as various support units (communications, logistics), etc. This specialization and role assignment allows the militia unit to conduct a complete offensive cyber operation from start to finish.

A Hierarchy model is the most likely option for a state sponsored entity, since it offers a more formalized and understandable structure, as well as relatively strong command and control ability. The control ability is important, as the actions of a state sponsored militia are by definition attributable to the state.

However, a Hierarchy model is not an automatic indication of state sponsorship. Any group that is cohesive enough to determine a command structure amongst them can adopt a hierarchical structure. This is very evident in Massively Multiplayer Online Games (MMOG), such as World of Warcraft or EVE Online, where players often form hierarchical groups (guilds, corporations, etc.) in order to achieve a common goal. The same approach is possible for a cyber militia as well. In fact, Williams (2007) suggests that gaming communities can be a good recruiting ground for a cyber militia.

While the state sponsored militia can be expected to have identified membership (still, it may be anonymous to the outside observer) due to control reasons, a non-state militia can consist of anonymous members that are only identified by their screen names.

4.2. Strengths

The obvious strength of a hierarchical militia is the potential for efficient command and control. The command team can divide the operational responsibilities to specialized sub-units and make sure that their actions are coordinated. However, this strength may be wasted by incompetent leadership or other factors, such as overly restrictive operating procedures.

A hierarchical militia may exist for a long time even without ongoing conflict. During "peacetime", the militia's capabilities can be improved with recruitment and training. This degree of formalized preparation with no immediate action in sight is something that can set the hierarchy apart from the Forum and the Cell.

If the militia is state sponsored, then it can enjoy state funding, infrastructure, as well as cooperation from other state entities, such as law enforcement or intelligence community. This would allow the militia to concentrate on training and operations.

4.3. Weaknesses

A potential issue with the Hierarchy model is scalability. Since this approach requires some sort of vetting or background checks before admitting a new member, it may be time consuming and therefore slow down the growth of the organization.

Another potential issue with the Hierarchy model is that by design there are key persons in the hierarchy. Those persons can be targeted by various means to ensure that they will not be effective or available during a designated period, thus diminishing the overall effectiveness of the militia. A hierarchical militia may also have issues with leadership if several people contend for prestigious positions. This potential rift in the cohesion of the unit can potentially be exploited by infiltrator agents.

Any activities attributed to the state sponsored militia can further be attributed to the state. This puts heavy restrictions on the use of cyber militia "during peacetime", as the legal framework surrounding state use of cyber attacks is currently unclear. However, in a conflict scenario, the state attribution is likely not a problem, because the state is party to the conflict anyway. This means that a state sponsored offensive cyber militia is primarily useful as a defensive capability between conflicts. Only during conflict can it be used in its offensive role.

While a state sponsored cyber militia may be more difficult (but not impossible) to infiltrate, they are vulnerable to public information campaigns, which may lead to low public and political support, decreased funding and even official disbanding of the militia. On the other hand, if the militia is not state sponsored, then it is prone to infiltration and internal information operations similar to the one considered at the Forum model.

Of the three models, the hierarchy probably takes the longest to establish, as the chain of command and role assignments get settled. During this process, which could take days, months or even years, the militia is relatively inefficient and likely not able to perform any complex operations.

5. Comparison

When analyzing the three models, it quickly becomes apparent that there are some aspects that are similar to all of them. First, they are not constrained by location. While the Forum and the Cell are by default dispersed, even a state sponsored hierarchical militia can operate from different locations.

Second, since they are organizations consisting of humans, then one of the more potent ways to neutralize cyber militias is through information operations, such as persuading them that their identities have become known to the law enforcement, etc.

Third, all three models benefit from a certain level of anonymity. However, this also makes them susceptible for infiltration, as it is difficult to verify the credentials and intent of a new member.

On the other hand, there are differences as well. Only one model lends itself well to state sponsored entities (hierarchy), although, in principle, it is possible to use all three approaches to bolster the state's cyber power.

The requirement for formalized chain of command and division of responsibilities means that the initial mobilization of the Hierarchy can be expected to take much longer than the more ad-hoc Forum or Cell. In case of short conflicts, this puts the Hierarchy model at a disadvantage.
Then again, the Hierarchy model is more likely to adopt a "peace time" mission of training and recruitment in addition to the "conflict" mission, while the other two options are more likely to be mobilized only in time of conflict. This can offset the slow initial formation limitation of the Hierarchy, if the Hierarchy is established well before the conflict.

While the Forum can rely on their numbers and use relatively primitive attacks, the Cell is capable of more sophisticated attacks due to their experience. The cyber attack capabilities of the Hierarchy, however, can range from trivial to complex.

It is important to note that the three options covered here can be combined in many ways, depending on the underlying circumstances and the personalities involved.

6. Conclusion

Politically motivated cyber attacks are becoming more frequent every year. In most cases the cyber conflicts include offensive non-state actors (spontaneously) formed from volunteers. Therefore, it is important to study these groups.

I have provided a theoretical way to categorize non-trivial cyber militias based on their organization. The three theoretical models are: the Forum, the Cell and the Hierarchy. In reality, it is unlikely to see a pure form of any of these, as different groups can include aspects of several models. However, the strengths and weaknesses identified should serve as useful guides to dealing with the cyber militia threat.

Disclaimer: *The opinions expressed here should not be interpreted as the official policy of the Cooperative Cyber Defence Centre of Excellence or the North Atlantic Treaty Organization.*

References

Carr, J. (2009) Inside Cyber Warfare. Sebastopol: O'Reilly Media.

Denning, D. E. (2010) “Cyber Conflict as an Emergent Social Phenomenon.” In Holt, T. & Schell, B. (Eds.) Corporate Hacking and Technology-Driven Crime: Social Dynamics and Implications. IGI Global, pp 170-186.

Krekel, B., DeWeese, S., Bakos, G., Barnett, C. (2009) Capability of the People’s Republic of China to Conduct Cyber Warfare and Computer Network Exploitation. Report for the US-China Economic and Security Review Commission.

Nazario, J. (2009) “Politically Motivated Denial of Service Attacks.” In Czosseck, C. & Geers, K. (Eds.) The Virtual Battlefield: Perspectives on Cyber Warfare. Amsterdam: IOS Press, pp 163-181.

Ottis, R. (2008) “Analysis of the 2007 Cyber Attacks Against Estonia from the Information Warfare Perspective.” In Proceedings of the 7th European Conference on Information Warfare and Security. Reading: Academic Publishing Limited, pp 163-168.

Ottis, R. (2009) ”Theoretical Model for Creating a Nation-State Level Offensive Cyber Capability.” In Proceedings of the 8th European Conference on Information Warfare and Security. Reading: Academic Publishing Limited, pp 177-182.

Ottis, R. (2010a) “From Pitch Forks to Laptops: Volunteers in Cyber Conflicts.” In Czosseck, C. and Podins, K. (Eds.) Conference on Cyber Conflict. Proceedings 2010. Tallinn: CCD COE Publications, pp 97-109.

Ottis, R. (2010b) “Proactive Defence Tactics Against On-Line Cyber Militia.” In Proceedings of the 9th European Conference on Information Warfare and Security. Reading: Academic Publishing Limited, pp 233-237.

Williams, G., Arreymbi, J. (2007) Is Cyber Tribalism Winning Online Information Warfare? In Proceedings of ISSE/SECURE 2007 Securing Electronic Business Processes. Wiesbaden: Vieweg. On-line: http://www.springerlink.com/content/t2824n02g54552m5/n

Young, S., Aitel, D. (2004) The Hacker’s Handbook. The Strategy behind Breaking into and Defending Networks. Boca Raton: Auerbach.

Towards Reversible Cyberattacks

Neil Rowe
U.S. Naval Postgraduate School
Monterey
California, USA

Editorial Commentary

There have been many arguments about the legitimacy of information warfare because of the challenge of controlling where cyber-weapons might go and what damage they might do. The challenge of controlling collateral damage is seen as truly quite large and beyond current capabilities. In this paper, Neil Rowe presents a provocative argument that cyber-weapons could be made to have reversible effects, which would change the ethical argument significantly. He contextualizes his analysis in an excellent review of recent events in cyber-conflict, which provides a strong platform on which he builds his conceptual case. He concludes by asserting that reversibility is even a desirable property in a cyber-weapon. It is an interesting argument. In the real world, bombs that have reversible effects might not have the intended effects: if buildings rebuilt themselves, people sprang back to life, and damage reversed itself, what motivation would there be to conclude a conflict? Yet perhaps in cyberspace, that very reversibility is a capability that might make the notion palatable from an international standards perspective.

Abstract: Warfare without damage has always been a dream of military planners. Traditional warfare usually leaves persistent side effects in the form of dead and injured people and damaged infrastructure. An appealing feature of cyberwarfare is that it could be more ethical than traditional warfare because its damage could be less and more easily repairable. Damage to data and programs (albeit not physical hardware) can be repaired by rewriting over damaged bits with correct data. However, there are practical difficulties in ensuring that cyberattacks minimize unreversible collateral damage while still being easily repairable by the attacker

and not by the victim. We discuss four techniques by which cyberattacks can be potentially reversible. One technique is reversible cryptography, where the attacker encrypts data or programs to prevent their use, then decrypts them after hostilities have ceased. A second technique is to obfuscate the victim's computer systems in a reversible way. A third technique to withhold key data from the victim, while caching it to enable quick restoration on cessation of hostilities. A fourth technique is to deceive the victim so that think they mistakenly think they are being hurt, then reveal the deception at the conclusion of hostilities. We also discuss incentives to use reversible attacks such as legality, better proportionality, lower reparations, and easier ability to use third parties. As an example, we discuss aspects of the recent cyberattacks on Georgia. This paper appeared in the Proceedings of the 9th European Conference on Information Warfare and Security, July 2010, Thessaloniki, Greece.
Keywords: cyberweapons, cyberattacks, reversibility, damage, cryptography, deception

1. Introduction

The U.S. military is concerned about defending against cyberattacks. Little progress has been made in the last few years in this defense, due to increasing dependence on networking and the spread of unnecessarily complex software products. Attackers have grown increasingly sophisticated, and are now predominantly members of large organized groups, either organized crime or government espionage. Militaries are increasingly wondering to what extent these cyberattack techniques could be used as nonlethal weapons (Rattray, 2001).

An emerging consensus is that many existing "laws of war" do apply to cyberconflict (Schmitt, 2002). This includes the Hague Conventions of 1899 and 1907 and Geneva Conventions of 1949 and 1977 (ICRC, 2007). Article 51 of the 1977 Additional Protocols of the Geneva Conventions prohibits attacks that employ methods and means of combat whose effects cannot be controlled or whose damage to civilians is disproportionate, and Article 57 says “Constant care shall be taken to spare the civilian population, civilians, and civilian objects”. So it is important to ensure this with cyberweapons.

These laws matter because of the practical difficulties in using cyberattacks effectively in warfare. As we have discussed elsewhere (Rowe, 2010), cyberattacks are less reliable than conventional attacks because they exploit bugs and flaws in software, and bugs and flaws are constantly being fixed.

Cyberattacks thus tend to be unnecessarily strong in an effort to ensure their success. This risks high collateral damage. The good news is that some cyberattacks are better than others in that the damage they cause is more easily reversible. Lack of reversibility is an important argument for banning weapons, as with the recent initiatives to ban land mines in warfare. This suggests we draw analogies to outlaw irreversible cyberattacks in international law and treaties.

1.1. The Georgia attacks

The cyberattacks on Georgia in August 2008 suggest a possible future of cyberwarfare; USCCU (2009) provides an excellent summary. Attacks were launched to coincide with a military invasion of Georgia by Russia (the "South Ossetia War"), and appeared to be well planned and timed (Markoff, 2008). They primarily involved denial of service against key Georgia Web sites, with some malware involved in support of this, plus some Web-site defacement. Some of attacking sites were known malware sites, some were new sites created specifically for the attack, some were "botnets" of otherwise innocent computers, and some were computers of people recruited to attack from social-networking sites. None of these were government or military sites.

The targets of the attack were government and business organizations in Georgia that contributed to its ability to withstand the conventional military attack which followed shortly thereafter. They included government agencies associated with communications as well as news-media organizations, apparently with the goal of making it difficult for Georgians to determine what was happening. Later attacks broadened the scope to financial and educational institutions, as well as businesses associated with particular kinds of infrastructure. These cyberattacks were clearly targeted at civilians, and were targeted quite precisely. A wide range of techniques were used in generally nonattributable ways in a well planned campaign. Apparently the attacks were designed (unlike the attacks on Estonia previously) to avoid international outcry.

Attacking primarily civilian enterprises is a clear violation of the laws of war (Walzer, 1977). Civilians are not supposed to be the primary targets of military actions unless they are substantially contributing to a tactical or strategic military asset. Civilian communications and media outlets are not military assets, and in fact can be adversarial to the military. This is different from the bombing of munitions plants during World War II, where the munitions were directly contributing to the war effort. So since the Georgia attacks were clearly correlated to a subsequent military incursion, they were clearly a violation of the laws of war. It is likely that the reason that military sites were not attacked was that they were better hardened against attack, so attacking them would be less cost-effective.

Denial of service and Web site defacement are relatively benign forms of attack compared to other possible cyberattacks. Once the attacks stopped, repair of sites was relatively straightforward; on this the attacks were relatively ethical. However, they still were not ethical. The government of Georgia could not inform citizens of what to do during the attack, and its ability to provide government services, medical services, and humanitarian activities then was greatly impeded. Some of the damage was permanent because of lost opportunities during the denial of service.

2. The damage of a cyberattack

Let us consider the main factors that affect the damage of a cyberattack. Cyberattacks can range from limited and controlled tactical attacks to broad and uncontrolled campaigns. This means their legal and ethical issues can vary considerably as well.

Collateral damage is a major factor in evaluating cyberattacks. This can cause needless suffering even if no one is killed. Concerns of this kind have limited U.S cyberattacks in the past (Markoff and Shanker, 2009). Collateral damage can be minimized by precise targeting. Such precision may not always be possible. Sites can change their names or shift (as in the case of Georgia) to another country, and self-propagating malware such as viruses and worms can autonomously spread beyond the initial targets.

An important difficulty with cyberattacks is in localizing them, something much more difficult than with conventional military attacks. This makes their effects difficult to repair. Computer systems and networks are complex. When something malfunctions, it may be difficult find the part of it that is responsible. Cyberattacks in particular will pick unusual targets within systems and do surprising things to them to obtain the maximum effect. Debugging of computer systems and networks is difficult, and many operators of computer systems lack detailed understanding of what they are running. The Georgia cyberattacks were focused primarily on the input to Web sites, which simplified their localization. But these attacks were clearly intended to be demonstrations. Most attacks will not be as easy to localize.

Another important factor in evaluating damage is its reversibility, the focus of this paper. If an attack can be quickly undone, this can be used to remove collateral damage, and it permits quick repair after the cessation of hostilities. It also helps achieve proportional response, a key aspect of the laws of war for counterattacks (Darnton, 2006), since an inadvertently too-powerful attack can be partially undone. Some proponents of cyberwarfare claim it is more reversible than other forms of warfare (Shulman, 1999), since damage to programs and data can be repaired by copying the original data over the damaged data. However, restoring programs and data by the victim can be time-consuming and requires well-trained staff (Dorf and Johnson, 2007) which is not always available. Cyberattacks also usually create psychological as well as physical effects, and psychological damage to a victim may not be easy to reverse. Also, attacks on time-critical activities may not be reversible. When a patient in a hospital is on a respirator controlled by a computer and the computer delays actions, the patient can die. Similarly, delaying many important activities of a government, and particularly a military, can cause plenty of damage. Nonetheless, using attacks that are mostly reversible is a step in the right direction towards the responsible conduct of cyberwarfare.

3. Techniques for reversible cyberattacks

Let us consider ways to enable cyberattack damage to be reversed by an attacker more quickly and better than by restoring from backup. These cyberattacks could be traditional outsider-based attacks from the Internet during which the attacker sends malicious packets to a victim that enable them to take over control of the victim's computer, or they could be attacks accomplished by a malicious insider. Note however that cyberattacks are crimes in most countries, as they amount to malicious vandalism of communications technology.

3.1. Cryptographic attacks

Cryptography is a systematic method for concealing information (Mel and Baker, 2000). Since information superiority is a key objective of warfare, concealing it can be an attack (Libicki, 2007). Then the attack could be repaired by restoring availability of the information.

An example would be encrypting key programs of a victim with a decryption key that only the attacker knows. Encrypted programs would be unusable by the victim until the attacker is willing to decrypt them. Valuable data such as sensor information can also be encrypted by an attack. Encryption can be accomplished by obtaining administrator ("root") access to a machine by any of a number of methods, and making changes to software and data. Such access can be obtained long in advance and then an attack can be triggered by an external signal. Rather than encrypting an entire piece of software, a simpler alternative is to insert a prolog or "wrapper" to programs that requires a user to enter a password known to the attacker before the program can be used. This is easiest if a program already requires a password, in which case the attacker could modify data to require the attacker's password instead.

Another alternative is to encrypt the data going to a victim, as discussed in section 3.3. Data is usually more vulnerable to modification than programs. Many secure networks encrypt their data in transmission, and this could be changed to use the attacker's key rather than the victim's. This could be done with administrator access to the machines doing the encryption, usually just the first and final ones through which the data passes (with "end-to-end encryption"), and could be accomplished by "rootkits" (Kuhnhauser, 2004). It could also be accomplished by modifying the hardware used for networking, replacing parts or whole computer systems with those designed by the attacker.

The main countermeasure for encryption-based attacks is restoration of the damaged code from backup. However, it may be difficult to determine what to restore because of the attack localization problem discussed above. Even when the attack can be localized, restoration can be difficult when properly trained personnel are unavailable, personnel are unfamiliar with the restoration procedure, or the restoration procedure is complicated (as it can be with complex software like operating systems). Restoration requires valuable time of system administrators that they did not anticipate using, and it might not be fast enough in a "blitzkrieg" cyberattack designed to quickly achieve objectives.

Encryption-based attacks could be easy to detect, since encrypted characters have statistical randomness very different from those of normal programs and software. Attackers who want their attacks to be visible to encourage negotiation would find this property helpful.

3.2. Obfuscating attacks

Computer systems are carefully designed entities. If we can disrupt their organization, they become unusable. So a class of "obfuscating" attacks could rearrange the software and data of a computer system, or map data values to new values in a one-to-one mapping, or insert extra data, in a way known only to the attacker. For instance, we could interchange parts of programs; we could add 13 modulo 256 to a set of designated 8-bit bytes; or we could insert random bytes into designated locations in programs. The plan for how we obfuscate can be arbitrarily elaborate if we record it carefully. Cryptographic methods are a special case of obfuscating methods, but the restrictions of cryptography are not necessary to make a system unusable. For instance, adding many random bytes could greatly increase the size of programs, something cryptographic methods do not do in their attempt to be space-efficient, but which works well as an attack technique given the typically small portion of occupied storage on most computer systems.

Anything can be targeted with obfuscation techniques, but the obfuscation can be more efficient if it targets critical parts of programs and key data. If the attacker wants their attack to be noticed, they can target highly visible parts such as the user interface. Just modifying the appearance of a window can make software ususable with little effort.

Obfuscating attacks can be undone by applying the reverse of the attacking actions in reverse order. So for instance if we interchanged two blocks of code, added 13 to each byte, and then added two bytes of "37" on the end, we can undo the effects by deleting the two end bytes, subtracting 13 from each byte, and then interchanging the same two blocks. Any operation performing a one-to-one mapping (an "isomorphism") on either the contents or location of data can be reversed by an inverse operation. This includes operations that add useless information since they effectively permute locations of the real information.

If the rearrangement is sufficiently complex, it would be virtually impossible for the victim to figure it out and reverse it, although unlike encryption, it could be reversed given sufficient time. Unlike encryption, obfuscation with interchanges and padding can be designed to provide the same statistics as the original system, and thus be difficult to localize. More than encryption, restoration from backup would be difficult and slow because the entire system would need to be restored if the modifications were well dispersed and the victim could not recognize them. Partial restoration could be worse than none at all because it could destroy some of the interchanged halves. Restoration can be made still harder if the attacker combines many techniques.

3.3. Withholding-information attacks

Another potentially reversible attack method directly withholds data. This is similar to blockading in traditional naval warfare and jamming in electronic warfare, both of which share the advantage of relatively reversible damage. Denial of service is an example of indirect denial of data by flooding a resource with false data so there is little time to process the true data. But denial of service is a relatively broad attack which risks much collateral damage.

A more precise way to withhold information is to use a "man in the middle" deployment: The attacker inserts their own hardware and/or software (perhaps by address hijacking) between the victim and the victim's intended communicants, or takes control of an existing machine on that route. Only information that the attacker allows will then pass from or to the victim. This could be accomplished by encrypting the information as suggested in the last section, so the victim gets or sends all their normal volume of data but no one can read it. Alternatively, if the volume of data is not large, it could be withheld from the victim and saved for restoration after the cessation of hostilities. Returning the data repairs some damage, since getting it late is usually better than not getting it at all, and facilitates tracking of secondary damage caused by the withholding. However, this will not reverse all damage, like physical damage from the failure of a computer system to prevent a subsequent irreversible physical attack.

If the "middleware" doing the diversion is designed to be highly selective, bandwidth may not be a problem. For instance, an attack on a sensor system might withhold only locations, which are easy to spot in text because they use standard formats. Or it might block the locations of attacker military units while reporting locations of casualties to permit Red Cross activities. Or a messaging system might only block orders down the chain of command, not reports going up, preventing the application of force while keeping the victim informed of what is happening. Man-in-the-middle deployments can be done with hardware, as by inserting a new device on the Internet connection to a computer. Or they can be done with software, by modifying the implementation of Internet protocols with the assistance of a rootkit.

An alternative way to withhold information is to misroute it. So a man-in-the-middle attack could deliberately change destination headers of Internet packets sent through it to that of a site it controls. If the corresponding correct destinations are stored somewhere, and the packets are stored at the new destination, the attack could be reversed. This has the advantage of eliminating storage at the man-in-the-middle device.

A countermeasure for man-in-the-middle attacks is to bypass the middle, much as blockaded countries can find new routes to conduct trade. Attackers can prevent this by attacking a "bottleneck" computer such as a server for a local-area network, or by exploiting key protocols for networking that must be used by a user. Firewall and intrusion-prevention computers, and TCP and HTTP protocols, provide good opportunities for such attacks. Almost as good are file and Web servers for a local-area network.

3.4. Resource-deception attacks

Another approach is to deceive a victim with illusory damage. Then "repairing" the attack means just revealing the truth to the victim. A simple way is to modify the victim's operating system to issue false error messages on any attempts to use the system for something important (Rowe, 2007). Most users take error messages seriously, so false error messages can be quite disruptive to them. Such messages raise no legal problems themselves, unlike man-in-the-middle attacks, since they happen not infrequently when the software lacks sufficient information to accurately diagnose an error. However, the necessary modification of the operating system is still a form of vandalism.

Resource deception can be implemented by modifying the operating system of a computer by a rootkit. One good way is through "software wrappers" on key components of the operating system and applications software (Michael et al, 2002). Normally the wrappers can behave transparently, passing on commands to the operating system and passing back re-

sponses. But in specified circumstances recognized by a system monitor, the wrappers can issue false error messages and other confusing information. Alternatively, hardware exceptions can be triggered by the wrappers, which can simulate serious errors.
Error messages can be made more persuasive using techniques from spam and phishing (Spammer X, 2004). Official-looking graphics and verbal manipulation can be used. Claims of authorization from authorities and experts, rewards for compliance, and threats for noncompliance can be cited. Creating an atmosphere of urgency will also help, e.g. flashing red letters saying "Security Violation -- Log out now." However, persuasion works less well when it coincides too closely with the attack, since an intelligent victim will likely infer a common cause. It would be better to begin deception well before the attack. Also, repeated deceptions lose effectiveness as the victim becomes familiar with them, so deceptions should only be used occasionally.

A countermeasure to resource deception is to reinstall the software generating it. But this is time-consuming. It may also be unnecessary because a clever adversary could modify an operating system in superficial ways that do not require reinstallation.

While automated deceptions do not damage data and programs to the extent of the previously mentioned attacks, they do create persistent damage in the form of increased distrust of computer systems by the victim. This can unfairly reduce their ability to use computer technology for a long time, and these effects can extend to a broad range. Trust is built up slowly, but distrust can increase quickly given a single act (Ford, 1996). Thus deception-based attacks may need to be used cautiously.

4. Additional factors contributing to reversibility

Not all cyberattacks following the above methods will be equally feasible or equally reversible. Other considerations are involved.

Methods for reversible attacks need precision in targeting to simplify their reversal as well as reduce their chances of collateral damage and disproportionality in attacking. Precision enables an attacker to focus on a few well-chosen military targets and better assess the effect of their attack. If the effect is too small, the attack can be increased; if the effect is too large, reversing the attack can be done even before hostilities cease.

Reversibility may decrease with time. For instance, a victim may close its Internet connections so that systems cannot be reached to repair them. Or an attack may be detected by the victim and repaired ineptly to make reversing impossible, as by loading the wrong backup copies resulting in incompatible software modules that will not work. These contingencies need to be addressed in attack planning. Reversal may also have a latency (time delay) that causes additional harm. For instance, if Georgia had surrendered midway during the campaign against it, it is unlikely that the attacks would have stopped for quite a while, since they were coordinated primarily at the planning stage and not during execution. Then Georgia would have incurred considerable damage after surrendering, a clear violation of the laws of war.

Another important factor is the ability of the defender to identify the attacker ("attribution"). It is desirable that the victim know this for a reversible attack since the attacker knows best how to reverse it. After all, anonymous attacks are typical of terrorism; a responsible country wants their attacks to be attributable to help achieve precise outcomes. A simple form of attribution is to consistently use a well-known source site. (Otherwise, just leaving the sites up for a while after the attack will aid tracing of their location.) More generally, an attacker can attach crytographic signatures to the attack code or data. Signatures can be embedded in unnecessary instructions in code or in comments in data; steganography (Wayner, 2002) can be used to conceal the signatures if necessary. Signatures can use the private key of a public-private key pair so that only the attacker can attach them.

5. Enforcement of reversible attacks

A question is what incentive a cyberattacker has to use reversible attack methods. A similar question can be asked about many other military technologies, such as conventional weapons instead of nuclear weapons. Some incentives in these cases come from international outcry at using unethical methods and the resulting ostracism of the offending state or organization. But more importantly, nations agree to laws of warfare, and unethical methods can violate those laws. Responses of the international community to such violations include sanctions, boycotts, fines, and legal proceedings (Berman, 2002).

A good incentive for reversible attacks occurs if the attacker must pay to repair the damage. Estimates of repair costs could be an important factor in the amount of reparations required to settle a conflict (Torpey, 2006). Reparations are also enforceable against non-state actors such as factions within a country. If a neutral party can enforce reparations, reversible attacks are advantageous to belligerents. The reversal methods proposed here can be initiated remotely, so territorial-integrity concerns that impede cleanup of damage of conventional warfare are less burdensome with cyberweapons. A related issue is the attacker proving that they have removed all traces of their attack, which is not difficult to do for the relatively simple attack techniques of this paper. For instance, an attacker that used signatures can prove that none remain on a system.

Another incentive to reversible attacks is if a victim is likely to respond in like kind. Then use of reversible attack could encourage an adversary to do the same because otherwise they would appear to be escalating the conflict (Gardam, 2004).

Cryptographic attacks can exploit three-party cryptographic protocols such as key escrow (Mel and Baker, 2000). In this, a neutral third party holds a key for deciphering an attack's encryption scheme. Similarly, in obfuscating attacks the "swap plan" functions like a key and could be held by the third party. A neutral third party like the United Nations could confirm signatures of attacks and assess damage, which could be more acceptable to the belligerents when done by a disinterested party.

A neutral third party could also provide selective or staged repair of reversible cyberweapon damage for belligerents that do not trust one another. The third party could alternate repair between two countries in stages so that none ever has a significant repair advantage over the other. A third party could try to calm crises by enforcing limited sanctions on the belligerents using the methods described above, that would allow food, medicine, and other forms of humanitarian assistance to be arranged across the Internet, while prohibiting activities that led to the conflict such as denial-of-service actions by either party to the conflict. Going further, a third party such as the United Nations could even employ reversible attacks themselves as a form of humanitarian intervention in a conflict to stop it, as for instance for a genocide. Reversible attacks then might be the more ethical than doing nothing.

6. Conclusions

All warfare aims at precise effects on its victims. Reversibility of attacks aids and supports precision. We have discussed four ways for implementing reversible cyberattacks, and some of the secondary factors that affect their reversibility. Reversible cyberattacks are clearly feasible, cost-effective, and some can be made undetectable. Thus reversibility appears to be a desirable property of cyberweapons.

An issue is whether the availability of reversible cyberattacks will encourage attacks. Reversibility, even if partial and delayed, lowers the cost to the attacker as broadly measured. However, any kind of attack introduces risks for the attacker, such as international outrage, sanctions, and counterattacks. Warfare still remains difficult to justify.

The views expressed are those of the author and do not represent those of any part of the U.S. Government.

References

Berman P. (2002) "The Globalization of Jurisdiction", University of Pennsylvania Law Review, Vol. 151 No. 2, pp. 311-545.

Darnton, G. (2006) "Information Warfare and the Laws of War", in Halpin, E., Trovorrow, P., Webb, D., and Wright, S. (eds.), Cyberwar, Netwar, and the Revolution in Military Affairs, Palgrave Macmillan, Houndsmills, UK, pp. 139-156.

Dorf, J., and Johnson, M. (2007) "Restoration Component of Business Continuity Planning", in Tipton, H., and Krause, M. (Eds.), Information Security Management Handbook, Sixth Edition, CRC Press, pp. 645-1654.

Ford, C. (1996) Lies! Lies!! Lies!!! The Psychology of Deceit, American Psychiatric Press, Washington, DC, USA.

Gardam, J. (2004) Necessity, Proportionality, and the Use of Force by States, Cambridge University Press, Cambridge UK.

ICRC (International Committee of the Red Cross) (2007) "International Humanitarian Law – Treaties and Documents", retrieved December 1, 2007 from www.icrc.org/icl.nsf.

Kuhnhauser, W. (2004, January) "Root Kits: An Operating Systems Viewpoint", ACM SIGOPS Operating Systems Review, Vol. 38, No. 1, pp. 12-23.

Libicki, M. (2007), Conquest in Cyberspace: National Security and Information Warfare,: Cambridge University Press, New York, NY, USA.

Markoff, J. (2008, August 13) "Before the Gunfire, Cyberattacks", New York Times, p. A1.

Markoff, J., and Shanker, T. (2009, August 1) "Halted '03 Iraq Plan Illustrates U.S. Fear of Cyberwar Risk", New York Times, p. A1.

Mel, H., and Baker, D. (2000) Cryptography Decrypted, 5th edition, Addison-Wesley Professional, Boston, MA, USA.

Michael, J., Auguston, M., Rowe, N., and Riehle, R. (2002, June) "Software Decoys: Intrusion Detection and Countermeasures", Proc. of IEEE Information Assurance Workshop, West Point, New York, pp. 130-138.

Rattray, G. (2001) Strategic Warfare in Cyberspace, MIT Press, Cambridge, MA, USA.

Rowe, N. (2007, May) "Finding Logically Consistent Resource-Deception Plans for Defense in Cyberspace", Proc. of 3rd International Symposium on Security in Networks and Distributed Systems, Niagara Falls, Ontario, Canada, pp. 563-568.

Rowe, N. (2010) "The Ethics of Cyberweapons in Warfare", Journal of Techoethics, Vol. 1, No. 1, pp. 20-31.

Schmitt, M. (2002) "Wired Warfare: Computer Network Attack and Jus in Bello", International Review of the Red Cross, Vol. 84, No. 846, pp. 365-399.

Shulman, M. (1999) "Discrimination in the Laws of Information Warfare", Columbia Journal of Transnational Law, Vol. 37, pp. 939-968.

Spammer X, (2004) Inside the Spam Cartel, Syngress, Rockland, MA.

Torpey J. (2006) Making Whole What Has Been Smashed: On Reparations Politics, Harvard University Press, Cambridge, MA, USA.

USCCU (United States Cyber Consequences Unit) (2009, August) "Overview by the US-CCU of the Cyber Campaign against Georgia in August of 2008", US-CCU Special Report, downloaded from www.usccu.org, November 2, 2009.

Walzer, D. (1977) Just and Unjust Wars: A Moral Argument with Historical Illustrations, Basic Books, New York, NY, USA.

Wayner, P. (2002) Disappearing Cryptography: Information Hiding: Steganography and Watermarking, Morgan Kaufmann, San Francisco, CA, USA.

Use of Information Sharing Between Government and Industry as a Weapon

Julie Ryan
George Washington University
Washington DC, USA

Editorial Commentary

In this paper, the problematic and persistent fact of life in the current world is considered: the fact that the infrastructures upon which information warfare is likely to be waged is neither owned nor controlled by geopolitical entities. Instead these infrastructures are mostly owned and controlled by very large multi-national corporations, whose loyalty to any one nation is not always possible to determine. This reality has led to many governments calling for "public-private partnerships", a structure in which information "sharing" occurs between the public entity and the private entities. The paper explores the not unlikely scenario of a very large multinational corporation using multiple partnerships in order to proactively protect its investment through the quite secret and surreptitious planting of a vulnerability through the auspices of the information sharing channels. The scenario is used to bring up the very tenuous ability of geopolitical states, with their sovereignty firmly grounded in physical space, to actually wage information warfare without the benign or not so benign consent of these corporate behemoths. The implications are somewhat sobering, if taken to extremes.

Abstract: governments have viewed Information sharing as a way to tap into the knowledge of the non-governmental enterprises which own and operate large

segments of critical infrastructures in order to develop concrete intelligence about security challenges. The effects of globalization and the inherent conflicts of interest create a potential for allowing the process to be used as a weapon of information warfare through abuse of the information sharing structure.
Keywords: Information warfare, critical information infrastructure protection

1. Information sharing

The challenges faced by governments associated with protecting critical infrastructures are complicated by the fact that large portions of the critical infrastructures are owned or operated by private industry. The United States (US) government as a way of tapping into the knowledge of the non-governmental enterprises, which own and operate large segments of critical infrastructures (Ryan 1998), proposed information sharing. The information-sharing concept was thereafter adopted by other national governments and corporations acting as trusted conduits (IACC 2003). The knowledge desired by governments includes information on vulnerabilities and attacks seen by the owners and operators of elements of the critical infrastructure. The promise in return to the providers is that the information will be kept secret but participants will be informed about attack types and discovered vulnerabilities. On its face, this appears to be a viable strategy for developing concrete intelligence about security challenges. However, there are inherent weaknesses to this approach that have the potential for allowing the process to be used as a weapon of information warfare. This paper examines the processes from a structural perspective and postulates potential hostile activities that may be enabled through abuse of the information sharing structure.

1.1. The perceived need for information sharing

In the 1990s in the United States (US), concern about protecting the critical infrastructures reached sufficient levels as to spur government action in the form of policy development, resource allocation, and organizational restructuring. Policies promulgated included Presidential Decision Directive (PDD) 62 Combating Terrorism and 63 Critical Infrastructure Protection. Resource allocation included budgetary set-asides for research and committees. Organizational restructuring included the creation of the National Infrastructure Protection Center (NIPC). These efforts also stipulated the development of information sharing and analysis centers (ISACs) through which “the voluntary participation of private industry [would be solicited] to meet common goals for protecting our critical systems through public-private partnerships" (US Government 1998). This recommendation sprung from an awareness that there was a vast reservoir of knowledge resident in the private sector that needed to be tapped in order for the government to understand the realities and needs of critical infrastructure protection (CIP).

1.2. Existing structures

The exact structural make-up of ISACs was left to the members of the critical infrastructure to decide. As a result, an analysis of existing ISACs in 2005 reveals a great difference in both structure and in participation restrictions. At this time, there have been thirteen critical infrastructures identified by the the US Government (US Government 2003 p 35), of which eleven are defined explicitly in The National Strategy for the Physical Protection of Critical Infrastructures and Key Assets. Of these, eight have existing ISACs, participation for which varies from ISAC to ISAC. Some allow any company even peripherally related to the core critical infrastructure to participate while others restrict membership through a variety of means, to include fee structures. For example, the Food ISAC allows membership by any company engaged in the production of food as well as those who supply products to retails stores that carry food products, as long as that company has filed a US tax return. Cost for membership in the Food ISAC is borne by the Food Marketing Institute. (FMI 2005) The Information Technology ISAC, on the other hand, requires a minimum $5,000 membership fee, due annually (IT-ISAC 2005). The IT-ISAC currently lists 22 corporations as members, with only two at the lowest membership level.

The ISACs that exist primarily are sponsored by governments and membership in the ISACs is limited to those who have some documented relationship with the sponsoring government. For example, the US sponsored ISACs require members to show that US tax returns have been filed. There are ISACs that are not government sponsored. For example, SAIC sponsors an ISAC that is worldwide in nature, appropriately named the World Wide ISAC. That ISAC charges $10,000 for membership, which does not appear to be limited by geographic location or national affiliation (SAIC 2005).
For the purposes of this analysis, only government sponsored ISACs will be considered. This simplifying assumption is necessary to reduce the complexity of the analysis, although the reader can certainly extrapolate to other ISAC structures.

2. Definition of weapon

It is useful to review the component elements of an abstracted weapon in order to contextualize the use and deployments of weapons. At an abstract level, a weapon consists of two general parts: the payload and the delivery vehicle. The payload is the part that accomplishes the desired effect while the delivery vehicle is the conduit by which the payload is transported to the target. The delivery vehicle contains the propulsion, navigation, and trigger for the weapon. Both the payload and the delivery vehicle may be in and of themselves complex; however, for the purposes of a simplified discussion, we consider them as single parts of the greater whole of the weapon.

The weapon may be used either directly or indirectly against an intended target. A direct use of the weapon would see the payload delivered to the principle target in order for the effect to be accomplished. An indirect use of the weapon would be for the payload to be delivered to a surrogate target with the intention that effects on the surrogate target would cascade to the intended target. An example of direct use of a weapon would be the delivery of a bullet to the heart of an enemy combatant in order to remove that combatant from a theater of war. An example of indirect use of a weapon would be the delivery of a bomb to a crowded shopping mall in order to induce an authority (such as a government) to remove soldiers from a theater of war. The intended effects of a weapon are varied depending on strategy and tactics but may include destruction, denial of use of a capability, influence on actions, or deception. Both direct and indirect uses of weapons may have unintended or collateral effects. Figure 1 shows this graphically.

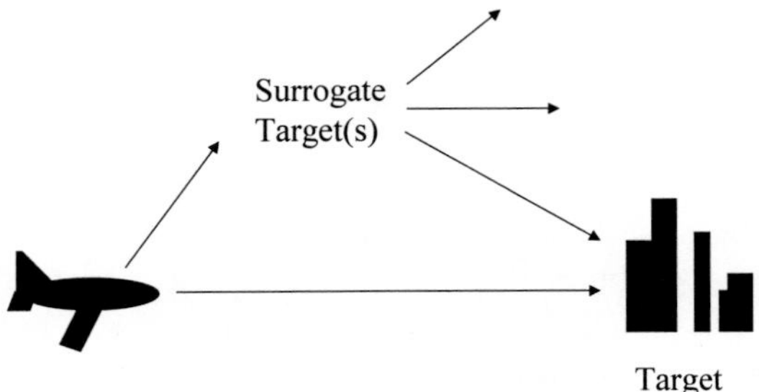

Figure 1: Direct and indirect weapon use against specific target

3. Information sharing as a weapon

In order to consider information sharing as a weapon, we must contextualize the process of information sharing as an abstraction. Once the process is abstracted to show the data flowing between companies and governments, then the use of the data flows as delivery vehicles for information warfare payloads may be examined.

3.1. Information sharing abstracted

Information sharing at its most basic consists of two streams of information supported by internal processing. One stream goes from the participant company through the ISAC and on to the sponsoring government. The second stream reverses that process. Each stream is considered at each node for decision processes related to external influences, internal constraints, and information sharing requirements, such as protection of critical data.

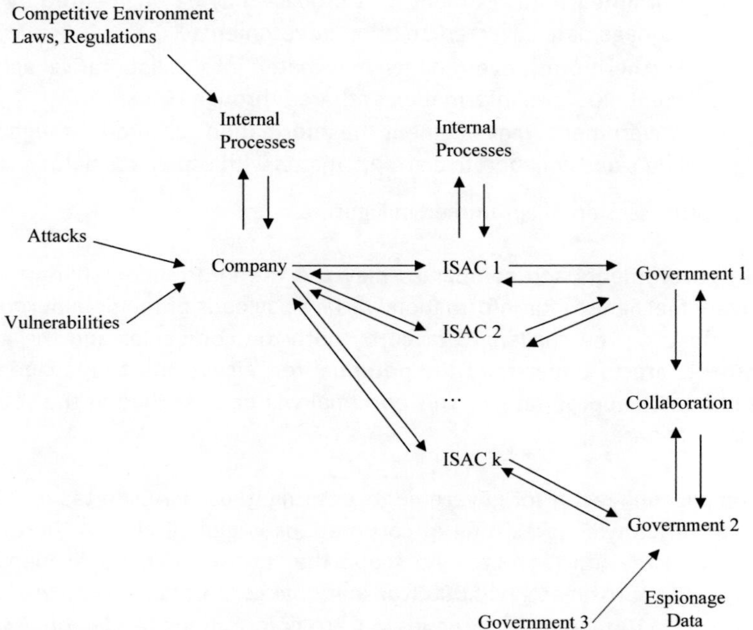

Figure 2: Information sharing data flows between companies and governments

The process can be described thusly:

- Companies 1 through i contribute information 1 through j to ISACs 1 through k.
- There is a many to many relationship between companies and ISACs: a company may participate in more than one ISAC and each ISAC needs the participation of many companies.
- Companies may participate in ISACs sponsored by more than one government.
- Each company has some internal processing aspect that supports the decision to either share or not share the information.
- Each ISAC has some processing method that supports integrating the shared information, protecting sensitive elements, and then sharing it with other ISAC participants.
- Additionally, for multiple ISACs sponsored by a single government, there is some processing function to take the collated information from each ISAC and combine it further.
- Within each government, this process may be augmented by espionage data collected on other governments.
- Furthermore, governments may enter into collaborative agreements to share information gathered through ISACs.
- Governments may augment the information gathered through the ISACs and collaborative arrangements with espionage data.

These processes are diagrammed in Figure 2.

Both governments and companies may use the information sharing as a delivery mechanism for information warfare payloads of multiple purposes and impacts. The challenges faced by both the companies and the governments are to understand the potential for misuse and to manage the resultant risk appropriately. This potential will be described in the subsequent sections.

A complicating factor for governments desiring to use ISACs to tap into the wealth of knowledge existing in corporations is globalization. There are companies of sufficient size and scope that transcend national identity. There are approximately 40,000 transnational corporations that exist. Of the world's 100 largest economies, 51 are corporations (Anderson 2000). Many of the largest corporations play influential roles in national and international politics, as evidenced by the attendees at the World Economic

Forum meetings held in Davos (WEF 2005) and participation in non-governmental organizations (UN 2005). This spread of influence, attention, and economic power indicate a lessening of controls from state authorities to corporate authorities and a rise in influence of corporate authorities on state authorities at all levels. This underscores the potential motivation for misuse of the information sharing processes.

3.2. Potential misuse and abuse in information sharing

The process of information sharing is in and of itself a possible delivery vehicle for information warfare payloads. All the elements of a delivery vehicle are present in the data flow process; the process itself provides a willing conduit for the delivery of the weapon. The triggering of the payload is the acceptance of the submitted data into the ISAC processes. The effects of the payload depend on the intention of the originator.

An example of how the information sharing can be used as a weapon is best described using a scenario. Company X is a corporation with a physical presence in 299 locations worldwide, which are contained in 120 nations. Company X participates in ISACs sponsored by 3 countries. In this scenario, the ISACs will be noted as ISAC-1, ISAC-2, and ISAC-3. Each of these countries have active espionage programs against each of the other countries. Company X has recently become concerned about strains in the relationships between two countries in which it does business. These hostile countries will be noted as Target 1 and Target 2. In order to control the situation, Company X devises a strategy in which it can create a covert ability to control the command and control systems of each of the country's militaries. The purpose of having this ability is to prevent the countries from going to war with each other.

Company X executes this strategy through the ISACs. Through ISAC-1, Company X submits technical details of an attack detected on its computer systems at a research laboratory. Along with the technical details of the attack, the Company provides information on how the attack was contained and rebuffed. Through ISAC-2, Company X submits technical details of a vulnerability discovered in its computer systems at a production plant. Through ISAC-3, Company X submits technical details of a different vulnerability discovered in its computer systems at a testing facility. For both vulnerabilities, Company X includes recommendations for mitigating the vulnerabilities. Each vulnerability is subtle and the recommended mitigations are extremely technical.

At ISAC-1, the data is accepted and placed into the database. Attempts are made to vet the data, but since no one else has reported the attack, no verification is possible. Laboratory researchers are able to reproduce the attack as specified by Company X, so the information is deemed reliable and is shared with other ISAC members and with Government 1. Government 1 has a sharing agreement with allies and shares the information with those allies, although the information is limited to protect sensitive information. In this manner, some limited information about the attack, blessed with the ISAC seal of approval, reaches the target governments.

The same process is repeated at ISACs–2 and –3. Governments 2 and 3 share this information only with Government 1, but Government 1 has sharing agreements with allies and so sanitized information about the vulnerabilities is promulgated. Again, the technical details reach the target governments.

A critical element of success in this strategy is that three separate pieces of information appear to come from different sources and come through different channels. Because of this, the ability of any of the ISACs, government analysis centers, and targets to detect a distributed attack is vastly decreased.

The target governments, being in a heightened state of alert, pay particular attention to protecting their information infrastructure. Each target government is known to be highly technically sophisticated and each has dedicated information warfare corps. The target governments take steps to protect against the specified attack and implement the recommended steps to mitigate the two vulnerabilities.

When the recommended steps are taken, a highly sophisticated synergistic vulnerability is introduced into the systems. This vulnerability is not detectable using existing scanners or analysis tools. In order to exploit this vulnerability, a series of capabilities must be invoked in sequence, requiring sophisticated knowledge of the presence of the vulnerability and the execution details. Company X now has control over both target information systems.

3.3. A real life example

The scenario described is not as far-fetched as it might seem. When there is a willing acceptance of data into a system, there is an open conduit for coercive data. Examples of this abound with Trojan-laden emails, but there is also a more specific example: the Super Bowl Attack conducted by Hughes Corporation against DirecTv pirates. The description of the attack

DirecTV began sending several updates at a time, breaking their pattern. ... The updates contained useless pieces of computer code that was then required to be present on the card in order to receive the transmission. The hacking community accommodated this in their software, applying these updates in their hacking software. Not until the final batch of updates was sent through the stream did the hacking community understand DirecTV. Like a final piece of a puzzle allowing the entire picture, the final updates made all the useless bits of computer code join into a dynamic program, existing on the card itself. This dynamic program changed the entire way the older technology worked. In a masterful, planned, and orchestrated manner, DirecTV had updated the old and ailing technology. ...

... One week before the Super Bowl [2001], DirecTV launched a series of attacks against the hackers of their product. DirecTV sent programmatic code in the stream, using their new dynamic code ally, that hunted down hacked smart cards and destroyed them. ... Some estimate that in one evening, 100,000 smart cards were destroyed, removing 98% of the hacking communities' ability to steal their signal. To add a little pizzazz to the operation, DirecTV personally "signed" the anti-hacker attack. The first 8 computer bytes of all hacked cards were rewritten to read "GAME OVER". (Michael 2001)

That technologists could devise such a strategy is not surprising, nor is it surprising that the attack took place. What is noteworthy, however, is that this electronic attack was launched by a large corporation against a set of individuals in a variety of countries. The implications to the concept of national boundaries and the physical protections afforded through distance are intriguing.

Of course, the potential for misuse is not limited to company participants in ISACs. Governments and other participants could misuse the sharing channels just as easily. What is intriguing is the potential for companies to use the channel to gain control or to exert influence on states, thus reversing the balance of power.

3.4. Probability of eEffectiveness

Having postulated the use of information sharing processes as a weapon, the next step is to point out how the potential impacts can be understood, from both a risk mitigation perspective and the potential for double cross operations.

In order to do such an analysis, it is useful to divide the information system into smaller functional elements and to define the model based on those elements. The model must include both physical and functional descriptions so that impacts to both physical and logical systems are described as a result of directed or cascaded actions. That abstraction provides an ability to describe target paths, direct effects, and interactive effects.

If necessary, the abstracted model can be nested to accommodate levels of complexity. The model itself could represent a simple network – a small number of networked computers – or it could represent a single module in a more complex system – an element in a complex command and control system. The information flow of interest is the flow of vulnerability and attack information and its effects on the functionality of the system.

The use of such a model would be to analyze an IW attack using the ISAC data on any of the targetable elements: the data itself, the access of the data from some storage medium, communication or transmission of the data, and of course the processing or manipulation of the data as well as the system administration. The probability of success of postulated attacks can be analyzed, as well as the potential for unintended impacts or cascades.

Each of the targets can be attacked with a weapon, so the two probabilities associated with the weapon must be considered: the probability that a delivery vehicle will successfully deliver the payload to the correct target, and the probability that the payload will successfully detonate. For a willing conduit, the probability of delivery is very high. For the purposes of analysis, it can even be assumed to be perfect, although that resists the real world knowledge of human frailty.

The statistical modeling of impacts is a great deal more difficult. For example, how is the loss of functionality quantifies in the case where deceptive data is interjected into a system? The types of system and the data use clearly impact this – in one system, an immediate loss of functionality could ensue as the processes report out of bounds outputs, while in another system, the result could be an insidious skewing of simulation outputs totally unnoticeable to an authorized user.

The use of a model to analyze attack possibilities can additionally provide benefit through the identification of second and third order effects that could be overlooked in more simplistic analyses. For example, an attack scenario can be modeled and then a second attack scenario modeled over the template of the result of the first attack. This process would provide information of two general sorts: first, identifying resilient pathways and logical functions; and second, identifying second order attack priorities. From the offensive point of view, this iterative modeling is useful to refine targeting strategies; from a defensive point of view, it is invaluable to identifying triage strategies to recover from attacks as well as identify vulnerabilities that could be made less vulnerable. Most importantly, however, such modeling clearly identifies intelligence data requirements, collection priorities and the operational essential elements of information. Additionally, it provides a user-friendly way of examining systems for synergistic or induced vulnerabilities.

This could additionally help to identify techniques, technologies and processes that could provide a significant defensive advantage to the information systems in question. Technological leaps forward such as distributed decision-making, groupware, and collaborative environments have proven problematic to both security controls and security configuration management. Most recently, the integration of USB-accessible storage devices in appliances from digital cameras to cellular telephones have caused security professionals to reassess security controls in an enterprise environment. These complexities prove both advantageous to attackers and annoying to defenders. A complex model for evaluating attack lay-overs can assist in developing defensive strategies for these complex environments.

4. Conclusion

The potential is real, the motivation may develop, and the impacts serious. A critical challenge in any situation where data comes in to a system is vetting the data for operational purposes (whether that be truth, accuracy, or some other set of measures). When information is specifically used for the defense of information systems, the requirement for such vetting becomes significant.

References

Anderson, Sarah and John Cavanagh (2000), Top 200: The Rise of Global Corporate Power, Corporate Watch 2000, http://www.globalpolicy.org/socecon/tncs/top200.htm, accessed December 3, 2005.

DHS (2005) Threats and Protection: Information Sharing and Analysis Centers, http://www.dhs.gov/dhspublic/display?theme=73&content=1375, accessed December 3, 2005.

FMI (2005) Food Industry - ISAC - Frequently Asked Questions, http://www.fmi.org/isac/faq.htm, accessed December 3, 2005.

IACC (2003) Sharing Is Protecting: A Review of Information Sharing, Information Assurance Advisory Council of the United Kingdom (http://www.iaac.org.uk/), http://www.niscc.gov.uk/niscc/docs/IAAC_NISCC_Sharing_is_Protecting_v21.pdf, accessed December 3, 2005.

Michael (2001) DirecTV's Secret War on Hackers, posted on SlashDot by michael on Thu Jan 25, '01 10:04 AM, http://slashdot.org/articles/01/01/25/1343218.shtml?tid=129, accessed December 3, 2005.

Ryan, Julie J.C.H., John Woloshok, and Barry Leven (1996) Complexities in Conducting Information Warfare, Defense Intelligence Journal, vol 5 no. 1 (Spring 1996): pp. 69-82.

Ryan, Julie J.C.H. (1998) The Infrastructure of the Protection of the Critical Infrastructure, Fall 1998, http://www.julieryan.com/Infrastructure/IPdoc.html, accessed December 3, 2005.

SAIC (2005) About the WW-ISAC, http://www.wwisac.com/about.htm, accessed December 3, 2005.

UN (2005) NGO Global Network, http://www.ngo.org/, accessed December 3, 2005.

US Government (1998) Fact Sheet: Protecting America's Critical Infrastructures: PDD 63, May 22, 1998, http://www.fas.org/irp/offdocs/pdd-63.htm, accessed December 3, 2005.

US Government (2003) The National Strategy for the Physical Protection of Critical Infrastructures and Key Assets, May 2003, http://www.whitehouse.gov/pcipb/physical.html, accessed December 3, 2005.

WEF (2005) World Economic Forum, http://www.weforum.org/, accessed December 3, 2005.

Terrorist use of the Internet: Exploitation and Support Through ICT Infrastructure

Namosha Veerasamy and Marthie Grobler
Council for Scientific and Industrial Research
Pretoria, South Africa

Editorial Commentary

The concept of cyberterrorism is one which is hyped by politicians and scorned by many technologists. In this paper, Veerasamy and Grobler point out the real use that terrorists have for the internet and other communications infrastructures: that of recruiting, that of fund-raising, and that of communicating between themselves. Numerous examples of how these activities are conducted are included. This paper builds upon the previous two by examining the role of non-state actors in competition and conflict in the modern era. This issue is a serious one for those concerned with national security because the goal of the terrorists is to undermine and unseat established governmental structures. Their use of the communications infrastructure is so far relatively benign, if one can consider raising and funding an army benign, but the potential is enormous. Through these actions, the terrorists show both an appreciation for the technological infrastructure and a fairly sophisticated imagination of how to use these technologies for their various goals. Should those goals and capabilities turn towards acts of armed aggression in cyberspace in the future, it may well be within their capabilities.

Abstract: The growth of technology has provided a wealth of functionality. One area in which Information Communication Technology (ICT), especially the Internet, has grown to play a supporting role is terrorism. The Internet provides an enormous amount of information, and enables relatively cheap and instant communication across the globe. As a result, the conventional view of many traditional terrorist groups shifted to embrace the use of technology within their functions. The goal of this paper is to represent the functions and methods that terrorists have come to rely on through the ICT infrastructure. The discussion sheds light on the technical and practical role that ICT infrastructure plays in the assistance of terrorism. The use of the Internet by terrorist groups has expanded from traditional Internet usage to more innovative usage of both traditional and new Internet functions. Global terrorist groups can now electronically target an enormous amount of potential recipients, recruitees and enemies. The aim of the paper is to show how the Internet can be used to enable terrorism, as well as provide technical examples of the support functionality and exploitation. This paper summarises the high-level functions, methods and examples for which terrorists utilise the Internet. This paper looks at the use of the Internet as both a uni-directional and bi-directional tool to support functionality like recruitment, propaganda, training, funding and operations. It also discusses specific methods like the dissemination of web literature, social-networking tools, anti-forensics and fund-raising schemes. Additional examples, such as cloaking and coding techniques, are also provided. In order to analyse how ICT infrastructure can be used in the support of terrorism, a mapping is given of communication direction to the traditional Internet use functions and methods, as well as to innovative Internet functions and methods.

Keywords: anti-forensics, internet, terrorism, ICT, propaganda, social-networking

1. Introduction

According to the Internet World Stats webpage, the latest number of world Internet users (calculated 30 June 2010) are 1 966 541 816 representing a 28.7% penetration of the world population (2010). Although this does not reflect a majority of the world population, it presents an enormous amount of potential recipients, recruitees and enemies that global terrorist groups can target electronically. However, terrorist groups' embracing of technology used to be an uncommon phenomenon.

In the book, *The secret history of al Qaeda,* an eye witness to the al Qaeda men fleeing United States bombardments of their training camps in November 2001 are quoted: *"Every second al Qaeda member [was] carrying a laptop computer along with his Kalashnikov"* (Atwan 2006). This scenario is highly paradoxical where an organisation utterly against the modern world (such as al Qaeda), are increasingly relying on hi-tech electronic facilities offered by the Internet to operate, expand, develop and survive. Especially in the early 1980s, some groups in Afghanistan were opposed to using any kind of technology that is of largely Western origin or innovation (Atwan 2006).

However, the world has changed. Technology has been introduced in most aspects of daily lives and the Internet has become a prominent component of business and private life. It provides an enormous amount of information and enables relatively cheap and instant communication across the globe. As a result, the traditional view of many traditional terrorist groups shifted to embrace the use of technology within their functions. In 2003, a document titled *'al Qaeda: The 39 principles of Jihad'* was published on the al-Farouq website. Principle 34 states that 'performing electronic jihad' is a 'sacred duty'. The author of the principle document calls upon the group's members to participate actively in Internet forums. He explains that the Internet offers the opportunity to respond instantly and to reach millions of people in seconds. Members who have Internet skills are urged to use them to support the jihad by hacking into and destroying enemy websites (Atwan 2006).

Keeping this principle in mind, the use of the Internet by terrorist groups has expanded from only traditional Internet usage to more innovative usage of both traditional and new Internet functions. This paper will summarise the high-level functions, methods and examples for which terrorists utilise the Internet. The examples and methods often provide for various functions and thus a strict one-to-one mapping cannot be provided. Rather, the examples given shed light on the technical and practical role that ICT infrastructure plays in the support of terrorism.

2. Functionality of the internet

Terrorists use the Internet because it is easy and inexpensive to disseminate information instantaneously worldwide (Piper 2008). By its very nature, the Internet is in many ways an ideal arena for activity by terrorist groups. The Internet offers little or no regulation, is an anonymous multimedia environment, and has the ability to shape coverage in the traditional mass media (Weimann 2005).

Whilst the Internet was originally created to facilitate communication between two computers, its functionality now extends to information repository as well. Figure 1 shows the general functions that terrorists may use the Internet for, with an indication of which type of methods are used for each functionality type.

- Recruitment – the process of attracting, screening and selecting individuals to become members of the terrorist groups; both web literature and social networking tools can be applied for this purpose.
- Training – the process of disseminating knowledge, skills and competency to new recruits with regard to specific topics of knowledge that may be needed during terrorist operations; social networking tools and anti-forensics methods are employed for this purpose.
- Communication – the process of conveying information to members of the terrorist group; social networking tools and anti-forensics methods are employed for this purpose.
- Operations – the direction and control of a specific terrorist attack; web literature, anti-forensics and fundraising methods are employed for this purpose.
- Propaganda – a form of communication aimed at influencing the terrorist community toward a specific cause; both web literature and social networking tools can be applied for this purpose.
- Funding – financial support provided to make a specific terrorist operation possible; fundraising methods are used for this purpose.
- Psychological warfare – the process of spreading disinformation in an attempt to deliver threats intended to distil fear and helplessness within the enemy ranks; both web literature and social networking tools can be applied for this purpose.

The Internet is the perfect tool to exploit in order to support terrorist activities. Not only does it provide location independence, speed, anonymity and internationality, but is also provides a relatively low cost-benefit ratio (Brunst 2010), making it a desirable tool. Figure 1 shows the complexity of terrorist groups' use of the Internet (as both traditional communication and information gathering tool) in innovative new ways. The Internet is also used as both uni-directional and bi-directional communication tool.

Although this list of functionalities is not exhaustive, it provides a better understanding of the need for specific methods to exploit the ICT infrastructure to support terrorist activities. The next section discusses the methods in more detail, and explains these with actual examples.

3. Exploiting the ICT infrastructure to support terrorist activities

For the purpose of this article, Internet exploitation methods are divided into four distinct groups: web literature, social networking tools, anti-forensics and fundraising. Figure 2 shows these groups with some examples of how the methods may be employed.

3.1. Web literature

Web literature refers to all writings published on the web in a particular style on a particular subject. Some of the types of web literature facilitated by terrorist groups include published periodicals and essays, manuals, encyclopaedias, poetry, videos, statements and biographies. Since web literature often takes on the form of mass uni-directional communication, this media is ideal for terrorist use in recruitment, operations, training and propaganda.

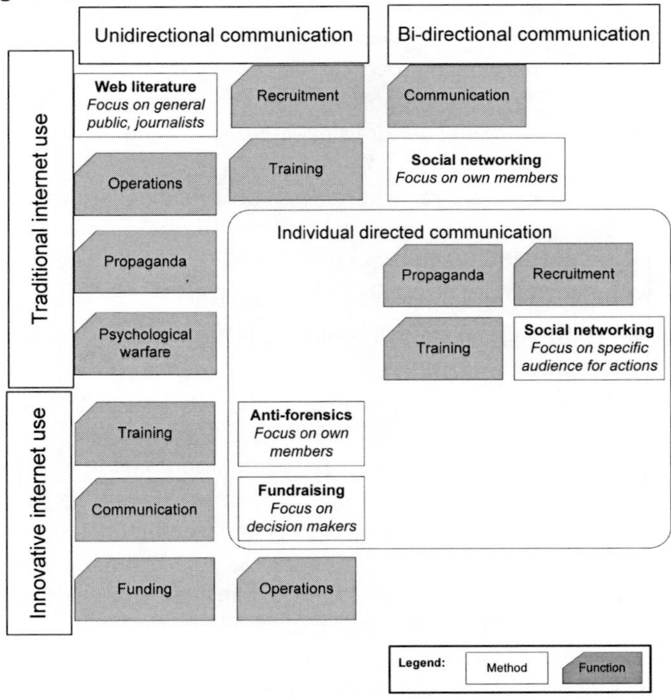

Figure 1: The Internet as terrorist supporting mechanism

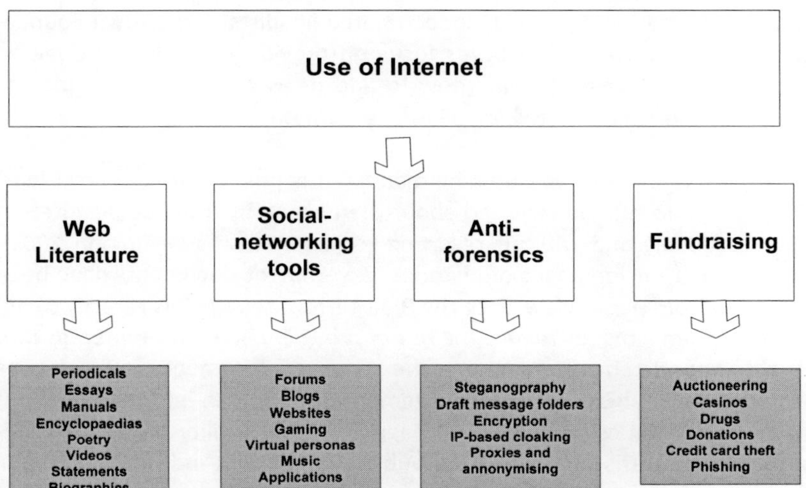

Figure 2: Examples of how terrorists may use the Internet

Radio Free Europe/Radio Liberty compiled a special report on the use of media by Sunni Insurgents in Iraq and their supporters worldwide. This report discusses the products produced by terrorist media campaigns, including text, audiovisual and websites (Kimmage, Ridolfo 2007). The distribution of text and audiovisual media is a traditional use of the Internet, with little innovative application. Text media include press releases, operational statements, inspirational texts and martyr biographies. Audiovisual media include recordings of al Qaeda operations in Iraq (Atwan 2006). Online training material can provide detailed instructions on how to make letter bombs; use poison and chemicals; detonate car bombs; shoot US soldiers; navigate by the stars (Coll, Glasser 2005) and assemble a suicide bomb vest (Lachow, Richardson 2007).

The use of *dedicated websites* within terrorist circles is prominent. By the end of 1999, most of the 30 organisations designated as Foreign Terrorist Organisations had a maintained web presence (Weimann 2009). In 2006, this number has grown to over 5000 active websites (Nordeste, Carment 2006). These websites generally provide current activity reports and vision and mission statements of the terrorist group. *Sympathetic websites* focus largely on propaganda. These websites have postings of entire downloadable books and pamphlet libraries aimed at indoctrinating jihadi sympathizers and reassuring already indoctrinated jihadists (Jamestown Foundation 2006). *Pro-surgent websites* focus on providing detailed tutorials to group members, e.g. showing how to add news crawls that provide the latest, fraudulent death toll for US forces in Iraq.

According to an al Qaeda training manual, it is possible to gather at least 80% of all information required about the enemy, by using public Internet sources openly and without resorting to illegal means (Weimann 2005). More than 1 million pages of historical government documents have been removed from public view since the 9/11 terror attacks. This record of concern program aims to *"reduce the risk of providing access to materials that might support terrorists"*. Among the removed documents is a database from the Federal Emergency Management Agency with information about all federal facilities, and 200 000 pages of naval facility plans and blueprints. The data is removed from public domain, but individuals can still request to see parts of the withdrawn documents under the Freedom of Information Act (Bass, Ho 2007).

Other examples of web literature and information collected through the Internet include maps, satellite photos of potential attack sites, transportation routes, power and communication grids, infrastructure details, pipelines systems, dams and water supplies, information on natural resources and email distribution lists. Although this type of information may not necessarily be useful in cyberterrorism activities, it can be used to plan traditional terrorism activities without actually going to the geographical location of the target. Some terrorist groups have recently been distributing flight simulation software. Web literature can thus be used in the initial recruitment campaigns by glorifying terrorism through inspirational media, as well as the training of members, propaganda and the operations of the terrorist group.

3.2. Social networking tools

Social networking tools focus on building and reflecting social networks or social relations among people who share a common interest. Some types of social networking tools facilitated by terrorist groups include online forums and blogs, websites, games, virtual personas, music and specialised applications. Social networking tools offer both uni-directional and bi-directional communications, and can be used for recruitment, training, propaganda and communication within terrorist groups.

Social networking and gaming sites often require new members to create accounts by specifying their names, skills and interests. Through the creation of these virtual personas, terrorist groups are able to gather information on potential recruits. Individuals with strong technical skills in the fields of chemistry, engineering or weapons development can be identified and encouraged to join the group. This type of information can be derived from interactions in social networking sites, forums and blogs where users share information about their interests, beliefs, skills and careers. Online gaming sites also provide a source of potential members. For example, terrorist groups identify online players with a strong shooting ability that might be indicative of violent tendencies. In some terrorist groups, this type of temperament would be ideal for operational missions.

In addition to traditional social networking sites like Facebook and MySpace, Web 2.0 technologies evolved to customisable social networking sites. West and Latham (2010) state that social networking creation sites are an online extremist's dream - it is inexpensive, easy-to-use, highly customisable and conducive to online extremism. Ning users, for example, can create an individualised site where users have the ability to upload audio and video files, post and receive messages and blog entries, create events and receive RSS feeds. If a terrorist group sets up a customised social site, they would have the ability to control access to members, post propaganda videos and even use the site for fundraising.

Another way of promoting a cause is with music (Whelpton 2009). Islamic and white supremist groups perform captivating songs with pop and hip-hop beats that often attract young influential teenagers. The lyrics of the music promote the cause and the catchy beats keep the youth captivated.

Other examples of social networking include chat rooms, bulletin boards, discussion groups and micro blogging (such as Twitter). The type of social networking used by terrorist groups depends on the group's infrastructure, ability and personal preference. For example, al Qaeda operatives use the Internet in public places and communicate by using free web based email accounts. For these public types of communication, instructions are often delivered electronically through code, usually in difficult-to-decipher dialects for which Western intelligence and security services have few or no trained linguists (Nordeste, Carment 2006).

3.3. Anti-forensics

Anti-forensics is a set of tools or methods used to counter the use of forensic tools and methods. Some of the identified types of anti-forensic measures include steganography, dead dropping, encryption, IP-based cloaking, proxies and anonymising. Since anti-forensic measures mostly offer targeted uni-directional communication, it is ideal for training, operations and communication within terrorist groups.

Steganography is a method of covertly hiding messages within another. This is done by embedding the true message within a seemingly innocuous communication, such as text, image or audio. Only individuals that know of the hidden message and have the relevant key will be able to extract the original message from the carrier message. The password or passphrase is delivered to the intended recipient by secure alternative means (Lau 2003). Although it is difficult to detect the modified carrier media visually, it is possible to use statistical analysis. The February 2007 edition of Technical Mujahid contains an article that encourages extremists to download a copy of the encryption program *"Secrets of the Mujahideen"* from the Internet (2007). The program hid data in the pixels of the image and compressed the file to defeat steganalysis attempts.

Another technique that would bypass messaging interception techniques is the use of virtual dead dropping, or draft message folders. Bruce Hoffman from Rand Corp. (in (Noguchi, Goo 2006)) states that terrorists create free web based email accounts and allow others to log into the accounts and read the drafts without the messages ever been sent. The email account name and password is transmitted in code in a chat forum or secure message board to the intended recipients. This technique is used especially for highly sensitive information (Nordeste, Carment 2006) and if electronic interception legislation may come into play.

Redirecting of traffic through IP-based cloaking is another anti-forensic technique. At a seminar in FOSE 2006, Cottrell (in (Carr 2007)) stated that: *"When the Web server receives a page request, a script checks the IP address of the user against a list of known government IP addresses. If a match is found, the server delivers a Web page with fake information. If no match is found, the requesting user is sent to a Web page with real information"*. From this, the expression cloaking as the authentic site is masked.

This also leads to a similar technique called IP-based blocking that prevents users' access to a site instead of redirecting the traffic.

Other techniques include the use of a proxy and secure channel to hide Internet activity. The Search for International Terrorist Entities Institute (SITE) detected a posting that encouraged the use of a proxy as it erases digital footsteps such as web addresses and other identifiable information (Noguchi, Goo 2006). The premise of this approach is that the user connects to a proxy that requests an anonymising site to redirect the user to the target site. The connection to the proxy is via a secure encrypted channel that hides the originating user's details. The well-known cyber user Irhabi 007 (Terrorist 007) also provided security tips by distributing anonymising software that masks an IP address (Labi 2006).

Another innovative use of the Internet is provided by spammimic.com. Spam (unsolicited distribution of mass email communication) has become a nuisance for the average netizen. Most people automatically delete these messages or send it to the spam folder. Spammimic.com provides an interesting analogue of encryption software that hides messages within the text of ordinary mail. It does not provide true encryption, but hides the text of a short message into what appears to be an average spam mail. Not only will the messages be disguised, but few people will take the chance to open the email in fear of attached malware. Thus, only the intended recipients will know about the disguised messages and decode it through the web interface (Tibbetts 2002).

3.4. Fundraising

Fundraising is the process of soliciting and gathering contributions by requesting donations, often in the form of money. Some of the identified types of fundraising methods include donations, auctioneering, casinos, credit card theft, drug trafficking and phishing. Since fundraising methods mostly offer targeted communication, it can be used for operations and funding activities.

Since the 9/11 terrorist attack, terrorist groups have increasingly relied on the Internet for finance related activities. Popular terrorist organisation websites often have links such as *"What You Can Do"* or *"How Can I Help"*. Terrorist websites publish requests for funds by appealing to sympathetic users to make donations and contribute to the funding of activities. Visitors to such websites are monitored and researched. Repeat visitors or individuals spending extended periods on the websites are contacted (Piper 2008). These individuals are guided to secret chat rooms or instructed to download specific software that enables users to communicate on the Internet without being monitored (Nordeste, Carment 2006).

However, malicious or disguised methods of fundraising are also possible. Electronic money transfer, laundering and generating support through front organisations are all fundraising methods used by terrorists (Goodman, Kirk & Kirk 2007). According to the Financial Action Task Force, *"the misuse of nonprofit organizations for the financing of terrorism is coming to be recognized as a crucial weak point in the global struggle to stop such funding at its source"* (Jacobson 2009). Examples of such undertakings include Mercy International, Rabita Trust, Global Relief Fund, and Help the Needy (Conway 2006). Some charities are founded with the express purpose of financing terror, while others are existing entities that are infiltrated by terrorist supporters from within (Jacobson 2009).

Other methods related to fundraising include online auctioneering to move money around. This involves two partners, known as smurfs, to arrange a fake transaction. One partner bids on an item and pays the auction amount to the auction house. The other partner receives payment for the fake auction item. There are also scams where users bid on their own items in an effort to store money and prevent detection (Whelpton 2009). In one specific auction, a set of second-hand video games were offered for $200, whilst the same set could be purchased brand new from the publisher for $39.99 (Tibbetts 2002). Although the ludicrously high selling price is not illegal, this item will only attract selected attention from a trusted agent. This allows terrorist groups to move money around without actually delivering the auctioned goods or services.

Online casinos can be used for both laundering and storing money. When dealing with large sums of money, terrorists can place it in an online gambling site. Small bids are made to ensure activity, while the rest of the money is safely stored and hidden (Whelpton 2009). Alternatively, any winnings can be cashed in and transferred electronically to bank accounts specifically created for this purpose (Jacobson 2009).

Stolen credit cards can help to fund many terrorist activities. For example, Irhabi 007 and his accomplice accumulated 37 000 stolen credit card numbers, making more than $3.5 million in charges (Jacobson 2009). In 2005, stolen credit card details were used to purchase domain space with a request stemming from Paris. When a similar request for nearby domain space was requested, shortly after the initial request, through another name in Britain, it was detected as fraud and the backup files of the initial site was investigated. Although the files were mostly Arabic, video footage includes insurgent forces clashing with American forces, depicting Iraqi conflict from the attacker's point of view (Labi 2006).

Drug trafficking is considered a large income source for terrorist groups. Fake Internet drugs are trafficked, containing harmful ingredients such as arsenic, boric acid, leaded road paint, polish, talcum powder, chalk and brick dust. In an elaborate scheme, Americans were tricked in believing they are buying Viagra, but instead they received fake drugs. The money paid for these drugs is used to fund Middle Eastern terrorism. The UK Medicine and Healthcare Regulatory Agency reports that up to 62% of the prescription medicine on sale on the Internet, without requiring a prescription, are fake (Whelpton 2009).

3.4.1 Other examples of the exploitation of the ICT infrastructure

Kovner (in (Lachow, Richardson 2007)) discusses one of al Qaeda's goals of using the Internet to create resistance blockades to prevent Western ideas from corrupting Islamic institutions. In some instances, Internet browsers designed to filter out content from undesirable Western sources were distributed without users being aware of it. Brachman (2006) also discusses jihadi computer programmers launching browsing software, similar to Internet Explorer that searches only particular sites and thus restricts the freedom to navigate to certain online destinations.

Another technique from the infamous terrorist Irhabi 007 was to exploit vulnerabilities in FTP servers, reducing risk from exposure and saving money. Irabhi dumped files (with videos of Bin Laden and 9/11 hijackers) onto an FTP server at the Arkansan State Highway and Transport Department and then posted links warning users of the limited window of opportunity to download (Labi 2006).

SITE (in (Brachman 2006)) discovered a guide for jihadis to use the Internet safely and anonymously. This guide explains how governments identify users, penetrate their usage of software chat programs (including Microsoft Messenger and Paltalk), and advise readers not to use Saudi Arabian based email addresses (ending with .sa) due to its insecure nature. Readers are advised to rather register from anonymous accounts from commercial providers like Hotmail or Yahoo!.

Cottrell in 2006 (in (Dizard 2006)) discusses the following emerging cloaking trends:

- Terrorist organisations host bogus websites that mask their covert information or provide misleading information to users they identify as federal employees or agents;
- Criminal and terrorist organisations are increasingly blocking all traffic from North America or from IP addresses that point back to users who rely on the English language;
- Another cloaking practice is the provision of fake passwords at covert meetings. When one of the fake passwords are detected, the user is flagged as a potential federal intelligence agent who has attended the meetings, which in turn makes them vulnerable to being kidnapped or becoming the unwitting carriers of false information; and
- Another method was used in a case in which hackers set a number of criteria that they all shared using the Linux operating system and the Netscape browser, among other factors. When federal investigators using computers running Windows and using Internet Explorer visited the hackers' shared site, the hackers' system immediately mounted a distributed denial-of-service attack against the federal system.

Sometimes communication between terrorists occurs through a special code developed by the group itself. By using inconspicuous word and phrases, it is possible to deliver these messages in a public forum without attracting untoward attention. For example, Mohammed Atta's final message to the other eighteen terrorists who carried out the attacks of 9/11 is reported to have read: *"The semester begins in three more weeks. We've obtained 19 confirmations for studies in the faculty of law, the faculty of urban planning, the faculty of fine arts, and the faculty of engineering."* The reference to the various faculties is code for the buildings targeted in the attacks (Weimann 2005).

Defacing websites are a popular way for terrorist groups to demonstrate its technical capability and create fear. These defacements often take the form of public alterations of a website that are visible to a large audience. An example of such an attack took place in 2001, when a group known as the Pentaguard defaced a multitude of government and military websites in the UK, Australia, and the United States. *"This attack was later evaluated as one of the largest, most systematic defacements of worldwide government servers on the Web"*. Another example is pro-Palestinian hackers using a coordinated attack to break into 80 Israel-related sites and deface them, and when al Qaeda deposited images of the murdered Paul Marshall Johnson, Jr. on the hacked website of the Silicon Valley Landsurveying, Inc (Brunst 2010).

4. Conclusion

The use of the Internet by terrorist groups has expanded to both traditional Internet usage and the more innovative usage of both traditional and new Internet functions. Global terrorist groups can now electronically target an enormous amount of potential recipients, recruitees and enemies. Terrorist groups often embrace the opportunities that technology innovation brings about in order to advance their own terrorist workings.

This paper is informative in nature, aiming to make the public aware of the potential that ICT infrastructure has in assisting terrorist groups in their operations and normal functions. These functions include all the processes from recruitment and training of new members, communicating with existing members, planning and executing operations, distributing propaganda, fund raising and carrying out psychological warfare. Due to the unique nature of the Internet, many of these traditional and innovative Internet uses can be carried out in either a uni-directional or bi-directional fashion, depending on the nature of the communication required.

Based on this research, in can be seen that international terrorist groups can use the Internet in most of its daily functions to facilitate the growth and operation of the groups. In a sense, terrorist groups can actively exploit the existing ICT infrastructure to advance their groups. This paper discussed specific instances and provided examples of this exploitation through web literature use, social-networking tools, anti-forensic techniques and novel fundraising methods. In conclusion, further research may be done to identify ways on how these innovative uses of the Internet can be used to counter terrorism attacks, and not only support their activities.

References

Atwan, A. (2006), The secret history of al Qaeda, 1st edn, University of California Press, California.

Bass, R. & Ho, S.M. 2007, AP: 1M archived pages removed post-9/11.

Brachman, J.M. (2006), "High-tech terror: Al-Qaeda's use of new technology", Fletcher Forum of World Affairs, vol. 30, pp. 149.

Brunst, P.W. (2010), "Terrorism and the Internet: New Threats Posed by Cyberterrorism and Terrorist Use of the Internet" in , ed. P.W. Brunst, Springer, A war on terror?, pp. 51-78.

Carr, J. (2007), Anti-Forensic Methods Used by Jihadist Web Sites.

Coll, S. & Glasser, S.B. (2005), "Terrorists turn to the Web as base of operations", The Washington Post, vol. 7, pp. 77–87.

Conway, M. (2006), "Terrorist Use' of the Internet and Fighting Back", Information and Security, vol. 19, pp. 9.

Dizard, W.P. (2006), Internet "cloaking" emerges as new Web security threat, Government Computer News.

Goodman, S.E., Kirk, J.C. & Kirk, M.H. (2007), "Cyberspace as a medium for terrorists", Technological Forecasting and Social Change, vol. 74, no. 2, pp. 193-210.

Internet World Stats 2010, May 27, 2010-last update, Internet usage statistics - The internet big picture: World internet users and population stats. Available: http://www.internetworldstats.com/stats.htm [2010, 06/08] .

Jacobson, M. (2009), "Terrorist financing on the internet", CTC Sentinel, vol. 2, no. 6, pp. 17-20.

Jamestown Foundation, (2006), Next Stage in Counter-Terrorism: Jihadi Radicalization on the Web.

Kimmage, D. & Ridolfo, K. (2007), "Iraqi Insurgent Media. The War of Images and Ideas. How Sunni Insurgents in Iraq and Their Supporters Worldwide are Using the Media", Washington, Radio Free Europe/Radio Liberty.

Labi, N. (2006), "Jihad 2.0", The Atlantic Monthly, vol. 102.

Lachow, I. & Richardson, C. (2007), "Terrorist use of the Internet: The real story", Joint Force Quarterly, vol. 45, pp. 100.

Lau, S. (2003), " An analysis of terrorist groups' potential use of electronic steganography ", Bethesda, Md.: SANS Institute, February, , pp. 1-13.

Noguchi, Y. & Goo, S. (2006), Terrorists' Web Chatter Shows Concern About Internet Privacy, Wash.

Nordeste, B. & Carment, D. (2006), " Trends in terrorism series: A framework for understanding terrorist use of the internet ", ITAC, vol. 2006-2, pp. 1-21.

Piper, P. (2008), Nets of terror: Terrorist activity on the internet. Searcher, vol.16, issue 10.

Tibbetts, P.S. (2002), "Terrorist Use of the Internet and Related Information Technologies", Army Command And General Staff Coll Fort Leavenworth Ks School Of Advanced Military Studies, pp. 1-67.

Weimann, G. (2009), "Virtual Terrorism: How Modern Terrorists Use the Internet", Annual Meeting of the International Communciation Association, Dresden International Congress Centre, Dresden.

Weimann, G. (2005), "How modern terrorism uses the internet", The Journal of International Security Affairs, vol. Spring 2005, no. 8.

West, D. & Latham, C.(2010), "The extremist Edition of Social Networking: The Inevitable Marriage of Cyber Jihad and Web 2.0", Proceedings of the 5th International Conference on Information Warfare and Security, ed. L. Armistead, Academic Conferences, .

Whelpton, J. (2009), "Psychology of Cyber Terrorism" in Cyberterrorism 2009 Seminar Ekwinox, South Africa.